The Therapist's Treasure Chest

A Norton Professional Book

The Therapist's Treasure Chest

SOLUTION-ORIENTED TIPS AND TRICKS FOR EVERYDAY PRACTICE

Filip Caby
Andrea Caby

Translated by Jenny Piening

W. W. Norton & Company

New York • London

Die kleine Psychotherapeutische Schatzkiste copyright © 2009
by SolArgent Media, Division of BORGMANN HOLDING AG, Basel

Die kleine Psychotherapeutische Schatzkiste, Teil 2, copyright © 2011
by SolArgent Media, Division of BORGMANN HOLDING AG, Basel

For information about permission to reproduce selections from this book,
write to Permissions, W. W. Norton & Company, Inc.,
500 Fifth Avenue, New York, NY 10110

For information about special discounts for bulk purchases, please contact
W. W. Norton Special Sales at specialsales@wwnorton.com or 800-233-4830

Manufacturing by Quad Graphics, Fairfield
Book design by Bytheway
Production manager: Leeann Graham

Library of Congress Cataloging-in-Publication Data

Caby, Filip, 1956–
[Kleine Psychotherapeutische Schatzkiste. English]
The therapist's treasure chest.
    volumes cm.
"A Norton Professional Book"—Part 2, t.p.
Includes bibliographical references and index.
ISBN 978-0-393-70862-2 (pbk.)
1. Psychotherapy—Practice. 2. Clinical psychology.
3. Psychotherapists. I. Caby, Andrea, 1962– II. Title.
RC480.C22 2014
616.89'14—dc 3
                        2014004402

ISBN: 978-0-393-70862-2 (pbk.)

W. W. Norton & Company, Inc.
500 Fifth Avenue, New York, N.Y. 10110
www.wwnorton.com

W. W. Norton & Company Ltd.
Castle House, 75/76 Wells Street, London W1T 3QT

1 2 3 4 5 6 7 8 9 0

If you want a wise answer,
ask a reasonable question.

Johann Wolfgang von Goethe

Contents

PART 4: SEEMINGLY HOPELESS: MASTERING PARTICULARLY
TRICKY SITUATIONS

A Note on the Text

We would like to begin by pointing out that, for the sake of simplicity, we have used the masculine form as needed throughout the text to avoid disrupting the flow of reading.

In the descriptions of the interventions, we often talk about the *patient*. This, of course, is synonymous with *client*. Because the idea for this book came from our everyday contact with patients, this term came most naturally to us.

We usually talk about the *therapist* or *counselor*, which is synonymous with *doctor* or *practitioner*. In many of the examples, therefore, we have used the words *counseling* or *therapy session*, and sometimes also *consultation*. All of these situations—even if they are in different professional contexts—have one thing in common: At the heart of the matter is a conversation between one or more people about a concern, and an expert who is being asked for advice.

This Treasure Chest has resulted from our daily work in practice and teaching, as well as from meetings with colleagues at conferences and further training courses over the course of many years. Initially, the ideas and methods were compiled specially for colleagues working in the fields of pediatrics and child psychiatry. In the process, we realized that other professional groups might find our suggestions beneficial, so users extended to psychologists, child and adolescent psychotherapists, family doctors and general practitioners, social workers, and teachers.

Most of the interventions described in this book can be used to the same extent in a therapeutic, teaching, or counseling context. The close proximity of these professional fields results in overlaps and gray areas that we have not tried to define in more detail. Rather, the focus is on the shared experiences and the creative potential of these different areas of work. In some cases, however, we indicate the boundaries between, for example, pediatrics and child and adolescent psychiatry. Some interventions are therefore marked with "Caution," because they cannot be applied freely.

The techniques we present in this book were generally tested and developed in the field of child and adolescent psychiatry, as well as pediatrics. Therefore, most of the work was with children, adolescents, and young adults but, in the context of family therapy, also with adults, couples, parents, groups, and teams. Methods that work well with younger children sometimes also work surprisingly well with older clients. Conversely, some ideas that we would not initially have dared to use with children worked amazingly well when we tried them with a younger age group. Thus, all of the interventions we describe in this book can also be creatively and imaginatively adapted and extended for use with other age groups.

We have also noticed that many of the interventions work not only in the context of individual therapy, family therapy, group therapy, and couples therapy but also in the context of teams. One example is the **Rewind** → **Reset** technique, which is a fantastic intervention for helping teams to resolve day-to-day conflicts and make a new start: By realizing what could have gone better, combined with a new appreciation of their conflict partner(s), clients are better able to express how they would like the situation to be played out next time based on a solution-oriented and resource-focused perspective.

Last but not least, we would like to expressly point out that the interventions described in this book are not a substitute for therapeutic training. Their purpose is to facilitate working with clients. All therapists and counselors continue to develop the techniques they have learned in the course of their working lives, adapt them to their circumstances, and often discover their own new strategies for dealing with particular problems. Conferences, seminars, and discussions with colleagues provide opportunities to exchange ideas, and it is often surprising to discover that similar concerns can lead to very different solution ideas, and vice versa. The conditions and concerns that we cover are particularly common problems or patterns of behavior that we have often treated successfully using the described methods. They are all just suggestions.

A Note on the Text

Acknowledgments

We would like to thank everyone who encouraged us to write *The Therapist's Treasure Chest*. We also thank our colleagues with whom we have worked for many years, whose ideas have inspired us and helped us in our daily work: Steve de Shazer, Insoo Kim Berg, Yvonne Dolan, Michael Durrant, Luc Isebaert, Kurt Ludewig, Jeff Zeig, the clinic and outpatient teams, and myriad others who cannot be mentioned in person. And, of course, the clients and patients, without whose cooperation, motivation, and courage many things would not have been possible!

We would also like to thank everybody who supported us—each in his or her own way—in bringing this book to print: our son Vincent for his help on the computer with photos and tables, our daughters Cheyenne and Laura for images and ideas, as well our editors, friends, and colleagues who were once again willing to read through the drafts. These include Nikolaus and Lisa Lohmann, Paul Adams, and especially Christian Benden for his expert advice on the topic of "Coughing and such . . . " and other pediatric issues.

We are always grateful to receive further suggestions, comments, advice, and so forth, and are available for lectures and seminars.

Finally, we would like to reiterate: Reading this book is not a substitute for professional psychotherapeutic training. Rather, it is designed to offer inspiration and stimulation.

Filip and Andrea Caby

The Therapist's Treasure Chest

Part 1
Opening the Treasure Chest

An Invitation . . .

. . . First, to be inspired and motivated by our experiences with different interventions: these were sometimes funny, sometimes moving, sometimes unexpected, and sometimes also confounding.

. . . Second, to try some of these interventions for yourself—and discover new ones. We can promise an exciting voyage of discovery.

In this Treasure Chest we have gathered all of our experiences so that they can make their way into the treasure chests of our readers.

Reasons to delve into this Treasure Chest

- Because the treasure reflects an abundance of experience
- Because it can speed up certain therapeutic processes
- Because it can help you come up with a new solution
- Because you simply want to discover what will happen
- Because you might be inspired
- Because you feel like trying something new

Exploring this Treasure Chest will be worthwhile if it fuels your creativity and if you can use the different interventions to develop more of your own. Perhaps you will use it because you don't know how to make headway, or perhaps you simply want to make your therapy or counseling work more enjoyable.

The treasures in this book can be applied anywhere and at any time: during a doctor's appointment or counseling session, in a clinic, in a social services context, or anywhere else they might be needed.

We hope you have fun rummaging around. There are surely many treasures still waiting to be discovered. Enjoy!

Contents of the Treasure Chest

This Treasure Chest is filled with a range of resources. Some speak for themselves: successes, abilities, resources. Others, such as exceptions and good thoughts, may need further explanation.

Contents of the Treasure Chest

- Exceptions
- Successes
- Abilities
- Good thoughts
- Resources
- Problem-free periods
- Spontaneous ideas

By "exceptions," we mean exceptions to the problem: When, as an exception, does the patient not have the problem? During these periods, the patient is obviously responsible for the problem not arising. By understanding which abilities and resources he is tapping into to create this "problem-free period," he is one step closer to solving the problem. It makes a lot of sense to probe deeper and to ask the patient what he is doing differently during these times.

"Good thoughts" include all spontaneous thoughts and ideas that arise, for example, from actively *doing* something.

The Structure of the Book

After a short theoretical introduction, the first part of the book provides an overview of basic questioning techniques and important advice on how to lead a therapeutic conversation.

The second part provides an overview of general as well as specific intervention techniques. In both Parts 1 and 2, the techniques and methods are divided into those that are used directly in the therapeutic interview and those that are recommended for use at home. In the latter case, the methods are to be discussed during the session and set as tasks for the client to do at home.

For the sake of clarity, the interventions are organized in the following format:

- Idea
- Method
- Tips

- Indication/contraindication
- Setting

Under "Idea" we provide a short description of the origins and principles behind the intervention, and under "Method," an exact description of how the technique can be implemented in practice. Under "Tips" we expand on or describe variations of the interventions. "Indication/contraindication" and "Setting" speak for themselves.

The third part of the book deals with specific indications. We present tried and tested approaches that we have found to be effective when dealing with common symptoms and disorders. The fourth part provides suggestions on how to make progress in some tricky situations frequently encountered by therapists and counselors.

The "treasures" are the interventions and tasks that we suggest can be used in these scenarios—of course, after careful observation and personal selection.

The Source of Our Inspiration

The ideas we provide here do not all stem from us. Some of them we picked up along the way and developed further; others we learned during our own professional training. It was not always possible to attribute each approach to the originator; some were probably developed simultaneously in different places in a similar form.

Many approaches and techniques were developed in the process of our daily work, became more established with repeated use, and finally took on a working form. Some ideas were inspired by our patients, who allowed us to try new ideas with them.

The Theoretical Framework

To help our readers understand the interventions in this book, we briefly outline the theoretical foundation of our work, which is systemic, solution oriented, resource oriented, and constructivist.

Systemic

We do not regard patients or clients with their problems in isolation but, rather, also take into account the bigger picture, which in its entirety is referred to as the *system*. The ideas presented here derive from this systemic approach. Because in recent years the term *systemic* has become something of a buzzword, with different meanings depending on the context, it makes sense for us to explain our definition.

Several decades ago, a paradigm shift took place in the thinking, research, and observations of some biologists: They no longer observed organisms in isolation but, rather, in interaction with their environments. Logically, they determined that as an observer of the system you automatically become part of this system.

As the person treating a problem system, you are therefore automatically part of this system and interact with it. This, in turn, means that when people decide to see a doctor, social worker, psychologist, or counselor, they have already changed their system by incorporating another person. Conversely, the treatment or counseling system is also changed in the process.

Just as these two systems influence each other, cause and problem influence each other as well. Thinking a step further: the solution to the problem logically influences the problem. Thereby, the cause of the problem changes too, breaking the pattern that maintained the problem in the first place: change comes about!

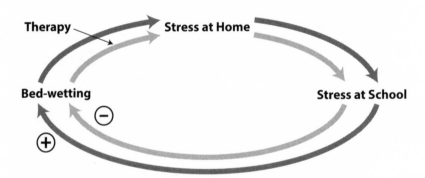

Figure 1: Bed-wetting: From a problem system to a solution system

Thus, a problem system increasingly becomes a solution system. The same people are involved, but they suddenly look in a different direction: away from the problem and toward a solution.

Solution Oriented

The practitioner should have a high degree of respect for the patient and for the patient's previous solutions.

For example, a family experiencing problems tried to develop a solution based on their situation. As a result, one member of the system could no longer cope, and his symptom revealed that the solution wasn't satisfactory for everyone (Watzlawick, 1999). Thus, a different solution, and a new perspective, was sought.

A goal of systemic therapy is to provide new perspectives on the system—in other words, to change the client's focus—so that other solutions become possible. Patients thereby extend their range of possibilities and can deal with their problems more creatively than before.

In practice, this means channeling existing problem-solving approaches and resources into further steps that will lead toward a defined goal (Vogt-Hillmann, Eberling, & Burr, 1999).

Resource Oriented

Resource orientation fulfills another objective of systemic therapy: members of a system are invited to discover—or rediscover—their resources. The therapist or counselor and the patient system embark on a joint quest for resources and solutions.

The therapist wants to turn his patients into problem-solving experts. To achieve this, patients need to draw on abilities that they know they have, as well as ones they have forgotten about or never registered. Thus, the task for the practitioner is to direct the focus of clients or patients away from their deficits and to steer them in the direction of their own resources (Durrant, 1996).

> When a mother comes to you with her child because that child has a psychological problem, she wants a solution from you. And you want her to find a solution—one that is different from the ones she's tried in the past. The mother would like for you to be the expert; you want her to become an expert. You are an expert in creating experts, and that is exactly what the mother wants. She wants you to turn her into an expert. But she doesn't know this yet.

Ultimately, the client's focus is simply realigned and directed toward new possibilities. *These possibilities lead to solutions.*

How a problem is sustained: Cybernetics

In the 1950s, after the birth of cybernetics, therapy-model creators began to ask a different question that led to different answers. Instead of asking, "What is the cause of the problem," they asked,

> *How is the problem being maintained?*
> *How does the problem influence the cause?*

From asking this, it is a fairly small step to asking,

> *What is the advantage of keeping the problem alive?*

These questions were inspired by the science of cybernetics.

Cybernetics is the science of control and regulation in living organisms, social organizations, and other feedback systems. Cybernetics makes it possible to reveal connections and interactions between complex systems. A universal characteristic of such systems is the ability, for example, to acquire, process, and pass on information.

According to Heinz von Foerster (1993), we speak of cybernetics when *effectors*, such as a motor, a machine, our muscles, and so on, are connected to a sensor or sensory organ, which in turn generates signals to act upon the effectors:

> It is this circular organization that sets cybernetic systems apart from others that are not so organized. . . . It looks as if these systems pursue a purpose.

Furthermore, according to Foerster, one of the significant advances in neuropsychology and neuropsychiatry was the change from

> looking at things out there to looking at looking itself. . . . It appeared that one could now dare to ask how the brain works; one could dare to write a theory of the brain. . . . What is new is the profound insight that it takes a brain to write a theory of the brain. . . . Translated into the domain of cybernetics: The cybernetician, by entering his own domain, has to account for his own activity; cybernetics becomes cybernetics of cybernetics, or second-order cybernetics.

In other words, second-order cybernetics is about the observer observing his own observations.

Asking yourself what the advantage might be of maintaining a problem enables you to consider the option that it might simply be better to keep the problem. This option, in turn, invites you to think about the speed at which change takes place, about the motivation of the individual people involved in the "problem system," or about the "problem behind the problem."

Constructivist

Constructivism is based on the principle that we construct what we know from what we experience. From a constructivist point of view, then, the individual's perspective is unavoidably personal. The observer can observe only in the light of his own experiences.

This has far-reaching consequences for the therapeutic process: Everything that we observe, we observe on the basis of our previous experiences. Others see the same thing, but in the light of their own experiences, which inevitably are not the same. Therefore, everyone observes the same thing but sees something different.

In terms of what they see and describe, patients are therefore always right, although they may describe the exact opposite of what the therapist or counselor sees. Of course, the therapist is also right, but there is little to be gained from two observers trying to convince each other of the validity of their own observations.

For the same reason, we find interpretations problematic, because interpreters ultimately have only their own experiences to fall back on and not those of the other person. An interpretation is useful only if it provides listeners with a new perspective and extends their horizon of possibilities.

There is also little point in offering suggestions and tips, because we can never know if they suit the context of the patient. The patient will decide if the tip is useful or not. On the whole, such suggestions have only very limited success.

The point of psychotherapy—and of this Treasure Chest—is to provide patients with ways and means of opening up new perspectives.

(Re)Constructing the past

When thinking about the past, we are inclined to see the past as written in stone. The saying "Coming to terms with the past" has negative undertones, because we need to come to terms only with things that were difficult or unpleasant. Of course, the facts cannot be changed, but the effect they have can. In order to successfully come to terms with something, it is necessary to draw on the abilities that we have today and to keep the goals that we want to achieve, or the perspectives that we want to open up, clearly in view.

A good metaphor here is a car ready for the scrap heap. Many people's pasts are comparable to a car that was once new, shiny, and fully functioning. Then things happen: the paintwork dulls, parts stop working, or the car is involved in an accident. The broken car is then assigned to the past, and seen from the perspective of today, it looks like a catastrophe.

The "coming to terms with this car catastrophe" can take many forms: you could write it off and take it to the scrap heap, or you could repair it, or you could keep the good parts in order to make one functioning car out of two broken ones. Thus, even when dealing with the past, there are numerous possibilities: to write it off and forget about it, or to accept it as fate and keep going, or to use parts of the past for the future. In the latter case, the future or, rather, the goal you are trying to achieve influences the way in which you look at the past: How can you, in the present, use the good spare parts from the past to create a better future? Or, to put it another way: How can you succeed in activating parts of the past for present purposes and even for bringing about future-oriented change? The opposite of "coping with the past" might be "making the past work for me today" or "activating the past."

Summary: The Approach of the Therapist

The therapist's approach should help strengthen the client's motivation and thereby encourage change; this always requires creativity.

The therapist needs to show respect, appreciation, and understanding for what came before (the previously attempted solution), as well as confidence and interest in the future (new solutions). Combined with a sense of partnership with the client, plus a little humor, this can create an atmosphere for developing a solution that acknowledges the influence that the solution and the problem continue to have on one another.

Various approaches to finding solutions, based on systemic and family-therapeutic models, are presented here in the form of tried and tested, easy-to-implement techniques.

The Therapist's Treasure Chest

Humor Works, Too

Humor has always played an important role in therapy. Titze and Eschenröder (2007) use the word *humor* as an umbrella term for all things funny or comical. For Freud it was a means for the ego to withstand suffering.

In psychotherapy, in particular, humor has to fit the client, as well as the therapist: It has to suit the client's cognitive abilities, cultural background, social circumstances, problems, and so forth. A prerequisite for using humor is having a good rapport with the patient.

But humor always serves the same function: It helps patients to relax, arouses their curiosity, opens up new perspectives, changes their problem-oriented focus, and boosts their confidence. *Laughter liberates.*

Humor works best when it is unexpected. Humor can even mark the turning point in highly fraught conflict situations.

Picking up on clients' metaphorical images can also be funny. With a little bit of drawing talent, you can even translate the humor into a visual caricature.

The "humor palette" contains as many different colors as the painter's palette. You just need to know which "color" is best suited to which situation.

A case example: Stories from Bruno

The first meeting with Bruno's family was filled with laughter. The long-standing strain that the family had been under was clear to see, but despite this—or perhaps because of it—their willingness to laugh was almost just as great.

Bruno's case history revealed that he spent a lot of time in his room, because that's where the computer was. But I (F.C.) was also interested in what else was in his room and discovered that he had two aquariums, one for fish and one for shrimp. Because of the time he spent at the computer, he spent only a few minutes each day taking care of these creatures. When asked what species of fish he had, Bruno replied that he didn't know exactly—he had started with two species, but now there also seemed to be some other kinds.

My answer: *It sounds as if you've bred a new species of fish. Your fish are obviously getting up to all sorts of mischief. It's like Sodom and Gomorrah in your room!* There were gales of laughter from the whole family, and the positive atmosphere tangibly increased the motivation for therapy.

Asked about the shrimp, Bruno was able to assure me that there was only one species but that their numbers had multiplied considerably. When I asked how shrimp multiply, he wasn't able to answer. Finding an answer to this question became the running gag of his subsequent stay in the clinic. And despite the magnitude of the conflict and the initial despair of the parents, he was able to leave the clinic after just three weeks.

Hypotheses: Useful or a Hindrance?

Working with hypotheses in a systemic field is contentious. Some therapists do not use hypotheses at all, suggesting they find them a hindrance. Others use hypotheses only in special cases, when they appear to be useful. As always, there is no one right answer.

The word *hypothesis* stems from the Greek word *hypóthesis*, meaning "basis," "supposition," "assumption." Thereby, it is an assertion that implies veracity but that has not been proven or verified. In statistics, a hypothesis is an assumption that needs to be verified with empirical data. From a scientific perspective, a hypothesis is an assumption based on scientific data that has yet to be proven.

Psychotherapy is based on an abundance of hypotheses, assumptions, and so forth. It is pointless to differentiate between a hypothesis and an assumption, since neither of them contains the proof that they are correct. With an assumption one imagines that things are the way they were assumed to be. A hypothesis is an idea about the way something could happen, or how it could be explained. An analytical interpretation is an assumption and also an idea for a solution.

A systemic hypothesis differs from a nonsystemic hypothesis in that it connects several elements of a system. Behavior, for example, is defined not only in terms of intrapsychic characteristics but also in terms of intrasystematic interactions (Backhausen & Thommen, 2006). Hypotheses have an ambivalent standing in the systemic field.

The point of hypotheses

We often regard hypotheses as a hindrance, and yet we frequently work with them: *Supposing your problem was solved . . . ?*

Hypotheses are useful when they **establish a sense of purpose** and **encourage action**. They explain things by relating phenomena to one another, thereby enabling new perspectives.

Hypotheses question the circumstances that gave rise to a particular personal philosophy and provide alternatives. They can be **invitations** to **change or widen the client's focus**.

When are hypotheses useful and when are they a hindrance? Which hypotheses should we avoid, and which ones should we use? From a systemic point of view, a hypothesis is more likely to be effective the more elements of a problem system it encompasses and the more it is able to connect the actions of the different elements involved.

For example, hypotheses are suggested to an individual patient so that he can, for example, choose the most suitable one or take away something useful or positive from each one. Or a hypothesis is used in a system to help the participants communicate their respective viewpoints. From a constructivist point of view, then, a hypothesis opens up new perspectives and possibilities for clients by enriching their respective perspectives with those of the others.

In short: A hypothesis is useful if it helps the patient and makes solutions seem more probable and achievable. Hypotheses are useless—and can even be harmful—if they are used to steer a client's thinking in a particular direction and to shape his outlook to conform to the hypothesis. A hypothesis makes sense only if it is also allowed to be wrong—and not if it is a prejudice that the therapist or counselor is trying to validate.

As a therapist, it is almost impossible to begin a conversation with a client without a hypothesis. You almost always have some preconceived ideas about the relational structures within a family or about the way a system functions. It is therefore good to know that you have these hypotheses in mind, in order to remain open and curious about things that deviate from your own hypothesis.

Another way of usefully applying a hypothesis in therapy or counseling is to ask the client why he thinks you have developed a certain hypothesis after observing him and his family. Through our actions, we cause the client to hypothesize about our behavior. In an analogy with second-order cybernetics, we could speak of a second-order hypothesis: a hypothesis about the hypothesis. (*See also* **Playing with hypotheses**, *page 161*.)

What Does Strategy Have to Do with Counseling and Therapy?

Jay Haley's (1991) solution-oriented approach to family therapy, also known as strategic family therapy, became well known for specific techniques such as **Paradoxical interventions** (prescribing the symptoms) and **Circular questioning**, as well for strategic analysis of the quality of the relationships between any two given members of a system.

A strategic approach involves destabilizing relationships to enable change. Take, for example, a triangular relationship among three people. Such triangular relationships inevitably comprise three two-person relationships (partners) that observe each other and are in turn related to each other. The relationship between two members of the system cannot be separated from the triangular constellation, and vice versa: Everybody influences each other.

Similarly, a relationship network of five people incorporates multiple pairs and several triangular relationships (Figure 2). One pair evaluates each of the other

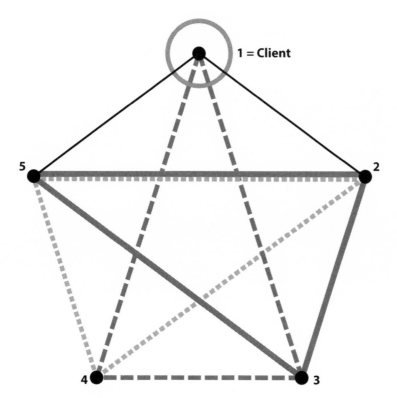

Figure 2: Five-person system

pairs within the triangles according to the quality of the relationships: good or prone to conflict? (In Figure 2, three of 10 possible triangles have been highlighted as examples.)

The question to ask in this situation is simply: *How would you judge this relationship? Or What are your hypotheses about the quality of the relationship? In your opinion, how is the relationship between A and B?*

With the strategic approach, the relationships are categorized fairly basically, as "good" or "not so good." This form of observation provides a good basis for initiating possible courses of action.

(**Note:** Psychotherapist Klaus Eickmann, at a seminar on family therapy in 1991, pointed out that approaching relationships in this tactical way may seem a little military, and thus may seem to place undue emphasis on *hypothesizing* about the quality of the relationships, but argued that this is strategically permissible as long as a resource- and solution-oriented approach is foregrounded.)

Figure 3 shows how triangular constellations can be categorized as either *stable* or *unstable*. A triangle is **stable** when there is a logical pattern to all of the relationships within a triangle: If I like both of my relationship partners in a triangle, it is highly probable that both of them also like me and each other. Another way of looking at it is: The friend of my friend is also my friend. But the following is just as stable: The enemy of my friend is my enemy, or, there is a strong possibility that the friend of my enemy will also be my enemy.

A triangle is **unstable** when the sum of the parts is not logical: The enemy of my friend is my friend, yet the enemy of my friend should also be my enemy, if I don't want to endanger my relationship with my friend. Anything else results in tensions. And the converse is also unstable: The enemy of my enemy is my enemy (see Figure 4)—a triangle system comprising only enemies cannot come to rest because there is permanent tension.

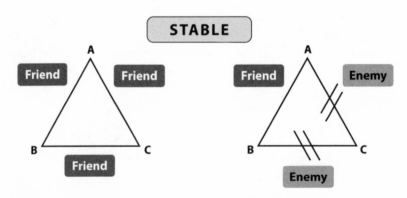

Figure 3: Stable relationship triangles

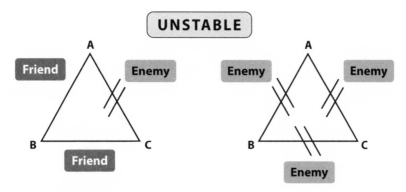

Figure 4: Unstable relationship triangles

Unstable triangles are subject to tensions and are more likely to incorporate the preconditions for change. From a strategic family-therapeutic perspective, unstable triangles can be advantageous. In stable triangles, problem systems can calcify, and the stability can become an obstacle to productive change.

A strategic approach involves destabilizing stable triangles to enable change. The best therapeutic interventions to use in this situation are ones that change the quality of the relationships in the existing triangle. The following systemic interventions can be used:

- Circular questioning
- Asking "coping" questions
- Solution-oriented observation tasks, for example, *Over the next two weeks, observe your relationship partner and focus on what you like about him as a partner.*

These or similar tasks or interventions make it possible to review the quality of a relationship and to automatically improve it. The structure of the triangle automatically changes, because the other relationship partner will have to adapt to the change, which in turn opens up new perspectives. Strategic family therapy—embedded in solution-oriented and resource-focused thinking—therefore makes it possible to mobilize blocked systems.

Of course, the point is not to turn good relationships into bad ones but, rather, to use solution-oriented interventions to improve crisis-ridden relationships. The focus of the relationship partners needs to be realigned in order to reconfigure the "family dance." We have found this strategic approach to be effective time and again.

More Structure, Please!

Important methods used in family therapy today developed out of structural family therapy (Minuchin, 1997) and can be incorporated in the form of structural interventions. Particularly important are the family structures per se (i.e., the generations—parents and children or parents and grandparents) and the boundaries between the generations or between the family and the outside world.

When working with families, Minuchin emphasizes the importance of checking whether the subsystems are adequately separated from one another. The subsystems represent the different generations in a family: the grandparents, the parents, the siblings. It is important for clear boundaries between the subsystems to be established and maintained—boundaries between the generations should not be blurred (see Figure 5). Boundaries can be directly observed in the way families divide up responsibilities, in the roles they assume, and in the way they communicate with one another. During therapy these boundaries can be changed and reformed through communication and with the aid of exercises; the family is newly "structured."

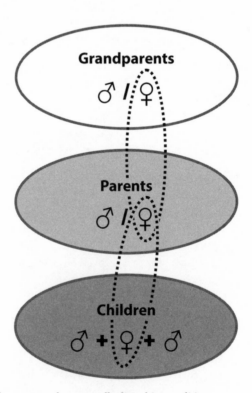

Figure 5: (Sub)systems and structurally disturbing coalitions

It is important to point out that in contrast to a constructivist approach, the structural family therapist approaches the task with his own idea of how a family should function. This is of course a deviation from our constructivist framework, although the structural perspective can be considered as one possible perspective. Furthermore, a resource of structural family therapy is required here: clarity—and with it, a strict, almost dogmatic approach.

When observing the structure of a family, it is important to keep the following in mind: Do the parents function as parents, or is one of the children interfering on the parent level? Is one of the parents in collusion with one of the children? In the latter case, neither the parent nor the child(ren) subsystem would be intact.

It is very common for the grandparent subsystem to become involved in the parent subsystem or for there to be a coalition between one of the grandparents and one of the grandchildren. In some families this crossing of the boundaries is an established part of the family dynamics and has become a matter of course.

One possible intervention is to share your own observation:

> *I would like to describe to you what I have seen. May I? I have noticed that every time I ask you something, your mom answers for you. Does that happen a lot?*

Usually a simple question like this is enough for the indirectly (circularly) addressed parent to feel directly addressed and to hold back from answering the next time the child is asked a question. This is the start of change!

Sometimes it is even necessary to provocatively ask whom the parent is married to: his or her spouse or one of the children? These *provocative questions* (which you should first get your clients' permission to ask) often lead the affected person(s) to see things from a new perspective and thereby instigate change.

A further possibility to clarify these constellations is to ask the family to do something during the conversation. For example, if parents are not convinced of the need to pull together to discipline a difficult child (maximum 12 years old), you could ask them to all stand up, with the child in the middle. Have both parents pull at one arm of the child—they will realize that they are both exerting themselves but that of course the child does not budge, because both parents are pulling in opposite directions. Then ask one of the parents to change sides and to now pull at one arm together with the other partner. The child has no other option now but to move in the direction of the parents. We have found this simple intervention to be very effective and more powerful than a thousand words.

Often the seating order of the family is enough to reveal what might be going on in the family.

Careful: It is good to observe these family constellations, but you should not be tempted to draw conclusions too quickly (see **Playing with hypotheses**, page 161).

An example: Family dynamics in seating order

A mother and her two sons came to therapy because the youngest son had been refusing to participate in school for some time before finally being admitted to a clinic. The parents had separated years ago but were clearly both still licking their wounds. At the first appointment with the mother and two sons—the eldest son and the father had not been included in the therapy so far—Son 1 was fairly detached from the proceedings. His mother explained that her two sons did not get along.

The seating arrangement was as follows:

Son 1 — Mother — Son 2

The mother sat in the middle between Son 1 (the elder) and Son 2 (the younger). There was constant physical contact between the mother and her younger son.

Intervention: *I would like you to all stand up and change places: Ms X, swap with your younger son, and Son 1, can you sit in your mother's seat? Thank you!*

Son 2 — Son 1 — Mother

After they had swapped places, the mother was asked, *How does that feel for you?* After considering the question, she answered: "It's more normal." The elder son said, "S'okay" and the younger son, "I like it!" The last response, in particular, was surprising.

As the session progressed, the brothers began to interact more, which was clearly a relief to the mother. The following week the patient attended the school at the clinic—from which he had been chronically absent—for the first time in weeks.

Sometimes it is good to give families the opportunity to experience what change *feels* like. This is best achieved through "movement improvisations." And almost as an aside, without the issue being addressed directly, the subsystem—in this case the sibling system—was restored. Intervening in the seating order is not a dogmatic decision of right and wrong but an offer to try something different with the option that it may turn out to be completely inappropriate. For example, Ben Furman (2011) often spontaneously invites his clients to demonstrate exactly the behavior that they are actually trying to change in the course of therapy.

Don't Be Misled by a Symptom

Doctors are trained to find symptoms, to make connections between symptoms and the results of tests and laboratory findings, to make differential diagnoses, and then to decide on particular therapies.

The counselor or therapist is confronted with a problem, and he may make a hypothesis from which he develops a therapeutic strategy. Experience may have taught him, for example, that certain symptoms or disorders arise only in particular family constellations.

Both approaches make sense, but they neglect the immediate context of the symptom. The areas to examine will emphasize the problem's context:

What does the symptom mean for the affected person?

What does the symptom mean for his environment?

Who benefits from it?

Who suffers the most?

How does the symptom affect daily routines?

How does the symptom affect family relationships?

A symptom gains significance from its context.

An example: Symptoms within context

John and Michael come to therapy with their respective mothers because they are wetting themselves.

John's mother is extremely upset and feels under pressure to solve the problem as quickly as possible. Michael's mother does not really have a problem but has realized that Michael's sister, who is three years younger, has not wet herself for a long time. She simply does not want to make the mistake of waiting too long to deal with the issue.

John's wetting problem has a completely different significance in his disciplined family than Michael's does in his more laid-back family.

This has far-reaching consequences for the therapy: John's wetting problem has to be treated completely differently from Michael's because the level of psychological strain they are causing in the two families is very different.

What's more, a diagnosis cannot be based on a single psychiatric or psychosomatic symptom. Any symptom can signify practically anything—which means that the diagnosis also depends on the context. For example, abdominal pain can mean that the patient is under too much pressure or is bored, it can indicate a traumatic experience, it can indicate constipation or a marital problem, and so forth.

> The symptom or problem is therefore nothing more than an invitation, on the one hand, to look more closely and, on the other hand, to find a solution.

The Art of Questioning

Without questions, there are no answers. Without questions, there is also no job! Any doctor/patient contact begins with: *What can I do for you?* This is a fairly innocuous question but there is more to it than meets the eye. It is similar to: *How can I serve you?* It is reminiscent of the earliest days of medicine, when the expert in the art of healing was a servant to the patient. With this question you become a kind of servant, a helper. In terms of this book, the question could be translated as: *How can I remind you that you are the expert? What can I do so that you know what to do?*

In terms of the effect it can have, questioning should not be underestimated. Questioning is part of therapy. The point of questioning is to steer the patient's thoughts in the direction of a solution. Steve de Shazer, founder of solution-focused brief therapy, completed therapies in which he only asked questions (de Shazer, 1989). Even if the purity of this approach might seem a little extreme, it clarifies that questioning is very effective.

But experience has shown that there are some rules that need to be adhered to when questioning.

Therapy starts with questioning!

Many doctors and therapists think it is a sign of their expertise if they ask lots of clever questions. Most questions that are asked in a medical or therapeutic context are aimed at filling gaps in knowledge: I ask so that I know more, so that I can gain a clearer picture of the symptom, so that I can assess the problem or the course of the disease, and so on.

If you work in a solution-oriented and resource-focused and constructivist way, you are intrigued by how people handle their problems. Your questions should express interest, curiosity, eagerness. On the other hand, the questions should also make clear that the patient is actively involved in creating his problem. A problem rarely comes out of the blue!

What Makes a Good Question?

The question is met by silence

If the client answers your question right away, it probably means he has answered the same question many times before, or that the question "only" served the purpose of filling in some gaps in knowledge with already familiar facts.

A good question is "beneficially disruptive" (Ludewig, 2005). That means it is surprising and unfamiliar and makes the patient look at the problem differently from the way he did before. It opens up new perspectives and extends the patient's context.

How do you "do" the problem?

The patient is invited to describe every step that led to his problem (de Shazer, 1997): Who does what when?

When a child has his umpteenth tantrum, it makes sense to probe deeper: Who said what, how, and when? Who reacted how, who reacted next? What did the child do? What did the father do at that moment? What did the mother do at that moment? Thus, a picture of the situation is established, and this often causes patients to smirk, because they suddenly realize that the problem always follows the same pattern. Questioning alone has aided progress!

Or, the question invites the patient to describe how he has dealt with the problem, that is, how the problem has affected family life, and what measures have already been taken within the family.

A case example: *How exactly do you do that?*

A father came to us with his five-and-a-half-year-old son, whose symptoms—impulsiveness, restlessness, and lack of concentration—seemed to indicate attention deficit hyperactivity disorder. He reported that because of this problem, the family had simply avoided "big events" and therefore hadn't really broached the issue of getting outside help.

Our next question, *How exactly do you do that?*, received the following answer: "We simply avoid situations that involve more than two people over and above our family. So if we have visitors, or if we are invited somewhere, numbers have to be strictly limited—otherwise the situation becomes unbearable."

By describing the way they dealt with the problem, the parents became aware of their increasing social isolation and agreed that school—which the boy was about to start—was going to be a daily big event.

It was clear that further measures needed to be taken.

The question makes the patient stop and think

The most important task of the therapist is not to understand too quickly. Patients usually feel in safe hands if somebody understands what they mean. The feeling of being in safe hands often means leaning back and relaxing—and although this is important for successful therapy, there also needs to be a certain amount of pressure. The patient must be in a position to develop new ideas for himself. He won't do this if he is too relaxed.

That is why the therapist has to work on both fronts. On the one hand, the client has to feel that he is in safe hands with the therapist. The therapist can express this by positively acknowledging the client's previous attempts to solve the problem, by showing interest in the patient's life stories, and expressing admiration for the way he has coped with his problem. On the other hand, the therapist wants to understand how the problem repeats itself—not in terms of repressed early-childhood experiences that manifest in dysfunctional behavior, but in terms of how the problem happens in concrete terms.

For the patient it is important that the therapist does not understand anything to start with. This "not understanding" leads the patient to put his thoughts in order and to get a feeling of how and in what contexts his problem arises.

A good question deserves a good answer

A striking feature of therapies we have observed is how many good questions go unanswered. This is why another important task of the therapist is to make sure that his questions are answered. Many patients have mastered the technique of pretending to answer: They say a lot but have not actually answered the question. Because the point of the question is to help the patient progress, it is the duty of the therapist to make sure that the question is answered. Otherwise, a question becomes part of the patient's former solution to the problem and does not lead to a new solution, let alone increase his sense of possibilities.

Ask permission to ask a question

Some questions can seem too close to the bone, too personal, unusual, or alienating. In order not to intimidate the patient, it is advisable—before ambushing him with such a question—to ask permission to ask it. The "asking permission" intervention strengthens the client-therapist bond and makes the client feel that he is being taken seriously.

What makes a good question?

- The therapist asks permission to ask the question.
- The question is met by silence.
- The question makes the patient stop and think.
- The patient gives a good answer to the question.

The Most Important Types of Questions

Some basic categories of questions are particularly important for a solution-oriented approach.

The most important types of questions

- What-else questions
- Scaling questions
- Coping questions
- Exception-seeking questions
- What's-it-good-for questions
- Questions that make a difference
- Hypothetical questions
- Aggravating questions
- Subjunctive questions
- Provoking questions
- The Miracle Question

What-else questions

The "what-else" question is used for more detailed probing in order to understand a situation better. By repeatedly asking this question, the patient provides a more detailed answer and gains a clearer picture of the problem he is describing—sometimes new insights come to light that can help the client develop a solution.

An example: *What else?*

Eight-year-old Lara comes with her mother for a consultation, because for some time she has been soiling herself. The girl is good at school, is in second grade, and loves dancing and ballet. She is clearly embarrassed by her problem and answers any questions connected to it very briefly and reluctantly.

Her parents have tried to send her to the bathroom for a quarter of an hour after every meal, but this hasn't worked. Lara says she doesn't like it there.

Tell me, what exactly don't you like about going to the bathroom?
It is cold there.
What else?
It is a bit scary because the ceiling lamp is very dim.

What else?

I do not like the fact that you cannot lock the door to the (guest) bathroom, and I worry that somebody might suddenly come in.

What else?

It also often smells bad.

What else?

While Lara continues to think, her mother—who has been silent up to now—joins in the conversation. She suggests that her daughter could use her parents' bathroom on the first floor, which is warm and nicely decorated.

At the next meeting a few weeks later, a beaming Lara proudly reports that her mother's idea was really great and that most days she no longer has a problem.

Scaling questions

You can ask clients to rate their problems on a scale of, say, 1 to 10, or 1 to 100, or even 1 to 1000, for example, to find out how the client perceives his stress levels or how much a problem troubles him. You could even ask, *How high or low would the scale have to go to reflect your personal stress level? Would it have to go into minus numbers?* This approach has lots of variations; for example, the client can then be given the task of trying to move one level up the scale, or to imagine how that might feel.

We return to the questioning technique of scaling in the **General Interventions** section (*see page 60*).

Coping questions

Coping questions are asked in order to express admiration for something great that the patient has done, but also to get the patient to recognize how he achieved what he did. Some examples:

- *How did you manage to cope with it for so long?*
- *How did you manage to finish your degree under those circumstances?*
- *If you would rate yourself at 4 at the moment, what did you do to get from 1 to 4?* (*see **Scaling**, page 81*)

These questions are designed to elicit information about the patient's resources and at the same time to show him that he has already used these resources successfully as a coping mechanism. The question shows respect and admiration.

Exception-seeking questions (*see also **Asking about exceptions**, page 79*)

It is rare for a problem to be omnipresent. It is therefore interesting to find out if there are times when the problem is not there, and how the client manages to stop the problem from arising. However, it is important not to make it too easy for the client. If he can answer the question with "yes" or "no," the conversation will probably end quickly. It is therefore advisable to pose the question as

Tell me about the days (situations) when it wasn't like that!

You are implying that there have been such days and inviting the client to think about them.

The what's-it-good-for question

With the question "What's it good for?" or "What's the point of that?" you are implying that there has to be a point to every form of behavior. This should make the patient stop and think about his behavioral patterns and his standard ways of reacting to situations so that he can create the conditions to bring about change.

This shifts the perspective from "It's always been like that!" to "Yes, and why?" The why question is frequently asked in other types of therapy. From a solution-oriented perspective, the why question is a backward-looking question, which tries to explain current behavioral patterns in relation to past circumstances. But children often show us how ineffective the question is, for example, when their parents ask why they tipped over the glass of milk yet again and they do no respond. The why question is usually completely redundant and a useless attempt at gaining rational control over things that cannot be controlled.

According to de Shazer, a problem is something that intensifies because patients keep trying the same solution, because no alternative approaches are available to them. Therefore, from a solution-oriented perspective, the question to be asked in relation to a persistent problem is not why but *What is it good for?* This gives new significance to the problem, and aspects of it may even be incorporated into a subsequent solution. Attempted solutions usually reveal many resources that the client can use to develop a new solution.

Questions that make a difference

In his preface to *More than Miracles* (de Shazer & Dolan, 2008), Varga von Kibèd writes: "As Steve and Insoo have shown us again and again, they never know before getting an answer what the meaning of their question was."

The reason to ask a question is not to gain information; that is, the aim of the question is not to find out particular things or to maneuver the client in a particular direction. A question is an expression of the therapist's curiosity, without it having a particular meaning from the outset. It is, in fact, important to free yourself from the meaning of a question. If, for example, you ask a question with a preconceived idea of the answer, you will inevitably perceive the client's answer insofar as it confirms your own expectations or hypotheses, with the result that you miss what else is being said, and what is not being said.

It is only when you listen precisely to what is being said, and how it is being said, that you hear what is really important. In this situation the client-therapist bond is important: You have to use the words of the client as precisely as possible and focus only on what he has already told you.

The significance of your question becomes clear only with the answer. That is why you can never know in advance how, for example, **The Miracle Question** will end (*see pages 32 and 87*). Steve de Shazer and Yvonne Dolan (2008) emphasize this time and again. It may be that the suggested miracle—that is, the disappearance of the problem—gives rise to another problem. Or the client comes because of Problem A but, after the miracle has been described, depicts Problem B. But that does not matter. *The client answers what he has heard, not what he has been told.* That is why the question becomes clear only once an answer has been given.

If an answer seems unrealistic, the client should be made to corroborate his answer in concrete terms: *How would that look?* or *Is that realistic in your opinion?*

"Let's say that . . .": Hypothetical questions

Questions should arouse the client's interest, make him curious, and invite him to join in the conversation.

Hypothetical questions are about gathering information and gaining a first impression of the client, in order to then formulate positive and resource-focused assumptions. Questions about the client's life—for example, his personality, his family, his career, his interests—can form the basis of hypotheses (Kindl-Beilfuß, 2008):

> *Judging from our conversation so far, I am assuming that you are a person who does not give up easily . . .*
>
> *Let's say we would continue with the treatment: Do you think you would be able to change anything else?*
>
> *If yes, what exactly would you change? How would you notice the change? How would others notice it? Would it change things for the better or worse?*
>
> *Which areas/aspects would continue to improve/get worse/stabilize?*

Questions of this kind are generally questions for opening up possibilities: *Assuming that . . .* or *What would happen if . . . ?*

Of course, clients also develop hypotheses about the clinic or practice where they intend to start therapy and, besides their specific concerns, often come with their own preconceived ideas and expectations.

Aggravating questions: "Could it be even worse?"

What can we do to aggravate a situation (Watzlawick, 1983)?

Sometimes helping clients requires an unusual approach. Questions that depict the problem or concern as worse than the way it was or is being experienced are an example of a provocative intervention, which usually involves some humor:

> *How could you make the situation even worse?*
>
> *Over the next few weeks, what could you concretely do to make the positive effects disappear again?*
>
> *What would have to happen to now really confirm all of your self-doubts?*
>
> *Who could contribute most to confirming your doubts? Who the second-most (and so on)?*
>
> *What would you have to do so that things really fall apart?*

Before asking an aggravating question, it is helpful to first gain the client's permission to take an unusual approach. These specific questions invite the client to reevaluate his current situation and to perceive it from a fresh perspective in relation to other experiences. You also make the client more aware of how he actually "did" his problem.

The power of the subjunctive

As an expert in the classic sense, we tend to use the indicative form: "That's the way it is," or "You have this problem because . . ."

We may be offering the patient an explanation of his problem, but we are explaining it in relation to our professional knowledge. However, it is likely that our knowledge does not correspond to the patient's problem context.

That is why we recommend using the subjunctive rather than the indicative form:

> *Could it be that . . . ?*
>
> *Perhaps I am mistaken, but it could be that . . .*

The subjective gives the patient the chance to consider whether what has been said corresponds to his context or not. It opens up new perspectives and can thereby lead to new solutions.

An indicative statement, on the other hand, closes down a conversation and simply reaffirms the role of therapist as expert, in the traditional sense.

May I provoke you? (Being polite never hurts!)

Whatever you do, ask for permission! The patient usually wants to cooperate with you, because you are trying to help him. He will only rarely say "no."

We return to this piece of advice frequently in the course of this book in relation to specific interventions. Asking permission makes patients feel respected and strengthens the client-therapist bond.

An amusing example: *Why is he allowed to do that?*

A few years ago, in the sauna at the gym, I (F.C.) was chatting with a professional carpet dealer. He began telling me about his youngest son, who didn't do things the way he wanted.

His older son was studying, helped out in the store, and didn't mind lugging carpets around. The younger son, on the other hand, came back home when he felt like it, took no interest at all in the family business, and was doing badly at school.

I could hear the question before it was even asked: "What can I do?" Because I couldn't really imagine having a therapeutic interview in the gym, I simply asked: "Why is he allowed to behave like that?"

This unleashed a new litany of examples of his younger son's dreadful behavior, which I responded to with the same question: "Why is he allowed to behave like that?"

As the hourglass in the sauna ran out, he thanked me and left deep in thought.

A year later, I was sitting alone in the sauna when the door opened and the carpet dealer came in. He recognized me right away. "Did I remember . . . ?"

I answered: "Yes, of course. How is your younger son getting on?"

"Fantastically!" After our brief conversation the year before, he asked himself: "Yes, why is he allowed to behave like that?" He had discussed this with his wife, and since then the son was no longer allowed to carry on the way he had been and had changed his ways. He was so happy!

Yet another year passed, and we met again—as if by arrangement—in the gym. The family was doing well.

What does this story teach us? Asking questions is often much more effective than giving direct advice. A question always fulfills two functions:

1. The questioner is curious and interested and wants to find out more.
2. The person being questioned said something that was interesting enough to prompt further questions.

The questioner has to decide whether to ask more questions or not. Either way, a dialogue has been established.

The Miracle Question

The Miracle Question is practically the hallmark of solution-focused brief therapy and most clearly reflects the thinking behind it. Based on our ongoing experiences, we would like to share some additional observations that strike us as important in relation to the Miracle Question (see **The Miracle Question**, page 87).

IDEA. Essentially, the Miracle Question asks the patient to imagine what life would be like if all his problems miraculously disappeared, and how that might happen. There are now many formulations of the Miracle Question (e.g., de Jong & Berg, 2008; de Shazer & Dolan, 2008). The aim of the Miracle Question is to get the client to imagine solutions based on his personal situation.

In contrast to when the Miracle Question was first developed, it is now standard practice to incorporate the client's context into the question. As a result, the relationship between the question and the context is emphasized from the start, and there is not such a big gap between the client's current reality and what he imagines after the miracle has happened. There is a greater chance that the developed solutions will work.

METHOD. Step by step, the Miracle Question technique might look like this:

(a) Preamble to arouse the client's curiosity:

> *Can I ask a rather unusual question?* or *Is it okay if I ask a question that requires a lot of imagination to answer?*

With this preamble you generate a "yes vibe" with the client, which in turn makes it easier for him to answer, and more likely that he will do so. (See *also* **Creating a "yes" vibe**, page 93.)

(b) The warm-up to the question: Before actually asking the question, you pick up on the client's situation by, for example, depicting how he comes home after work and has a rest or gets some other things done. Or—with the client's help—you outline his usual daily routine.

This is followed by the Miracle Question, and begins with *You are tired and go to bed . . .* and so on.

Tips. In order to avoid getting exaggerated or flimsy answers, the question(s) should relate to the actual problem situation.

Afterward, it is a good idea to give the client a little break. The client has time to immerse himself in this "solution zone," the therapist has time to switch on his antenna and to carefully listen to what the client is saying and how he is saying it. The rather hypnotic effect of the question should not be disturbed by a rushed approach. Only in a calm atmosphere will you pick up on the nuances, the practical aspects of the miracle, the concrete things.

For example, it is not important to know what others will do differently when the miracle occurs but, rather, how the client himself contributes to others doing things differently—and, in turn, how the changes in others bring about change in the client.

The aim of the question is always to suggest that the client is able to change his behavior, so that the gap between the miracle and the implementation of the miracle is as small as possible.

This in turn means that the result of the miracle should then be implemented in very small, concrete steps.

The Miracle Question then really does cause a miracle (de Shazer & Dolan, 2008).

Types of questions

- What-else questions
- Scaling questions
- Coping questions
- Exception-seeking questions
- What's-it-good-for questions
- Questions that make a difference
- Hypothetical questions
- Aggravating questions

Other Good Systemic Solution- and Resource-Focused Questions

Other types of question have resulted from our daily practice and can be adapted to a variety of situations. However, from our clinic-based experiences, the most important of all systemic solution-oriented questions are still the following:

How will you know that . . . ?

. . . it was worthwhile?

. . . things have changed?

. . . you are doing something differently?

Of course, there are many variations of this question. All of them work best when accompanied by subsequent questioning along the lines of *what else?*

In the process, various issues can be more directly addressed, such as the client's motto for life or his wishes for the future or for his family or friends:

Which motto has influenced you and even helped you get ahead?

What do you do to recharge your batteries? Who or what, particularly, helps you when nothing seems to be working anymore?

What reasons are there to nonetheless feel confident?

The 10-minute question

What will we need to have spoken about for you to say, at the end of the session, that it was a worthwhile 10 minutes?

Summary: When is a question a good question?

- If it cannot be answered right away.
- A good question triggers new thoughts and ideas in the client, who then needs time to *think them through*. Questions that can be answered like a shot have missed their mark or were answered without thinking.
- A question—at least in a therapeutic context—should open up *new perspectives* or act as a catalyst for change. In the language of psychotherapy: questions have to be disruptive.
- A *disruption* is a changed mental state, which through a combination of surprise—triggered by some kind of change—and the opening up of a new perspective gets the patient thinking in a solution-oriented way. In psychotherapy it is important to create disruptions regularly but sparingly, so that new solutions become possible.

The Therapist's Treasure Chest

As systemic, solution-oriented, and resource-focused therapists, whatever we do or don't do, ask or don't ask, we are always working toward increasing the client's sense of possibility and self-efficacy—because it could be that he will find the solution himself!

Using Metaphors: What Has Amtrak Got to Do with Psychotherapy?

Tom Levold (2006) describes the use of metaphors as a way of transferring the structural, visual features of particular areas of experience to other areas of experience. A "dialogue" develops between an image giver and the image receiver, with the goal of making the receiver able to grasp and implement the image of the giver. The image giver may also be able to broaden the image receiver's horizon of possibilities.

An example: The chameleon metaphor

During the live supervision of a family therapy session followed by a reflective team discussion, the team picked up on the word "chameleon," which the mother had used to describe her eight-year-old son Joshua when she realized that he would make good progress during his therapy in the clinic but always lapse back into his old behavior at home—like a chameleon.

The reflecting team began to discuss the advantages and disadvantages of a chameleon and asked themselves whether perhaps the reason Joshua changed his behavior like a chameleon was to secure his survival in the family.

When the family reflected on this theory, the mother picked up on the metaphor and realized that she, too, used chameleon-like strategies and from then on was better able to understand and accept her son's behavior.

In resource- and solution-focused approaches, using metaphors is effective only if the resources of the metaphor are emphasized in order to make the metaphor available to the client. The client is thereby presented with new resources to supplement his existing ones. According to Levold, the metaphor creates a bridge between the problem as it is experienced (nonverbally) and a verbalized solution.

Levold argues that metaphors help us think about certain subjects or issues selectively: We channel our thoughts with the help of a particular image. In terms of therapy, this means that the more obvious the metaphorical structuring of a problem is, the more readily the metaphor will be received and reapplied, and the less room there is for alternative perspectives. We must make the most, then, of even simple metaphors. For example, part of a chameleon's resilience comes from its ability to adapt to its environment. A person who is described as a chameleon for relapsing into destructive behavioral patterns when at home (a problem) is also, in a different sense, being labeled resilient and able to confront problems by being adaptable, which can be considered a solution. The metaphor, by this internal contradiction, may seem broken and less useful. But consider that the chameleon also has very different abilities that could contribute to the solution of a problem. Simply adapting to the problem is usually not enough to solve it. For example, the relative safety that the chameleon achieves by using his adaptability—for better or worse—allows the chameleon to make the problem feel less threatening and to gain time to think about other solutions. Thus, even the gray areas of a simple metaphor can be therapeutically brought into consideration in the search for a solution.

The Art of Not Understanding: Nonsolutions Are Also Solutions

One of the most important tasks of the therapist or counselor is not to understand too quickly. This issue comes up again and again in seminars and discussions with colleagues—a reason to look at it in a bit more detail. How do we actually *not* understand?

Even if you have absolutely understood how the client's problem is happening at home, it is important to communicate to him that you have not (yet) understood it, for example, with such questions as

> *I still haven't quite understood—could you explain it to me again?*
>
> *I've understood a lot already, but I haven't quite grasped the part about . . .*
>
> *I'd like to go through it with you again so that I can be really sure I've understood it. Can you explain it to me one more time?*

These questions have the effect of redirecting the client's focus and making him concentrate on specific details of how he does things. This technique is also used in home-video training, in which video sequences are closely analyzed to reveal strengths of the system.

The detailed questioning results in the patient analyzing the way he does things, and he may begin to question or change things himself. Rotthaus (2005) also calls it "exacting":

> "What *exactly* do you mean by that?"
>
> *Exactly which ideas occur to you in relation to this? And how exactly could you use these in the future?*

In other words, it is important to take time and analyze the situation closely with the client.

By not understanding, you also change the client's attitude: Instead of depicting his situation emotionally, he is invited to analyze his own behavior and processes in minute detail and to achieve an objective, unemotional distance.

It is therefore far more important that the patient or system understand the family dynamics than whether the therapist does. The way in which a family learns to deal with its problem can be described using the metaphor of a dance: After initially painstaking work at the beginning, when the steps have to be carefully practiced, the dance eventually flows of its own accord. Later, mistakes in the step sequence can be picked up on and corrected only by analyzing the steps that were actually danced. Similarly, we all dance a variety of dances in our everyday lives.

The Art of Making a Connection: Therapeutic Communication Techniques

Who's Leading Whom?

Grabbe (2010) philosophizes that the term "leading a therapeutic discussion" is actually misleading, because it suggests that one person is leading and everyone else is following: "Actually everyone comes together and creates something new! Perhaps *mis*leading a discussion makes more sense?"

A therapist will often have more success with this approach than if he gives directives. Ultimately, it is not the therapist's solution that will help the client, but his own—one that suits his context and personal reality.

As an expert in communication techniques and intervention methods, the therapist is responsible for the structure; he can dictate the framework and ensure that a solution is reached in the end. But the client remains the expert when it comes to his problem, and therefore also the expert in finding possible solutions. The client's topics of conversation may lead the therapist astray and take the conversation in unexpected directions. The therapist is curious to find out where the conversation is heading, becomes immersed, and ends up giving the client more space to express his concerns. The solution-finding process can be embarked on together.

Establishing a Bond with the Client

Establishing a bond with the client is vital not just in psychotherapy (Mrochen & Bierbaum-Luttermann, 2007). This ability to "connect" is equally important in counseling, coaching, and other advisory roles. It comes down to establishing a relationship with the other person on an equal footing. A successful therapeutic relationship starts with establishing a bond. A variety of factors contribute to achieving this:

- Creating a pleasant and relaxing atmosphere in the room
- Being in tune with . . .
    - ° the body language of the client
    - ° his tone of voice
    - ° the speed at which he speaks
    - ° his mood (how well does the therapist adapt?)
- The client's age (you speak completely differently to a child than to an adolescent!)

Being a good observer is extremely important for establishing a bond. It will occur automatically if, rather than judging yourself to be an expert, you keep an open mind and listen to what the client tells you before discussing—and helping him to implement—his ideas for change. Without careful observation, this would not be possible.

Body language can also be important for connecting with a client. For example, the best place to approach a child might be in the toy corner, sitting on the floor—this is the only way of talking to the child at eye level. During a conversation, body language can also be used to connect with the client. Sometimes the patient may feel provoked; sometimes it will stir him into life. A man who is slouching will notice that the therapist has adopted the same pose—he will be surprised, and the foundations for change will have been laid.

Children also react with great interest when a doctor suddenly behaves exactly the way they do—a rapport has been established!

Therapeutic settings: When do we work with whom?

Children

Whoever comes, comes. Furman (2011) regards the therapist as a host, and the client can decide together with the therapist who else will be invited and formulate an appropriate invitation. If the client is an adult, there is a good chance that he will come alone. However, it is not unusual for him to allow his girlfriend, partner, spouse, or parent(s) to come with him. Ultimately, the client decides.

It is different with children, however. Usually the mother accompanies the child to the first meeting, although it is becoming increasingly common for both parents to come with their child or for both parents to come without the child. Sometimes the parents come with their child(ren) but assume that the child(ren) will not be involved in the discussion. This is usually because the parents want to avoid forcing their children into the limelight.

In rare cases, the adults insist that they should first speak with the therapist alone, while the child waits to be invited to join in. We have had different experiences with this approach but have usually found that when they are excluded, children paint a far more dramatic picture of what is being discussed than is actually the case.

Other parents come with the assumption that they themselves will not be involved and that only the child goes in. If, on the other hand, parents come to the initial meeting without the child, the child should be included in the next session unless, for some reason, the child has absolutely no interest in coming.

The Therapist's Treasure Chest

Working with circular methods enables the absent person to be included, so that it is possible to do therapy with someone who is not even there. We started to invite into the consultation room everyone who came along. An interesting question to ask right at the start of the session is how the family decided who was going to come along.

Adolescents

If you ask adolescents if they would prefer to have a one-on-one conversation, or would rather have their friends with them, they are often surprised by the suggestion but quick to take up the offer.

The client's teachers, social workers, and so on, who instigated the meeting in the first place, will usually be willing to be included in the subsequent therapy process if asked.

By the second meeting, the client should definitely also attend, and the family can decide who else will come. At the next meeting the same subject can be brought up again: How did they decide who would come this time?

But it is the same at the second meeting: Whoever comes, comes. And the person who is absent is often the most important one.

By at least the age of 14, adolescents are entitled to a one-on-one meeting. Parents are not always the best therapy partners for adolescents, and adolescents rightfully feel the need to work things out for themselves.

In a one-on-one meeting with an adolescent, is important to emphasize that what they tell you will not leave the four walls of the consultation room. It is vital to provide this safe environment, although with the caveat that if self-harming or the harming of others becomes an issue, you will be forced to involve the parents or guardians. It might be the case that a series of one-on-one meetings reveal important issues to do with the client's family environment, making it necessary to include this environment in the therapy. This needs to be discussed with the client. A possible intervention might be:

> *Since I have assured you that I will not pass on what you have told me without your permission, I now need your advice! To find a satisfactory solution, I think it is important to include certain other people. How can we do this? In your opinion, who could this person or these people be?*

It is also permissible to adapt the setting.

Siblings

Parents and siblings are particularly important when working with families. Brock (2010) describes the concept of drawing on the multiple relationships in families with several children. By including siblings in the psychotherapeutic setting, he sees an opportunity to integrate more perspectives and to explore innovative solution approaches.

Despite issues such as sibling rivalry and envy, relationships between siblings can be used as a resource (Vogt, Hubert-Schnelle, & Clavée, 2010). Sibling dynamics can be addressed in family drawings or in work with genograms.

Peers

The inclusion of peers is usually an important socialization instrument for children and adolescents. Friends and classmates of the same age encourage the development of personal interests and are part of the process of breaking away from the parents. Together, peers develop private language codes, explanatory models, and solution strategies that can be used to provide support in problem situations (Lenz, 2008). We frequently fall back on this in our day-to-day psychiatric work with children and adolescents.

A case example: Oliver

Oliver, a tall 16-year-old, had already turned up to several individual, group, and family therapy sessions. Every time he turned up, his attitude was a mixture of "I'm coming because I have to" and "Let's see, maybe something will come out of it . . . "

However, everyone involved was unanimous that no changes had come about: Oliver was still "never in the mood for anything"—particularly not school; he experimented with alcohol and drugs and seldom stuck to rules. The situation within and outside of the family threatened to escalate, so the option of inpatient treatment in a clinic was increasingly discussed—an option that was vehemently opposed by Oliver.

Finally, Oliver agreed to the suggestion of inviting his friends along. His parents agreed to inform the parents of the respective friends and to ask their permission. Out of five invited friends, three turned up to the next session.

At the beginning of this joint session, after the original idea of inviting his friends had again been elucidated, Oliver agreed to briefly describe his situation.

The therapist then asked his friends: *What would you advise Oliver to do now?* After briefly considering the question, they made the following suggestions:

- He should talk to his parents.
- He should make sure that he doesn't cause any more trouble.
- We'll have to talk about it, because I've got exactly the same problem at home.
- We could talk to his parents about it.

When Oliver was asked which of the suggestions he would act upon, he smiled and said: "The best thing would be for all four of us to sit down with our parents, but since that won't work, I suppose I will have to come next time with my parents."

Therapist: *Which next time do you mean?*

Oliver: "Well, next session."

The next session did not result in a complete turnaround, but Oliver felt more confident about addressing difficult issues like violence in the family, his expectations of his parents, and his own willingness to make compromises.

Involving friends in therapy is still relatively unexplored territory. It is already an accepted fact that, in group therapy, the other members of the group are more helpful than the therapist. In contrast, involving a patient's friends in therapy is still a rare exception.

We were reminded of this when we worked with a patient's classmates in the setting of a "reflecting family" (see **Reflecting positions**, page 143).

In terms of possible therapeutic or counseling settings, other options include texting with adolescents and conversing with the parents, particularly fathers, via e-mail. And probably we will soon all just be Skyping in any case!

Structuring the therapy

Starting therapy

"A magic force dwells in every beginning." This quote, from the poem *Stages* by Hermann Hesse, illuminates how new beginnings invite change and how the course of life, with its inevitable twists and turns, can be positively utilized.

But it is not just each new stage of life that invites change; the start of a therapy or treatment process does, too. You start something new, are given the opportunity to find out what could be changed, and perhaps also leave familiar things behind.

The resources of everyone involved can be creatively and diversely drawn upon if the client and therapist keep these opportunities in view and explore them in a safe and secure environment. According to de Shazer and Dolan (2008), it is sometimes even possible to directly address changes that have come about before the first meeting:

> *Have you noticed any changes since you made today's appointment?*

There are many different ways to start off the conversation, depending, among other things, on the personality of the client. It is always important to define a framework for the conversation, to clarify wishes and goals, and to give the client the feeling that you are taking his concern seriously and that he is being given the space to express himself, even in the case of rushed, unprepared meetings.

At the beginning of every conversation, we find it useful to outline how the available time could be used most productively and to ask the client what ought to be addressed in the given time, in order for him to feel at the end that the session was worthwhile:

> *What would have to happen during this session for you to feel that it was a success?*

Pauses and silence

De Shazer (1989) frequently reiterated that pauses were the most important part of a conversation. By not immediately answering a question or coming up with a further question, there is time to linger on or supplement what has been said, or for further ideas to develop.

Even when clients (and therapists/counselors) find them hard to endure, pauses or prolonged silences are a useful strategy to address issues in more depth.

Another approach (de Shazer, 1997) involves asking the client to consider how he might answer the same question a few years down the line:

Do you think there will be a more important issue in your life?
Do you think your problem will be as important to you then as it is now?

It can also be very helpful to have short interruptions in the conversation, to break up a conversation at a certain point for a few minutes, particularly during first meetings or in crisis situations. The therapist also needs breaks in the conversation.

As a therapist or counselor, silences can also be hard to bear: inevitably you think that you have to immediately continue with the next sentence, with the result that you lose yourself—and the client—in an ocean of words. Rather than focusing, you end up diluting what you have just said, and the client looks at you blankly or goes into an unintentional trance.

At the start of their training, therapists and counselors are taught tricks such as taking along a notepad to organize their thoughts while listening, or making notes simply to fill the pauses. However, something that worked well to begin with does not always work in the long term: writing can act like a barrier, the connection to the patient is lost, and the process takes on an undesired formality.

Writing is useful and valuable when key points are made or interventions are being fleshed out, or important biographical details have to be recorded—but it can be counterproductive to indiscriminately write everything down. Writing is also useful when it is done with the client, for example, on a big piece of paper in the middle of the table, for noting down important key points or resources.

A pause in the conversation can be therapeutically effective! Good questions are distinguished by "the pause that follows," which is necessary in order to think about the question. But even simple sentences sometimes need a pause in order to have the desired effect: If you can assume that all sentences spoken in a therapeutic context are meaningful, they also need space in order for their meaning to unfold. And space, in this context, means time.

In our role as advisers, we are often not convinced ourselves by what we are saying, and we show this by immediately starting a new sentence after finishing the last one . . . Whether it is regarded as a mechanism of speech or a natural part of talking, the issue of inserting pauses into conversations is an important one, so there is no need to fear the pause.

The client's concern is the therapist's job. Therapists often feel that in order for a therapeutic conversation to be called *work*, it needs to involve talking. The therapist feels almost under pressure to talk as much as possible, regardless of whether the client actually wants to hear what the therapist has to say.

However, if you see it as your job to get the *client* to work, you will realize that the purpose of what you do or say is to get the client to think, to do things differently, to develop new ideas, and so on.

Over time, we have found that the motivational aspect of our therapeutic work has grown in importance. And consequently, the pauses in conversations have become increasingly important. Only by pausing after a sentence is it possible to think about what has just been said.

It is only very occasionally necessary to talk at length in therapeutic settings. One reason might be to tell a story that—followed by a pause—serves as an example or motivation for the client. Another reason might be to put the patient into a trance or to explain certain complicated procedures (psychoeducation).

Sometimes a therapist begins a monologue when he does not know how to proceed, and before the patient starts to realize that the therapist is at a loss, he simply continues to talk. Or even worse: the therapist or counselor cannot bear the silence anymore himself and starts to talk about something randomly.

The subsequent pause is an invitation to the client to think about a sentence or question and to self-reflect, and it provides the therapist with an opportunity to show he is interested. It is also an opportunity to think about further therapeutic steps or to strengthen the bond with the client by showing an interest in his answer and giving him the space and time to really think about the answer. It also shows that you respect your own words, as well as the client's answer and his ability to develop his own ideas.

Inevitably, some conversations don't go as planned, to the point where you might think it would have been better if it hadn't taken place at all. If you do not have a third-party observer at your disposal to watch the proceedings from next door, you have to adopt this metaposition yourself and, if required, abandon or terminate the conversation.

There is nothing wrong with realizing that, *if we continue like this, it will only end badly!—Let's talk about this again later* . . . This kind of conversation can be continued in the next session or after a suitable break. The **Rewind** → **Reset** intervention (*see page 181*) also works well in this kind of situation.

Concluding/reflecting on a conversation

At the end of each session, there should be a brief summing up of the conversation. Either the therapist/counselor or the client can do the summing up:

What has this discussion confirmed for me?

What did I find inspiring or new?

What ideas might I take away with me?

Also not to be forgotten is the classic, solution-oriented "standard task" after the first session (de Shazer, 1989):

> *Between now and the next session, please make a note of everything about your life/your family that should stay exactly as it is!*

Communication techniques with children and adolescents

Depending on their mood and the baseline situation, children and adolescents often have many creative ideas and solution suggestions. Even if parents or other caregivers are not initially convinced about immediately including (all of) the children in the discussion, this approach is worthwhile and usually works.

Bonney (2003) attributes even young children with problem-solving abilities and a high degree of creativity. This is confirmed on a daily basis in our work. Simply by allowing them to be present in a meeting gives children the opportunity to follow the issues and concerns, to ask questions, or to interpret issues from their own point of view.

Therapeutic background and environment

It can basically be said of all forms of therapy and counseling that creativity and imagination, as well as a high degree of flexibility and openness, can be a wonderful engines for creating optimal framework conditions.

Sometimes this special challenge begins with the very first contact (Delfos, 2004). Some children are extremely shy or come to the first session with deep-rooted anxieties. If they have settled in the waiting room and even begun to show an interest in their environment by, for example, picking up a toy, it is a good idea to include this toy in the subsequent meeting.

In extreme cases, initial contact can even be made in the waiting room, as long as there are no other clients waiting and you are not likely to be interrupted. In some cases the floor is better than any kind of chair or seat, particularly if it is comfortable for playing and chatting.

If you have the opportunity to choose or design a room that will be used for meetings with children, adolescents, or families, then a sufficiently spacious room should of course be a priority.

When it comes to the interior design of the room, less is more, but certain pieces of furniture can make the room seem warm and welcoming. One of our colleagues frequently deals with chronically ill adolescents and has found that they often choose to sit somewhere where they can withdraw from direct eye contact. This can be achieved, for example, by having a hanging chair attached to just one spot on the ceiling, so that it can swivel. The client may prefer to turn to the wall and talk to the wall instead of the therapist. If the therapist also turns to face the wall, it is still possible to have a conversation.

Young children also love to be able to hide or avoid eye contact—in which case pop-up tunnels, armchairs with reclining backs, and so on, make this possible.

A mixture of open shelves—preferably higher up the wall—and, if necessary, lockable cupboards also create an environment in which it is possible to work with all age groups and a whole range of behavioral issues.

There are children who remember everything about their visit, for example, where to find particular toys or pens and paper, and who love the ritual of rediscovering and using them during each visit.

Too much wall decoration should be avoided—experience has shown that it can be very distracting. However, some pictures, for example, of a landscape, a road, or a figure, can be useful for starting a conversation—they can work as icebreakers and can help to get the patient's thoughts flowing.

Having a section of the wall hung with pictures drawn by clients motivates many children to also produce something that can be hung there. If there is not enough space for this (which is often the case), the following suggestion can be made:

> *I would love to hang your picture on my wall! Next week you can decide if you want to take it home with you or give it to someone else as a gift.*

Some children and adolescents are very proud when their work is copied or photographed and the photo then kept in their file. This also makes it possible to return to and discuss the pictures at a later date.

Children—and sometimes adolescents—often use objects or materials available in the room to express their ideas or feelings. Paper, pens, modeling clay, toy figures, and building blocks are particularly effective. Together with the client, you can also "draw" feelings on paper, cardboard, and so on.

A case example: Saskia

Eight-year-old Saskia comes to an appointment with her father because she is being bullied in school. She describes how she has regular arguments with other children and that she has hardly any friends in her class and spends most afternoons on her own as she doesn't have anyone to have a play date with.

During recess, the other children won't let her join in with their games. Those children who did spend time with her were put under pressure by other kids and abandoned her.

The father adds that his daughter is extremely upset about the situation, and meetings with her teacher have not helped.

While the therapist is talking to the father, Saskia wanders over to the toy corner. She finds some modeling clay and asks if she can make something with it. She tries out various shapes and finally creates two figures having a conversation and brings them back to her seat.

At the next meeting, the clay figures are used to talk about the subject of "feelings" and to discuss different types of body language. These two malleable figures can be quickly reshaped to display affection or rejection.

But even the most perfect room is not a substitute for the therapeutic relationship; it can only help to facilitate the therapy.

Suitable materials for working with children and adolescents

- Rag doll or stuffed animals
- Paper, rolls of wallpaper
- Colored pens, crayons
- Modeling clay
- Wooden or plastic figures (but preferably without removable small bits, particularly if very young siblings are present!)
- Wooden blocks in different shapes and sizes
- Hanging chair in which you can swivel around
- A little table or desk
- A children's rug or "children's corner"
- Pop-up tunnel, tents, or folding chairs

Helpful rules for communicating with children and adolescents

You may find the following suggestions helpful, depending on the age and stage of development of the child or adolescent.

Communicate at eye level. Adults can make it easier and less intimidating for children by communicating with them at eye level. For example, with Ben, a frightened seven-year-old, the conversation finally took place on the rug in the toy corner. After racing toy cars around for a while, the boy opened up a little, even if he vigilantly avoided eye contact.

A case example: Justin

Justin, who was 11 years old at the first meeting, had decided not to speak, so communication had to take place in different ways. At the beginning of the session, the boy didn't move from the door of the consultation room. When invited to come into the room, he reacted with a hostile expression, shrugged his shoulders, and stayed where he was.

The therapist then explained that they had 45 minutes at their disposal that they could spend in a variety of ways. He then went and sat down at his desk in the corner of the room and began to read through some papers. At this point Justin gradually moved away from the door and into the room, looking at various things, including a picture, a glove puppet, and a game. Finally he stopped at the couch table, on which there was a board game, and began to occupy himself with this.

When the therapist saw this, he asked the boy if he felt like playing. Justin nodded almost imperceptibly, but still did not say anything. The two of them set up the game and played without exchanging a word, but with an occasional smile, shaking of the head, or nod. At the end of the session, the therapist praised Justin for his persistence in not talking, and when he asked the boy if he would like to come to the next session, Justin nodded and used a handshake to say goodbye.

At the next session, Justin impressively managed to "discuss" his concerns using only the words "yes" and "no"—a huge step forward.

Communicating in age-appropriate language . . . and sometimes even nonverbally. With younger children, in particular, it is important to choose your words so that they are age appropriate and easy to understand. Sometimes it is a good idea to adapt the speed and volume of your voice to the client's; sometimes whispering is even helpful. Either it helps to form a bond with the child, or it arouses the child's curiosity.

It is often easier to make progress, particularly in a first meeting, by drawing or playing rather than talking, as in the case example with Justin. Depending on the child's age and an initial appraisal of his development, you can try a pantomime or practice juggling (with an emphasis on practicing, not mastering the skill), laugh, scribble, drive toy cars around, look out of the window, or drum a rhythm—whatever seems appropriate and takes the child's fancy. Trying something out together and then both deciding against it works well, too. Doing magic tricks can also break the ice.

Not talking about the problem. During the first meeting, the focus is on everything except the problem. Breaking the ice, getting to know each other, perhaps discovering shared interests, playing or drawing together, are often more effective invitations than directly discussing the concern or asking why the client has come to see you. In extreme cases, insisting on "verbal" communication can even have an adverse effect.

Don't just ask questions—answer them, too. Children and adolescents are often curious about what awaits them. To begin with, you can talk about how these consultations or sessions normally work, how long they take, the sort of things that are discussed, and how you can work on issues together (Delfos, 2004, 2007). Sometimes it is also important to openly express your own concerns:

> *Up to now I only know that . . . and I'm asking myself how I can help you. Perhaps you can give me a clue about what needs to happen and what we need to talk about so that your parents/ teachers feel that you don't need to come and see me anymore.*

Provide room for unusual concerns or behaviors. Innovative approaches are required when children or adolescents come to a consultation full of aggression, anger, or resistance—for example, pattern breaking, doing something unusual, or asking the client for his opinion.

Bring time and patience: One thing at a time. If children (like adolescents or adults) are asked too many questions at once, they often don't answer any of them.

Answering a question very quickly can also be a strategy to fend off further annoying questions, and the answer is unlikely to have been thought through.

Inspire trust. In a one-on-one discussion with a child or adolescent, it is not unusual for significant information to arise that will require the inclusion of the family or system at a later date. However, the child has told you this information in confidence, and that is exactly how it should be treated. Nonetheless, the child or adolescent can be asked how he thinks the therapy should continue (as suggested by Duncan & Miller, 2003).

Seeing from the child's perspective. In order to understand certain unusual behavior or specific subject matter, the perspective of the child or adolescent is very important. Good rapport and respect are just as important as neutrality and openness.

In certain situations, for example, when dealing with trauma, it is particularly important to deal openly with the issue and to be understanding of the client's behavior, which may at first glance seem inappropriate (Pfeiffer, 2008).

Helpful rules for communicating with children and adolescents

- Communicate at eye level
- Communicate in age-appropriate language
- Communicate nonverbally
- Don't talk about the problem
- Don't just ask questions—answer them, too
- Provide room for unusual concerns or behaviors
- Bring time and patience: One thing at a time

- Inspire trust
- See from the child's perspective

Communication techniques with people with intellectual disabilities

The psychotherapy of clients with intellectual disabilities has always played a subordinate role in the psychotherapeutic landscape. Too often there is still an assumption that psychotherapy will work only if the client is in a position to understand the subject matter of a discussion in the traditional sense, or to deal with his problem on a cognitive level. It is also assumed that to do therapy, let alone psychotherapy, with a person with intellectual disabilities requires special measures, without these ever being spelled out.

A distinction is rarely made between different levels of intellectual disability, with the result that the person's unique character traits go unnoticed. Furthermore, people with intellectual disabilities are often immediately treated differently from people without disabilities.

Yet it is these children, adolescents, and adults who teach us to become creative and flexible: Instead of speaking, we sometimes have to play, take a walk, use body language, draw, and so on. We inevitably have to expand our personal therapy repertoire and our personal style to find a therapy medium that works for us:

> People with intellectual disabilities often show us very directly and overtly, even physically, that they don't know themselves, their strength, their bodies, that they can only partially express their feelings, that they find it difficult to form and maintain relationships. They also clearly show us what they have experienced: that they have elicited rejection or over-protection, that they have attracted attention through being different, that they have been disappointed and abandoned, that they have had to deal with too many separations, that they now find it difficult to try new things and trust new people. (Färber, 1983)

All encounters that take place in the context of psychotherapy and counseling are about establishing a relationship with the client, on the one hand, and professional expertise, on the other. Striking the right balance between the two determines the effectiveness of the therapy, regardless of the clinical picture being treated. Intellectually disabled clients have as much right to this as clients with personality disorders or adjustment disorders.

In reference to his experiences with systemic solution-oriented approaches with disabled clients, Sickinger (2000) emphasizes—like de Shazer—the particular importance of "client orientation" to turn "complainants" and "customers" into clients who are motivated to become actively involved in the problem-solving process.

The psychotherapeutic treatment of people with intellectual disabilities is also about integration, but this should not be confused with pedagogical, development-oriented measures and exercises, although admittedly the boundaries between therapy and pedagogy are becoming increasingly blurred.

Psychotherapy ultimately creates the conditions in which, for example, pedagogical measures can be effective. And in this respect, psychotherapy with an intellectually disabled person does not differ from psychotherapy with a "normal" person. A good foundation can be laid only if there is mutual trust between client and therapist—and this requires mutual acceptance of the other person's abilities, limitations, and needs.

The client-therapist bond is therefore extremely important.

Communication techniques in crisis situations

A crisis therapy session can refer to meetings that do not take place under normal circumstances and that are characterized by resistance, or to meetings during which a crisis arises and threatens to escalate.

A few important ground rules apply in these situations: honesty and authenticity on the part of the therapist, a high level of transparency and openness in discussing the issue(s), and the maintenance of a professional distance at all times while also establishing—and maintaining—a bond with the client.

Stories from Bruno (*see page 11*) is a case example of many things including rapport, patience, and so on. **The waiting game** is another amusing case example from Bruno, which could have ended differently.

A case example: The waiting game

One day Bruno, a tall 16-year-old, was announced as an emergency. He was a computer addict, and his parents' attempts to prevent him from playing more computer games had failed because he had physically attacked his mother and demolished everything in the house. His father had to restrain him physically. He was brought by force into the clinic by the police, although without being told that he had been brought to a ward for children and adolescents in need of protection—that is, a closed ward. The parents had reached the end of their rope and felt there was no other option open to them or their son.

While he was being admitted, Bruno quickly understood that he had been "had" and began to lash out at his parents again. The situation looked like it might spiral out of control. The therapist called to the scene was informed by the parents that Bruno was capable of not budging for hours.

The therapist decided to go into the room as a "silence expert" and tried to greet Bruno with a handshake, which Bruno rejected. He turned his back to the therapist, and the therapist sat down in such a way that he could see Bruno's face in the mirror. Bruno made it easy for him, because he did not move from the spot. The therapist sat and said nothing but was able to observe the young man's facial expressions. After about 15 minutes the therapist said to him: "Your parents have told me that you're good at waiting. Do you know what the advantage of waiting is?" Bruno listened attentively but did not answer. A few more minutes' pause: "The advantage of waiting is that nothing happens. Do you know what the disadvantage of waiting is?" Bruno continued to listen attentively, shifted his weight onto the other foot and remained silent. "The disadvantage of waiting is that nothing happens." After another 15 minutes the therapist got up, stretched his legs, and sat down again. He asked: "By the way, have I told you what the advantage of waiting is?" In the mirror Bruno flashed a smile. "The advantage of waiting is that nothing happens. And did I tell you what the disadvantage of waiting is?" Bruno's smile broadened. "The disadvantage of waiting is that nothing happens."

Bruno had to pull himself together but did not change his position: He remained standing. A quarter of an hour later he was asked the same questions again, and this time he found it more difficult to keep his composure. The therapist got up, approached Bruno, who immediately tensed up again. The therapist backed off and sat down in order to reply to e-mails at his computer! Now and then he would repeat the questions. Another 15 minutes and the same scenario: Bruno's smile turned into a laugh. During the next hour the therapist repeated the procedure a few more times, and Bruno's laughter became increasingly unreserved. When the therapist then also began to croak like a frog now and then, the spell was broken and Bruno snorted with laughter but stayed in the corner.

When he was told that both of them were being forced to work together, although the therapist had not invited him and Bruno had not expressed any desire to come to the clinic, Bruno left the room without any trouble and spent a quiet night.

The alternative approach would have been to use force, which, however, would have put a severe strain on the therapeutic relationship from the start. Good crisis management in this kind of situation requires good knowledge of your own resources. In this kind of situation, in particular, it is important to come across as

The Therapist's Treasure Chest

genuine, to maintain a professional distance, and to show empathy without becoming overbearing.

You can use your own resources to bring out the client's resources—or vice versa. Bruno's ability to sit tight aligned with the therapist's ability to wait patiently and silently. Bruno's open, expectant expression showed the therapist that he was ready and willing to be surprised by what would happen: the perfect basis for asking an unusual question.

The question worked wonders at a time when Bruno was probably expecting to be forcefully taken out of the room. The question made the situation more unusual and opened up the perspective for Bruno to escape unscathed, because this was not a fight but a mutual dialogue.

In every crisis situation it is important to convey to the client that you will get through the situation together.

Professional distance

Professional distance is achieved through a combination of physical distance and a clear indication that you are there for the client. In situations that threaten to spiral out of control, it is important to keep an overview and to react appropriately.

Rapport

Remember, you can show rapport by

- Adapting your own speed to the client's
- Responding to his emotional strain
- Using the client's choice of words and speed of talking

This rapport in itself creates a disruption that unsettles the client and makes him more open to further interventions.

Convey a positive message slowly and a negative message quickly

Sometimes you have to convey something painful to a client. In this scenario it is important to have established an atmosphere in which it is possible to say what has to be said. At the same time, you should not be overly considerate, as this can end up having the opposite effect.

Dragging out a piece of bad news is not only tortuous but also leaves many questions unanswered because the patient or parents can sense that not everything is being said. If you have to inform parents that their child has special needs or a learning disability, and the parents have high expectations of their child, it is a good idea to convey the negative message quickly.

Caution: *It is easy to make a mistake—it does not help much to harshly spit out a piece of bad news; on the other hand, it also does not help to confuse things by evading the issue.*

Sometimes you may feel it is necessary to say something like: *It could be a laboratory error . . .* or *We need to wait for the results of further tests . . .* Or *It is so rare it seems very unlikely . . .* But when you have objective and unequivocal evidence, it makes absolutely no sense to beat around the bush.

When, for example, a child's schooling is at stake, and it is clear that the child will not make the grades to get placed on an advanced learning track, as the parents would prefer—especially if there is nothing the parents want more—it is our unavoidable duty to point out that there will be problems.

If during a therapy or counseling session it becomes clear that the child's welfare is at stake, it is also important not to hide the fact. However, in this scenario it might be expedient to call upon other experts to make an assessment before deciding on a further course of action.

If unpleasant decisions need to be conveyed, for example, if a child needs to be taken into care, there is no point in fudging the issue.

However, if you are offering praise, it is important to do so in small portions over a longer period, because this creates a more constructive atmosphere!

When have you reached your limit? Be honest and pass the buck

Sometimes, despite every good intention, a solution to the problem cannot be found, or the problem is too overwhelming from the start.

The ideas and suggestions in this book are tools to help you make progress in your day-to-day work and to solve psychological problems that have not yet become entrenched. If the interventions you use have no effect, there is no point in continuing.

In most cases, this is an indication that a psychodiagnostic assessment is required or that the buck needs to be passed on to a qualified specialist. If interventions do not lessen the burden on the client, then he should be referred elsewhere or you should consider more intensive measures such as a semiresidential or residential treatment.

If as a therapist or counselor you have the feeling that you are not making progress, you should not waver for long but refer the patient elsewhere. You are doing neither yourself nor the client a favor by hesitating, because if you feel under pressure, you will not come up with good ideas, and the more entrenched a problem becomes, the harder it is for the subsequent therapist or psychiatrist to work on a solution with the client.

Part 2

The
Interventions

Introduction

This part of the book describes individual interventions and discusses their purposes and applications. In a sense, this section can be read as a kind of instruction manual, but the reader can of course adapt the ideas to his particular needs or system requirements. For example, it is useful to find out about clients' or families' everyday lives in order to integrate elements from their everyday routines, hobbies, or other pastimes into the therapy, and in order to establish a good relationship with the client(s).

Some interventions are grouped together; others stand alone. We have tried to make the descriptions as short and to-the-point as possible and to convey the most important aspects of each intervention in one to a maximum of three pages.

The interventions are organized in the following format:

Idea

Method

Tips

Indication/Contraindication

Setting: family, individual, group, or couples therapy, and/or teams

We wish you every success and hope you enjoy trying out new interventions. And don't be surprised: they work!

General Interventions

Direct Interventions in Conversation

Metaphors

IDEA. From a neurophysiological point of view, working with metaphors is comparable with an anchoring of abilities. The fact that certain states of mind or emotions, problem situations, or solution constructions are connected with a metaphor can mean that the mere mention of the metaphor can create a solution atmosphere or strengthen the client's feeling that an ability is within his grasp.

Besides its anchoring function, introducing a metaphor also enables a change of perspective. This surprising moment causes confusion and thereby opens up new ways of seeing. It has a positive influence on the therapeutic relationship. The reaction to, or effect of, a metaphor is acted out in the right hemisphere of the brain and enables a connection to be made with the level-headed left hemisphere of the brain.

Milton Erickson has cultivated this technique with impressive results in many fascinating examples (Rosen, 2009). One of the most unforgettable stories is of the girl with the countless freckles, who hated herself and the whole world because of her appearance. When she was presented to Erickson by her mother, he immediately and aggressively accused her of theft. She was of course angry and confused, but also curious. Then he explained that she had "stolen" all of the cinnamon cookies, cakes, and buns from the kitchen—you could see it in her "cinnamon face."

METHOD. Metaphors can arise from two sources: from the client, or from the therapist. In both cases, the specialist abilities of the therapist are required.

Working with clients' metaphors. Many families talk about themselves in metaphors. It requires a good deal of rapport on the part of the therapist to register, act on, and develop these metaphors. Metaphors are usually used only in one direction and, unlike a coin that has only two sides, a metaphor usually has more. Metaphors can be used in a variety of ways. Using the example of the chameleon (see **The chameleon metaphor,** *page 36*):

- *Were chameleon-like qualities already apparent before?*
- *If yes, which ones, and who used them for what purpose?*
- *If you were really a chameleon, what would you now do differently?*
- *What else is being a chameleon good for?*

In another story from Bruno, Bruno's mother used the following image to visualize her son's behavior: *I think our son's brain is in his stomach and not in his head.*

The metaphor "Where is your brain at the moment?" was then used spontaneously at many points in the therapy and lightened the mood. One of the subsequent sessions began with a spontaneous declaration by Bruno's family (this time spoken by the father): *I think today we've all got our brains in our heads!*

Introducing metaphors to clients. It is a creative achievement of the therapist to be able to turn what he observes into a metaphor. Metaphors can be taken from many different fields, for example, the human body, health, illness, animals, plants, architecture, games and sports, money and business, cooking, or eating and drinking. Metaphors can be used to help visualize actions and perceptions. They invite the client to move away from wallowing in his problem to think about it in more concrete terms.

An example from family therapy

A father, mother, and their 14-year-old adopted daughter were at loggerheads about how much freedom she should be given. She had already put her parents to the test during a three-week absence during which her father, in particular—a very respected but also difficult man, because of his blunt personality—had taken all legal and some not-so-legal courses of action to find his daughter. His daughter had also been indulging in legal and not-so-legal substances and found herself in some dangerous situations. The girl was admitted to the clinic as an inpatient and released after six weeks. During this time, her father lashed out at the therapist treating his daughter because he feared that not enough was being done for his daughter—because during his daughter's three-week absence, he felt that he had been left in the lurch by the police, the youth welfare services, and the court. In the second family-therapy session after her release, the conflict between the daughter and father was carried out openly, while the mother watched the squabbling pair in silence. In the middle of a heated argument, the therapist interrupted the discussion and asked the mother: *Mrs. Z, I would like to make a quick observation. I imagine you must be feeling like the sausage between the two halves of a hotdog bun. Would you agree?*

The mother laughed and, astonishingly, the father and daughter laughed, too. The hotdog became the family's running gag. The mother suddenly felt herself strengthened in her role as "equalizer" and began to open up more and more from one session to the next.

TIPS.

- In order to work with metaphors, you need to have a good bond with the client(s). The images that patients use in conversation are a rich source of metaphors. The fact that these images are linked with emotions and often remind the person of sensory experiences mean they have a big impact.

- On the other hand, metaphors that are introduced by the therapist will have a powerful effect if they represent solutions and are in tune with the emotional world of the patient. Here it is helpful to combine metaphors with humor.
- When introducing a metaphor or using a family metaphor, it is always a good idea to ask for permission to do so.
- If you think that a metaphor could be useful but nothing occurs to you, you can always refer to the 12,000 metaphorical idioms listed in George Nagy's *Thesaurus of English Idioms* (2006).
- It should, however, be noted that not every client will understand or latch on to every metaphorical construct—in which case it doesn't make much sense to pursue it. You could come back to it at a later date if you have the feeling that the client might then embrace it.
- Drawing a metaphor on a piece of paper is often more effective, because it can be given to the client to take away with him. The drawing is surprising, relaxes the situation, and has what it takes to become a running gag or reference point throughout the entire therapy.

INDICATION. Metaphors can be used with almost any kind of indication. It is not absolutely necessary to combine the use of metaphors with humor; emotional proximity and deep sorrow can also be captured metaphorically.

When working with mentally disabled people, it is also a good idea to occasionally try working with metaphors.

CONTRAINDICATION. None, as long as you ensure that everybody in the system "gets" the image and is able to appreciate that a metaphor is not meant literally but can help them to see things from a different angle.

SETTING. Individual therapy, family therapy, group therapy, couples therapy, teams.

Metaphors you can use

- Sports metaphors
- The car metaphor
- The ball-point pen metaphor
- The switch metaphor
- The mountain metaphor

- The balloon metaphor
- The "filling station" metaphor

A case example: A soccer metaphor

Malcolm, a 14-year-old boy—not very tall, but brawny—returned for another crisis meeting just five days after his first emergency outpatient appointment at the clinic. He was brought in because he had injured a nurse in his residential facility—she had to go to the hospital with a broken nose and several cuts. After the first session it was agreed to move Malcolm to another unit and to have a follow-up session in the near future.

In the second residential facility, the nurses were so afraid of Malcolm that they had not told him when his next session was going to be. When the time came to take him, the situation looked like it would spiral out of control, so after another fight, Malcolm returned to the clinic for a crisis intervention.

In the clinic it soon became clear that he would not be able to stay at his current residential facility, as the intensive-care unit there was already over-filled. During the meeting at the child and adolescent psychiatry clinic, Malcolm announced that he absolutely did not want to stay there, and that if he was made to stay, he would beat everyone up.

A therapist was asked to join the meeting, and after he had introduced himself, he picked up on Malcolm's last threat and described it as "the old way," which had the effect of creating an environment dominated by fear: *I know that when others are afraid of you, you initially feel very powerful, but it doesn't help you achieve anything. You are now in the psychiatric clinic for the fifth time* . . . (Before his most recent appearance he had already been treated three times as an inpatient.) *I think we all agree that this is not the right path to take anymore.*

Because Malcolm looked at the therapist attentively without saying anything, the therapist knew that Malcolm was no longer on the defensive. So the therapist asked him, *Do you have any hobbies?* Malcolm responded, "Football!" *And do you have a favorite team?* "Ravens!" *Ah—they're not doing too well at the moment.*

Malcolm knew right away what he meant and talked about the team's financial problems. *What are the Ravens doing at the moment that you could also do?* Malcolm looked surprised. *Will the Ravens make the playoffs this year?* "Yes!" Malcolm answered.

Right! How do they manage to be in so much debt and still play well? "They exert themselves." *Right! And what does that require?* "All the players have to give their best. They work together and want to be the champions!"

What do you have to do to become a champion? "Exert myself." *And what does that mean?* "Go to school and get an education."

Do you have an idea how that could work? "Nope." *Then let's think about it together over the next few days.* "No, I'm not staying here."

And why not? "Because I don't want to. And if I have to stay here I'll smash everything up."

That's the old way. I think we have to ask your dad now. (Malcolm's father had sole custody of his son.) *He has to help us decide.*

The father decided over the phone that his son should be admitted to the clinic, and when the son was told, he was obviously surprised about the decision. He started to cry, and when he was asked if he had anything to say, he answered in a voice choked with anger: "I'm going to beat my dad up."

After a short pause, Malcolm asked: "How long do I have to stay here?" *How long do you want to stay?* "Not longer than a month! I want to spend Christmas with my mom and New Year with my dad ..."

"Do you have a football field here?" *Yes, why?* "I have to go out for 10 minutes now." *Okay, but remember, you're playing a six-point game at the moment, like the Ravens. If you come back you can take the lead. If you high-tail it, you'll lose the game and miss the playoffs!*

"I won't disappear."

After six minutes Malcolm came back to the ward and started his therapy.

Sports metaphors

TIPS. Sports metaphors work really well in a variety of situations, from talking with parents about implementing rules and repercussions to analogies with goal scoring. For example,

> *What, in your opinion, is most important to be able to score a touchdown? ... And if you compare that with school? You said it requires a lot of effort to concentrate and to understand the techniques. I agree. And what about the suggestion of your teacher to work really hard on your math so that you don't have to repeat the year ... ?*

The car metaphor

There are many metaphors that can be used with hyperactive children. Our favorite is the Ferrari metaphor. We like to describe to the parents that they have a Ferrari in their garage with a 360-horsepower engine, but nobody dares to drive the car. These cars are very powerful but you have to know how to handle them. They are extremely sensitive and difficult to brake, and turning the steering wheel even slightly too far can spell danger. Nemetschek (2006) also used the racing car metaphor in his therapy of ADHD children.

The ball-point pen metaphor

Beaulieu (2010) likes to use the metaphor of the ball-point pen, which you can click open or closed. You have to open it in order to write with it. By clicking it open and closed a few times during the conversation, you link it with the question: *Is your mind currently open to what you want to achieve?*

The switch metaphor

The switch metaphor works well with children up to 10 or 11 years of age. Many parents already use the metaphor, for example, when they say they wish their child had a switch to turn them on or off. Parents just want a break but can't find the switch.

TIPS. These switch or button metaphors work especially well with children if they are combined with a drawing. The children are absorbed by this fun drawing task and in the process actually turn off their own switch!

This metaphor can be integrated into an observation task to complete before the next session, in which the parents have to guess when the child's switch is on or off.

The mountain metaphor

A distant goal that does not seem easy to reach can be visualized as a hike up a steep mountain and down the other side. To have reached the summit suggests a successful approach. But what did this require? Courage, stamina, food and drink—these kinds of answers are a good basis for staying with this image:

> *We can pack a rucksack with provisions that will help us during our ascent—what would we have to pack? A hiking stick would also be a good idea, and people to keep us motivated. Taking a break in a pretty spot with a stream to drink from would be great . . . But if somebody is standing, overawed, at the foot of the mountain and feels as if the mountain is getting higher and higher, then you can tell them that they don't necessarily have to go over the mountain. You can also walk around it. The goal is the same— and must not be lost sight of.*

The balloon metaphor

- A balloon can correspond to a wish or a dream—it can drift up to the sky, or it can also burst.
- It can serve as an example of how certain things need to be handled very carefully, so that they don't pop.
- The balloon can also be a measure of how to slowly and steadily expend energy, or how to quickly deflate a difficult situation or issue.
- It can act as a counterpart to one's own motivation or energy level: *You've described how run-down you feel and that you feel deflated—what would have to happen in order for this balloon to regain its shape and perhaps rise up again?*

The filling station metaphor

This metaphor works well as a psychoeducational intervention for obesity: a person is a highly complicated mechanism and our body somehow controls all of the thousands of processes going on inside us.

We have numerous "control systems" regulating these processes. For example, our nervous system is constantly checking and regulating our hormones. So, when there is not quite enough of a certain hormone, the body ensures that more is produced.

One can imagine it a little bit like a filling station: *Have you ever filled up a car with gas? Have you seen it being done? Did you notice what happened to the fuel dispenser when the tank was full?* This leads into a description of how the fuel dispenser has a cutoff valve that stops the flow as soon as the tank is full.

- *What would happen if this mechanism stopped working? The tank would overflow and you would have to quickly intervene.*
- *This is more or less what is going on in your body at the moment. You are supplying it with too much fuel, and the cut-off valve is somehow broken. Your body no longer registers when it has had enough. And you keep on eating and the fuel has to go somewhere, so it is turned into fat . . . If you had to think of a way of repairing the cut-off valve, what could you do?*

Many adolescents will be quick to explain that it is all about noticing when you are full—and that you do not have to refuel every 12 miles but can wait until the tank is more or less empty.

This metaphor can function as a useful visual aid throughout the therapy and in our experience has always made sense to clients.

The Therapist's Treasure Chest

Other frequently used metaphors

Ultimately, there is hardly anything that can't be used metaphorically. You just have to do it.

- A task can feel like an *obstacle race*.
- Life can be like a *river* or *path*, a *spiral* or a *journey*.
- In many cases the image of a *gate* or a *door* works well.
- Clients might feel like a *ship* on a stormy ocean.
- A relationship might resemble a **dance**.
- A problem can seem like a *cliff*, a *wall*, a *hurdle,* or an *obstacle*.
- Everyone is familiar with the metaphor of taking a *load* off their mind.
- A new perspective can be like a *bridge*.
- A solution might be a *break in the clouds* that finally lets the sun through again.
- Helper figures might be experienced as *icebreakers* or *diggers* that clear the way and make room for new perspectives and possibilities.
- The image of a *juggler* who has to keep all the balls up in the air for the performance to succeed, works well for a stressed multitasking working mother.

And the client can also be invited to describe his feelings and state of mind metaphorically. For example, a single father compared himself in his current situation to a *marathon runner*. In subsequent meetings the conversation revolved around how it was possible to get in shape for such a challenge—and whether it was even worth attempting. The man decided that he needed a coach to help him master all aspects of his life, but particularly to ensure that he was getting enough rest, as this was something he wasn't able to achieve on his own. Finally he was able to develop some good strategies for himself with the help of an imaginary helper figure—a famous athlete.

Activating and working with resources

Discovering resources

As discussed in preceding sections, it is very important to work on a solution that uses the client's existing resources. In diagnostics, therapy, and counseling, there is an increasing emphasis on looking at the client's existing resources; in addition to reducing the problem behavior, the focus is also on uncovering and consolidating skills and abilities. In crisis situations, in particular, resources can be used in the context of stabilizing interventions and exercises.

Having resources is important, but it is often difficult to discover them. It is often simpler to get a client to think about how he would like to be in the future. He may feel that he cannot achieve a new solution with his current resources. However, if the situation is approached the other way around, that is, if he imagines the problem has been solved in the future and he discovered new resources in the process (see **The Miracle Question**, *page 87*), it seems much less daunting and can be tackled with much more confidence. The following questions can then be asked:

How will it be when you are happy again?

How would you like to be in the future?

What will you do differently?

It is important to aim high, because ambitious goals make it easier to take small steps.

All of our clients have resources. Usually they are aware of some of them and completely unaware of others. How do we find them out?

Resilience or resources?

Challenging circumstances can lead to a person's existing abilities being further developed and—depending on the situation—can also lead to new skills and abilities being discovered (Rutter, 2000). The "resilience" concept is a resource-focused model for explaining mental toughness, focusing on a person's personal ability to master and actively implement problem-solving strategies when dealing with stress, challenges, and difficult life situations. In other words, *resilience* comes to the fore when dealing with problematic situations; in the process, existing *resources* are used and new ones developed.

These resources are found partly in the individual himself—in qualities like self-esteem, optimism, the ability to actively solve problems, or self-efficacy—and partly in the person's family and/or social context, for example, emotional security and encouragement within the family, appreciative and supportive parents, structure, a secure relationship with at least one person, positive role models and learning experiences, or stable contact with one's peers (Lenz, 2008).

According to Levold (2006), resilience is a resource that emerges in a person's interaction with a problem. Let's take this a step further: resilience can be actively enhanced by strengthening the client's resources and using them to weaken the problem.

Resilience can therefore come to the fore only in connection with a problem—without a problem there can be no resilience. This begs the question of whether a person can know if he is resilient or not if he does not have a problem.

People who are regarded as being very resilient are usually confident and have good social skills, active coping strategies, and good self-control. Developing these abilities is also a vital aspect of solution-oriented and resource-focused therapy.

Working with resources can also lead to an improvement in resilience and makes it easier to cope with a crisis than it would be without these resources.

Techniques for activating resources

- The resources family tree
- The resources barometer
- The resource bowl of cherries
- The resources team
- The resources salad
- The resources interview
- Resource memory
- The resources bandage
- Guessing resources
- The resources rug/laying out resources
- Drawing resources
- The resources timeline
- Resources roulette

Activating resources

After establishing which abilities and knowledge a client already uses to master everyday situations, it is possible to continue using these abilities to work on finding solutions to his existing problems (de Shazer & Dolan, 2008).

Ways of influencing this principle include developing the abilities and positive characteristics of the client and his environment, motivating the client and the system, awakening the client's desire to even want to bring about change, and establishing a stable therapeutic relationship in which the expectation of success is strengthened (Döpfner, Banaschewski, & Sonuga-Barke, 2008).

The activation of resources as described by Döpfner and colleagues is particularly important in the multimodal psychotherapeutic treatment of children and adolescents, as the activation has to come from outside, requires a sufficient degree of motivation, and incorporates the patient's entire system.

Lenz (2008) argues that the social resources of children of ill parents need to be activated in a targeted way if there is insufficient support within or from outside the affected families. He emphasizes the importance of establishing support networks as well as group therapy.

A further aspect besides the (re)activation of existing resources is the fostering of new strengths and abilities.

An example: Sebastian

Sebastian is nine years old and having difficulties finishing his homework and tasks at school on time. He is of average ability and motivated but is cause for concern because of the amount of time he needs to complete his work.

During the first meeting with his parents he is shy but interested and open to the suggestion of a one-on-one chat during the next session. During this meeting he is given the task of writing his name on a piece of paper and thinking of an ability starting with each of the letters of his name (*see **Working with the child's name**, page 122*). These abilities should be ones that he is proud of, or that other people would describe as good abilities.

Sebastian thinks for a while and makes some initial suggestions such as "sporty" for the "s." After he has written the word above the letter, he asks: "Can I write something down that I don't have yet but would like to have?"

What ability would you would really like to have? asks the therapist. "*I would love to be brave.*"

Even braver? How brave are you already? "Well, I'm not really brave at all . . . but I wish I were!"

How would things be different if you were brave? "I wouldn't care so much when I make a mistake or don't write neatly. And I would finish quicker . . ." he responds.

METHOD. Schemmel and Schaller (2003) emphasize the importance of resources in a psychotherapeutic and psychosocial context. As they point out, focusing on resources is in fact neither a new technique nor a unique one, but it is worth

The Therapist's Treasure Chest

looking more closely at some methods for teasing out resources in different contexts, so that they can be used more effectively when working with clients. Here are a few examples and useful interventions.

The resources family tree: Based on a genogram—a systematic instrument for illustrating family history—you can get the client to produce a resource-focused family tree either during the session or as homework (Andrecht & Geiken, 1999). Instead of dates of birth and death, the focus is primarily on the abilities that these people exhibit(ed) in their working or private lives.

Sometimes there are family myths that can benefit the patient. A family doctor may already know about these myths and can use them in the consultation. Sometimes it is a good idea to invent a myth: *The Meyers have always been very brave!*

The family tree reveals many other abilities. The abilities that are uncovered are then linked to the question: *Where are these abilities in you?*

The resources barometer: The patient chooses from among the many resources that come to light in the family tree that might not otherwise have occurred to the patient, or that he wishes he had, and rates the extent to which he uses this ability at the moment: from 0, "not at all," to 10, "always."

A very shy child, for example, might rate his or her "courage" ability as level 2. The question is then: *What will you do differently when you get to level 3?*

Whatever the patient suggests can then be set as homework: *Do things as if you were at level 3!* Resources are thereby activated or reactivated.

TIPS. When working with children, it is a good idea to give the parents an observation task: "By the next session, I want you to make a note of other resources that you discover in your child."

When working with adolescents or adults, the most important thing is to motivate them to observe themselves—or to observe others, and to decide which resources they wish they had themselves.

INDICATION. Finding and reinforcing clients' strengths and abilities is one of the basic techniques of a solution-oriented and resource-focused approach, which is why it can be used with any type of problem.

CONTRAINDICATION. People suffering from depression often struggle with this task. But in the right circumstances it is still worth a try!

SETTING. Individual therapy, family therapy, group therapy, couples therapy.

The resource bowl of cherries: Even if life isn't a bowl of cherries, therapy or counseling can be. With a little help, clients begin to discover their resources and to name them.

What they don't yet know is that they also have resources that they don't know they have. With the simple question, *Which abilities would you like to have?* you provide the proverbial bowl of cherries and the ideas start to flow.

METHOD. As described in **The Art of Questioning** *(see page 23)*, a simple question can have a big effect. The simple question, *Which abilities would you like to have?* sets in motion a cascade of questions, at the end of which the client may realize that he already has the resource he desired. Here are some examples of similar questions.

A cascade of questions

Which abilities do you wish you had?

How would you notice that you have this ability?

Was there ever a time when it felt a little bit as if you already had this ability?

What would other people start to notice if you had this ability?

What do you have to relearn?

TIPS. If somebody is depressed, he usually can't see the point in doing something. It is best to try to get through to the depressed client on a cognitive level. He is suffering because much of what used to be is no longer there. So the client often knows that he has to relearn, for example, to smile, have fun, be creative, and so on.

With depressive patients, the bowl of cherries can be presented differently, with the question, *Which abilities would you like to get back again?*

INDICATION. All indications.

CONTRAINDICATION. None.

SETTING. Individual therapy, group therapy, family therapy, teams.

The resources team: Based on **The inner team** *(see page 163)*, you can also put together a soccer or baseball team, with players that are the client's already existing or still-to-be-developed resources.

Depending on how challenging you want to make it, certain players can be moved forward or swapped with reserve players who are waiting in the sidelines for their chance to play.

METHOD. The real or desired abilities are written on little pieces of card and, depending on how many there are, are arranged into a soccer, basketball, or baseball team on the table, or sorted into smaller groups.

The therapist discusses with the client which particular situations or challenges he currently has to cope with. Together, therapist and client think about which abilities would be particularly helpful for dealing with the situation.

This team can also be kept for the next challenge. Therapist and client then consider whether the same resources are needed or whether one of the substitutes should be brought into the game.

The coach may, of course, change the strategy at any time, in which case other abilities may be needed.

TIPS. If all else fails, you can also use the special resources of the client's favorite soccer/baseball/basketball team—a fan's inner team also has the abilities of his favorite team.

With younger children you can also use **Glove puppets** (see *page 118*) to represent the team in combination with the puppets' particular strengths.

INDICATION. For coping with every kind of challenge.

CONTRAINDICATION. None.

SETTING. Individual therapy, group therapy, family therapy, couples therapy, teams.

The resources salad: Recognizing, acknowledging, and classifying each other's talents, strengths, and abilities are a big challenge not only in family systems and teams.

In certain group situations, the topic of "abilities" can be purposefully introduced and playfully implemented; depending on the group dynamic, it opens up a variety of possibilities for exploring issues in more depth and for further reflection.

METHOD. Each member of the group or system writes down one of his particular abilities on a piece of card, without letting anybody else see what he has written. The cards are then laid face down on the table or floor, or put in a box or basket, and mixed. Each member of the group then pulls out one card and shows it to the others. As well as explaining the resource, he has to decide whether he has this resource himself. Everyone in the group can also think of situations in which this resource would be particularly valuable, or how it could be developed.

In the second half of the session, the group should work together to think about whom the respective resources might fit, that is, who might have written them down and whom they might belong to. The members of the group or system should also be invited to say whether they, too, would like to have this resource and to give examples of situations in which they might need it.

INDICATION. Systems that complain a lot (families that have frequent arguments; groups who do not seem to value each other, and so on). As it is presented here, this intervention should not be used in an individual or couples therapy setting; it would need to be modified significantly.

CONTRAINDICATION. *Careful:* With clients suffering from depression, or groups or family systems with clear schisms and partisanships, this intervention can be counterproductive. In these cases it is important to first establish a "yes" vibe in relation to working with resources, before the group members can work with each other constructively (see *Creating a "yes" vibe, page 93*).

TIPS. This intervention works particularly well in combination with **Circular questioning** (*see page 85*).

SETTING. Family therapy, group therapy, teams.

The resources interview: Schiepek and Cremers (2003) describe resource interviews in group settings that serve the purpose not only of activating resources but also reflecting on and evaluating them. They can also stimulate a resource- and ability-focused state of consciousness.

METHOD. The members of a group or family are directly asked about their resources. As well as finding out which abilities each of them is contributing, the focus is also on the value of these abilities for the group as a whole.

> Which strengths do you have as a family that could help you in this situation?
>
> Which abilities might also be helpful?
>
> Can you describe a situation in which you have already successfully used your abilities?

TIPS. A resource interview can be visually represented with the help of Post-it notes or a flip chart; pie charts and other visual aids can also be tried.

With children and adolescents, resource interviews can also be carried out using the "finish the sentence" method. For example,

> My favorite game is . . .
>
> The things my brothers and sisters like about me are . . .
>
> At school my best subject is . . .
>
> My parents think it's great that I . . .

INDICATION. Works with any kind of problem or concern.

CONTRAINDICATION. A prevailing mood of depression.

SETTING. Group therapy, teams, family therapy, couples therapy.

Resource memory: Here the idea is to discover resources and link them to future goals in order to open up new possibilities. Resource memory works particularly well in decision-making situations. Sometimes patients have to make a decision but don't feel in a position to do so, or feel paralyzed. Resource memory works by initially concentrating on three resources and asking questions in relation to these: *In terms of the decision you have to make, how would things look in five (or more or less) years if you had used these abilities?* Or, *Does this ability apply more to decision 1 or decision 2?* This method is particularly effective with older children, adolescents, and adults.

METHOD. First, find the resources. The client is asked to name his resources, and these are all written down on pieces of card or paper. The list of resources is compiled from the resources the client sees in himself, the resources that other members of the group or system—as well as other people—see in the client, observations of the therapist, from anamnestic data, including particular interests or hobbies, the client's life story, job, and so on.

Next, link the resources: The cards are then turned over and shuffled, and the patient is asked to pick three cards. These are turned over and discussed, with the aim of getting the client to think about what else might be possible with these three abilities. (Ideally, try and play at least three rounds.)

If an important decision has to be made, you can ask if this resource is better suited to the one or other option, and why? Finally, a decision emerges on the basis of the resources. The respective cards can be left lying face up or turned around again and reshuffled. With every round, three cards should be turned over and reflected upon.

Questions that can be asked about the resources include the following:

How will things look (in a particular time) if you use these resources?

Which of these resources speaks for option 1, and which ones for option 2?

If you had to advise somebody who had these resources, which decision would you advise him to make?

A case example: John

John, 17 years old, was admitted to a clinic following a psychotic break in reaction to an overwhelming situation that was triggered by his family setup and stress in his job. His parents had never been married; he lived with his mother and was the focus of her life. His father tried to put up resistance, which led to the fact that the son was pulled back and forth.

John was working as an apprentice in a small bridge-building company, without really having any regular working hours. During his treatment as an inpatient, he made a relatively quick recovery and was free of his psychosis.

But minimal amounts of stress led to symptoms closely resembling psychosis, so that his treatment had to be extended.

He did an internship in a major company that offered vocational training and was soon torn between his mother and father again: His mother wanted to have him back home again, but his father said: "You'll never get another chance to do your vocational training in a firm like that!"

In order to make a decision, we did the resource memory intervention, and the following resources, among others, emerged: persistence, loyalty, flexibility, conscientiousness, punctuality, openness—and several more.

At the end of the resource memory exercise, John said: "Many of my abilities seem suited to the big firm, but I am very loyal and would like to go back to my old company. That is most important to me. That's clear to me now."

TIPS

- This intervention is particularly good with adolescents and in general in helping make a decision.
- With children, variations include memory cards with symbols, drawings, or collages, which the therapist or counselor can help the client to create if necessary.
- Resource memory can also be used with groups, families, and teams.
- It can also be repeated after a certain amount of time (six months, a year).

CONTRAINDICATION. Usually too difficult for preschool children, but sometimes possible if the resources are drawn or visually represented in another way.

It can be a challenge with clients who are very negative or who have no motivation or ideas. In this case it is best not to use straight away—this method is too good to waste and can be saved for a later date.

SETTING. Individual therapy, family therapy, group therapy, couples therapy, teams.

The resources bandage: With younger children especially, it is important to anchor the resources that have been discovered and to get them to use them outside of the consultation room. Making the ability visible, for example, in the form of a bandage, has proven to be very helpful in such situations, and is a way of prescribing the ability.

METHOD. Ask the client: *What could you really do with between now and the next session? Which of your abilities do you think you will particularly need?* You can either use a normal bandage and, for example, draw the resource on it, or use the "magic method" of sticking on an invisible bandage that only the patient knows about.

You can make it even more exciting by writing the resource on the skin and sticking a bandage over it. The parents can be given the task of trying to find out what is hidden beneath the bandage.

TIPS. This intervention is most suitable for children.

INDICATION. If you need a quick intervention and you want to anchor a resource.

CONTRAINDICATION. None.

SETTING. Individual therapy, family therapy, group therapy (children).

Further ideas using resources: Here are some further ideas for discovering and activating resources.

Guessing resources. Each member of the group or family thinks of a resource and writes it down (or draws it) on a piece of paper that he keeps folded up. The other members of the group try to guess each other's resources by asking questions or getting the person in question to act out or pantomime his resource. This approach works especially well in children's group therapy and in families.

The resources rug/laying out resources. Resources are written down or drawn on big pieces of card or paper and, depending on their size, are laid out on a table/ board or on the floor like a rug. You can then move from resource to resource and reflect on each one: *In what situations do I use this resource already? In what other situations might I use it?*

Drawing resources. Clients are given the task of drawing or painting their abilities, or modeling them with clay, in order to remember them:

Draw something that you wish you could do!

Between now and next week could you depict your most important abilities in a drawing?

For example, a young boy didn't really like drawing, so instead used a special movement of his hands and head to show his strengths. He practiced these movements a few times and learned to use them when he needed to remind himself of his abilities.

The resources timeline. Resources can be added to biographical timelines: *Which of your abilities did you really rely on at the time? How did you manage to master the situation?* You can also look for the shared resources of a family by using a single line for the whole family, or by placing the individual timelines next to each other and using the shared resources as intersection points.

Resources roulette. Resources are compiled playfully and allocated according to chance. With a little imagination you can equip a game of roulette with resources instead of numbers. The resource "chosen" by the ball should be practiced by the client in the coming weeks, and his family/friends should try and find it out.

Asking about exceptions

IDEA. According to de Shazer (1998) the term *problem* determines the term *problem free*. Possible solutions emerge in the space in between.

For therapy to be motivating and resource focused, it is a good idea to look for the exceptions to the problem or client complaint—periods or instances in which the problem has not been, or is not, an issue—as these often contain the key to the solution.

Asking about exceptions suggests that there are times when the client successfully uses his resources to prevent the problem from arising.

METHOD. Clients are almost always able to come up with examples of exceptions to a problem. From this alternative perspective they may realize, for example, that the pain is not normal, and that in fact the exception is the norm. And in this "normal" space lies the solution, which is usually not as complicated as the client imagines.

Of course, the "How?" question must also be addressed: *How did you manage to prevent the problem from arising during this problem-free time?*

It is important to ask the patient what he does, or what methods he uses, during these problem-free periods, because this puts him in control of the situation. Hearing himself describe what he did suggests that he can find the solution himself!

In the case of a child skipping school, rather than asking about the times when he *doesn't* go to school, you could ask: *When—and above all how—did you manage to go to school?* Or if somebody has a complaint that is apparently omnipresent, some good questions are:

When was it different?

How was it during those times when things were better?

I presume you don't have these pains all the time? How is it different when the pain isn't there?

And asking about exception(s) to a rule can never hurt.

Caution: *It is also important not to ask a question that can be answered simply with "yes" or "no."*

TIPS. You should not be deterred too quickly with "I don't know" or a similar response. Here, too, the basic rule applies: *A good question deserves an answer.* Also, be persistent! The patient's well-being is at stake.

And incidentally, no problems are omnipresent. However, as a therapist or counselor you will often experience that a client believes that a problem is "always there" until you probe deeper: *Problems tend to fluctuate. What is it like when the problem is less severe?* or *What is it like on those days that are a little different (better) than the others?*

Asking about exceptions to the rule can also be effectively combined with an external observation task. Exceptions are often much more obvious to others than to oneself: *What is it like on those days when your husband copes better than usual? What do you do differently?*

In the worst-case scenario—for example, with a depressive patient—the patient might not come up with any ideas. Then an external observation helps: *What might other people (who are close to you) perhaps also see?*

Asking a *circular question* (see **Circular questioning**, *page 85*) is also worth a try: *How would other people in your life answer this question if they were here?*

INDICATION. For all problems that subjectively overwhelm the patient. This does not mean that a problem has to be present all the time. For example, it also works well with patients who suffer from panic attacks: *Can you think of a time when you didn't have a panic attack when you thought you would have one?* This question works with almost every problem: It surprises the patient and forces him to think in a new direction.

CONTRAINDICATION. None.

SETTING. Individual therapy, family therapy, group therapy, couples therapy.

The Therapist's Treasure Chest

Scaling

IDEA. The transition from illness to health is a continuum and not an all-or-nothing proposition (Antonovsky, 1997). Because there are no objective criteria in psychotherapy (as yet) for measuring the success or failure of treatments, the wonderful technique of scaling was invented. It enables the client to evaluate his current situation and make progress, and it can be integrated into **Circular questioning** (see page 85).

Using this method, therapeutic advances can be made in big or small steps. Scaling is a good way of evaluating how much health has already been achieved and how much illness is *still* there.

METHOD. The task: *Imagine a scale of 1 to 10. If 1 is when you feel at your very worst, and 10 is when all your problems have disappeared and you feel at your best, where on the scale would you place yourself at the moment?*

Starting with 1 can suggest that some progress has already been made—starting with 0 can also work in some cases, for example, if you are working with a suicidal patient or with patients who are literally debilitated by anxiety or a phobia (Caby, 2001). Here, too, words can construct realities (Hargens, 2003).

TIPS. *Circular scaling:* Ask the question, *If I was to ask your mother how close you are to achieving your goal, where would she put you on a scale of 1 to 10?*

If a patient is undecided or grades himself badly, it is worth asking the question: *Where would your best friends put you on the scale?* If this answer is different from the patient's own: *What can they see that you can't see?*

Establishing therapy goals. Some patients have a clear vision of how their lives would be if their problem was gone: They are usually able to describe what they would do differently if they were one or two levels up the scale. Others are unable to do this; in this case smaller steps have to be negotiated:

What would you do differently if you were at level 5½ and not 5?

What would you have realized if you had said 5½?

This enables the patient to advance in very small steps and allows for a progressive approach over a number of sessions. Scaling tasks are particularly useful if you are working within a narrow time frame. The client not only establishes where he is on the scale but *proves* it with examples of his own actions. He thereby puts his progress into concrete terms and can continue to build upon it.

In a residential or day unit setting, scaling is used as a group-dynamic intervention, going hand in hand with **Circular questioning** (see page 85). So-called *group barometers* are established: *Who will work on which abilities over the coming week? And where are you on your scale?*

You can also use the scaling system more specifically:

Which of your abilities do you want to work on before the next session? How much do you use this ability at the moment on a scale of 1 (hardly at all) to 10 (all the time)?

And what would you do differently if you were one number higher up the scale?

This intervention focuses on this one ability and conveys your confidence that the patient is able to develop it.

Scaling helps to make complex aspects of clients' lives more concrete—for the therapist as well as for the client.

Scaling also helps the patient to see the nuances between the extremes. It may not even be desirable to want to reach 10, but the following questions can work well: *On what day did you get closest to 10? And what did you do differently on that day that you would rate it so highly?*

Variations on scaling can also be applied, such as **The rubber band** (*see page 137*).

INDICATION. Scaling is suitable for all symptoms and conditions that are in a state of flux. Almost all states of mind can be scaled. With patients suffering from depression, it may be necessary to take very small steps.

An example: Antonia

Sixteen-year-old Antonia is in residential care for the third time because of severe self-harming. She cuts herself with a knife and inflicts burns on herself.

While talking she reveals a sense of humor but repeatedly says that she cannot say what she feels when she harms herself.

She answers many questions with "No idea," or "I don't know," and yet her despair is written on her face.

Diagnostically it is a borderline disorder.

Through scaling, she finally finds a way of tapping into her feelings: She lists a surprising range of feelings and rates them on the scale.

This scaling is the beginning of the actual therapy. Later, Antonia is also able to name and scale positive feelings. Through scaling she very slowly develops the confidence to confront her feelings (see Figure 6).

Therapy often involves finding what motivated the client to seek therapy in the first place. This can be scaled, too.

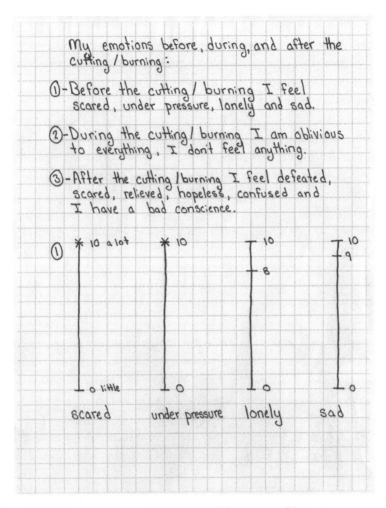

Figure 6: Scaling by a 16-year-old girl with a self-harming problem

Another type of scale that can contribute to the success of a therapy is the *willingness scale*: *How high would you rate your willingness to actually do something to achieve your goals?*

The *confidence scale* can also contribute to evaluating the chances of success of a therapeutic process: *How confident are you that you will achieve the goals that you have set yourself?*

CONTRAINDICATION. None.

SETTING. Individual therapy, family therapy, group therapy, couples therapy.

Reframing

IDEA. Reframing in psychotherapy is equivalent to what the Belgian surrealist René Magritte did in painting: He changed the context of the objects and thereby changed their meaning.

Magritte painted a gigantic flower in a much too small room: As an observer you are initially surprised, and it is only on second glance that you notice that something isn't—or is—right.

Reframing in psychotherapy means seeing things differently or from a new perspective. When problems are given a different—that is, new—frame, they suddenly look very different! The context gives the symptom its particular significance (Hargens, 2003).

METHOD. During a session with a client, it can be very helpful to provide him with a different "frame" or context. This can be done seriously or humorously, but it should always serve the purpose of surprising, stimulating, or opening the "other eye."

Here are some examples:

- With their profusion of ideas, ADHD children ensure that things never get boring.
- Depressed people teach us the art of being thoughtful.
- Arguing couples show us the vitality of their relationship.

TIPS. In order to use this reframing technique in therapy, it is a good idea to try it out in a non-work-related context first. For example, the weekly trip to the supermarket suddenly takes on a new meaning when it is reframed as a ritualistic start to the weekend!

INDICATION. With a little practice and delicacy, it works almost all the time—unless the patient does not understand it due to his cognitive abilities, although, seen from another perspective, this allows the patient to really take his time and immerse himself in the process of understanding.

CONTRAINDICATION. None.

SETTING. Individual therapy, group therapy, family therapy, couples therapy.

Circular questioning

IDEA. Circular questioning incorporates absent or attendant members of a system (e.g., a family) in the therapeutic process, without addressing them directly but rather by asking the respective member(s) to answer on the other person's behalf (Simon & Rech-Simon, 2001).

It is a perfect technique to clarify the constructivist aspect of systemic therapy and to use it! When a client or patient makes a judgment on what the other person would say, he is automatically incorporating his own judgment, because you can only judge from your own point of view. Therefore, it is not the *difference* of opinions that is surprising but the *similarities*.

Ultimately this kind of questioning leads to better mutual understanding, and also gives the therapist or counselor insights into the system and its conflicts or resources (von Schlippe & Schweitzer, 1999).

Those involved are also often surprised by the circular answers!

METHOD. The therapist asks such questions as

If your father was sitting here now, how would he answer the question?

If your husband had been here, would he have said something different?

When I ask your mother in a moment how you are, what do you think she will tell me?

TIPS. Sometimes it helps to emphasize this technique with visual allusions. For example, for an absent member of the system whom you would like to include in the conversation, you can point at an empty chair in the circle or even place an extra chair in the circle.

Circular questioning is a good way of incorporating children and adolescents in a conversation, and they often provide interesting perspectives that up to that point may not have been the focus of the conversation.

With younger children you can also, for example, bring the child's doll into the conversation.

Circular questioning can be effectively combined with other methods.

INDICATION. Can be used almost always.

CONTRAINDICATION. None.

SETTING. Individual therapy, family therapy, group therapy, couples therapy.

Circular parenting

IDEA. This is a variation of **Circular questioning**. Parent-child conflicts often involve just one parent—usually the mother. With single parents there isn't even a choice.

In either case it is useful to have a virtual parenting partner on hand who can be called on for advice. In the case of married couples, this is relatively straightforward; the mother asks herself: *What would my husband say if he were here now?* Or she reminds herself of things they both agree on.

An alternative would be to actually call the other parent or guardian for some pedagogical reinforcement.

From the perspective of a single parent, too, it can be useful to imagine a partner who can be interviewed using the **Circular questioning** technique. He or she can even be given a name, for example, Archimedes: *If Archimedes were here, what would he advise you to do now?* In this way you create an external "repository" of theoretical parenting knowledge that can be drawn upon when needed.

The Miracle Question

IDEA. Insoo Kim Berg and Steve de Shazer (see de Shazer, 1989) developed the Miracle Question to help clients envision the solutions to their problems.

When things are going badly, or even when they are going well, the therapist gets the patient to imagine the future in which the problem has been solved and then to think backward from the future to explain how he solved the problem.

The patient often realizes for the first time that a solution is possible.

METHOD. The Miracle Question should always be introduced as something unusual and shrouded in secrecy and could be formulated as follows:

> *Imagine: Tonight you go to bed early and fall asleep. Soon you are sound asleep, and while you are sleeping, a miracle occurs. And the miracle is this: all your problems have disappeared!*
>
> *But you were fast asleep and have no way of knowing that this miracle has occurred! When you wake up the next morning, what little thing do you think you will notice that makes you realize that a miracle has occurred and your problem has gone?*

As the patient begins to answer, it is important to emphasize his active participation:

> *What will you do differently when the miracle has happened?*
> *What will you do differently at breakfast, while you're brushing your teeth, getting dressed, while going to school, at school, when you come home, and so on?*

And:

> *What will other people notice?*
> *Who will be the first person to notice that the miracle has occurred?*

It is important to envisage the changes in concrete terms!

TIPS. You should allow plenty of time after asking the question. The patient will be surprised by the question and will need time to think. He will be in a solution zone and need to think himself into the task.

Some patients immediately dismiss the question and say things like "There are no miracles" or "I don't believe in miracles." This can be avoided by first asking the patient's permission to ask a rather unusual question.

If the patient's skepticism remains, then you can say:

And what if miracles really did occur?

But you of all people deserve a miracle.

Maybe you'll come back in two weeks and tell me that a miracle really has occurred!

You should ask the question only if you have sufficient time and a harmonious relationship with the patient.

Afterward you should not forget to ask: *What else will change . . . ?* and *What else . . . ?*

INDICATION. The question works best with patients who are really motivated to do something about their problem.

In the words of de Shazer, the patient should be a "client," not a "complainant" or a "customer." The *complainant* comes to share his woes—and usually to complain about others, but not because he wants to change something. The *customer* is interested and comes to gather information so that he can decide at a later stage if this is the right thing for him. The *client* is on a mission and wants to solve something.

CONTRAINDICATION. When the therapist or counselor uses the question mechanically and lets the client get away with a few wishy-washy platitudes.

Caution: The question is so unique that it should not be squandered. It is a form of hypnosis, and should therefore be used carefully and in exactly the right conditions— the question needs time and space!

SETTING. Individual therapy, family therapy, group therapy, couples therapy.

Externalization (narrative therapy)

IDEA. Externalization, or narrative therapy (White & Epston, 1990), enables the client to perceive a problem at a distance so that it becomes more tangible: An enemy outside the gate is easier to fight than one that has infiltrated and become mixed up with one's own resources!

The mere act of externalizing separates the problem from the personality of the child or adolescent who is experiencing the problem (de Shazer & Dolan, 2008). The technique of externalization pushes the problem away and enables the client to close ranks against it.

The key point of externalization is to make the problem more concrete. It becomes easier to comprehend and less threatening, and the patient is given the feeling that he can interact with the problem.

METHOD. There are several ways of externalizing.

Blow the problem away, allowing bubbles loaded with the problem to fly away

The *tea-bag trick* (explained on page 90)

Create a second entity—for example, with anorexics we work successfully with the model of the healthy and the ill entity: *With whom am I talking at the moment?* or *What percentage of the whole person is the healthy part today? And what will we have discussed so that afterward it is 5 percent more?!* and constantly make clear with whom you are currently talking, with the ill or the healthy part of the person.

Transfer pain to a (horrible) soft toy or another object through beaming or blowing

Find a helper figure (see also **Cartoon therapy**, page 125)

Glove puppets to act out conflicts outside of the "self" (see page 118)

Worry dolls that can disappear under the pillow and take away the problems at night (see **Dream catchers and worry dolls**, page 188)

The *backpack of cares,* a bag into which all worries and cares can be stuffed, which you can take for a walk and occasionally put down

Ask questions, such as *What could you give your problem as a gift to put it in a more positive mood?* or *Can you make a cooperation pact with it?* (a strategy often used in politics!) or *Does the problem also have some advantages, and is it worth joining forces sometimes?*

TIPS. Instead of being ruled by a problem, the patient can personify or objectify it, thereby making it more tangible.

An example: A big box of fears

A patient suffering from anxiety suddenly improved when we came up with the idea that this anxiety was so annoying that it should be locked away.

The patient immediately had the idea of building a big box in which she could sometimes lock away her fears. She made the box look like a house, where her fears could go and temporarily live when they got too annoying.

The patient could thereby take time out from her fears and really felt liberated during these times. The box also had a little door, which she could open if she wanted to let her anxiety back out.

The *tea-bag trick* works as follows: you take a typical tea bag, fold it apart without tearing it, and empty out the contents. The bag is now twice as long and looks like a small roll of thin paper. You stand this roll upright on a little plate or saucer and set it alight at the top. Get ready for a surprise!

Drawing the problem as homework is another externalization technique. The client can see the problem, which makes it less threatening. Things that you cannot imagine are always harder to fight than things that you can imagine in concrete terms.

You can get the patient to converse with his problem, to enter into a dialogue with it. This allows the patient to think about whether the problem might also have some useful resources and whether it is worth joining forces to solve further problems.

With a little imagination you can use almost anything! Patients are unbelievably creative when it comes to finding solutions through externalization.

INDICATION. Externalization techniques are easy to use and in our experience have proven to be particularly useful with families under large amounts of strain who no longer have a clear picture of their problem, every type of anxiety, pain syndromes, and problems of all kinds.

CONTRAINDICATION. None; works for children as well as adults!

SETTING. Individual therapy, family therapy, group therapy, couples therapy.

Provoking

IDEA. Like all other interventions, the aim of provoking is to instigate change by increasing the client's sense of possibilities. By provoking the patient, you want to irritate him, arouse his interest, and open his eyes to alternatives.

METHOD. This method involves occasional, selective provocation in order to draw the patient's attention to his self-created blockages or dead ends.

One of the most effective methods is to reflect back to the patient what you have observed in the conversation. Clients are often cooperative enough to demonstrate the reason why they are there during the session. This shows the trust they are putting in the therapist or counselor.

Examples: Provoking

A child is asked a question and the parent answers. And this does not happen once but again and again. The therapist/counselor asks, *Excuse me, but can I just describe to you what I am seeing?* (The question is usually sufficient on its own to bring about change!) You describe exactly what you have observed, and without having addressed anyone in particular, a changed form of communication becomes possible.

A father talks proudly about his daughter and does not notice that she is in the middle of puberty and trying to assert her independence. He thinks that everything that she does is great, which is causing her to feel exasperated. The therapist/counselor asks, *Mr. XY, do you mind if I provoke you?* The father responds: "Sure, go ahead!" *I'm wondering if you would also praise your daughter if she tried to hurt you?*

With a classic dysfunctional family, with no clear hierarchies and a four-year-old son who is given no boundaries and does what he wants, including insult his mother, the therapist/counselor asks, *Excuse me, can I ask who is in charge here?* Usually the father answers. *And why do you let your son insult your wife—or is your son doing that on your behalf?*

Provoking the client is advisable if nothing else works—sometimes people have to be shaken up a bit and confronted with the way they are behaving. When a person is so confident in his behavioral approaches that he no longer notices the needs of those around him, it is necessary to provide alternative perspectives.

The aim of provocation is to make the person pause for thought, so that he begins to see things differently; otherwise, change wouldn't stand a chance. This is the only way of giving the patient the opportunity to develop alternatives and broaden his sense of possibilities.

TIPS. Always ask for permission to provoke the client!

It is worth asking more rather than less frequently, because some of things that we do as a therapist provoke the client even when it isn't our intention.

INDICATION. Only for experienced therapists in a trusting therapist-client relationship based on mutual respect.

CONTRAINDICATION. None.

SETTING. Individual therapy, family therapy, couples therapy.

Creating a "yes" vibe

IDEA. Certain types of questions are simple and effective ways of getting the client to say "yes." Creating a "yes" vibe provides a good basis for further interventions and immediately puts the conversation on a more positive footing.

METHOD. Ask questions that can be answered only with "yes" or questions to which you already know the answer, such as

- *You've had to wait a long time to get an appointment?*
- *You've already done a lot to try and solve the problem?*
- *You've been very patient, haven't you?*
- *You have two other children?*
- *You tried calling recently?*

INDICATION. Can be used at any time, but particularly in difficult discussions or conflict-ridden constellations.

CONTRAINDICATION. None.

SETTING. Individual therapy, family therapy, group therapy, couples therapy.

Rituals

IDEA. Welter-Enderlin (2004) regards rituals as extremely important because they convey a sense of belonging and orientation in an ever-changing world.

The advantage of working with rituals is that most people are familiar with rituals from their everyday lives, patients rarely object to using them, and they allow room for (creative) maneuvers.

Rituals offer support and security and provide structure in times of upheaval or anxiety. Talking about rituals can help to reanimate something that has been lost or almost forgotten, and to reestablish a stabilizing force in everyday life.

Method. Working with rituals is an established approach in systemic therapy and counseling. Not only are rituals an important part of the daily routine in clinics, they can also be incorporated into a variety of methods for treating outpatients.

In group therapy with children, adolescents, and adults, as well as in work with families, they give structure to the sessions and provide clients with a sense of dependability.

Asking about *already existing rituals* is just as important as *initiating new rituals*, for example, in a patchwork family that still has to establish new daily routines.

When you ask clients or families about their everyday or special rituals, you will often find that they are either unaware of them, or really do not have any significant rituals. The conversation then normally leads to exploring potential daily rituals together. Here are two examples:

(1) A young single mother comes with her five-year-old son and eight-year-old daughter. Both children are very lively, and there is frequent conflict—getting them to eat regular meals is particularly difficult, and usually she only succeeds by feeding them in front of the TV. The neighbors have already complained about the noise, and at the boy's kindergarten the teachers have reported that he is often tired and can't concentrate.

When asked about the family's daily routines and rituals, the mother replies that in the morning she often has difficulties getting them out of bed and in the evening getting them to go to sleep. When asked to describe mealtimes, she apologetically explains that there is not enough room for a dining table.

For the next session, she is given the task of concentrating on the methods with which she has already had some success in the evenings and turning them into a fixed bedtime routine.

In the next session the mother discusses the new bedtime routine and also reports on another new idea inspired by her daughter's suggestion of having a picnic in the park: They now eat on a blanket in the living room, which the children really enjoy. And in the next few weeks she will be getting a second-hand folding table for the kitchen, at which family meals will be eaten in the future.

(2) A family has been living in a new house for several months. The father has brought his 12- and 14-year-old daughters into the marriage, and the mother her eight-year-old twins and a dog. Although everybody had looked forward to living together, it is turning out to be more stressful than expected. The family members have very different expectations regarding everyday routines, and the children are trying to play the adults off against each other.

During a conversation with the whole family, the children and parents draw a picture on the topic of "How we eat our meals together." While they are drawing, they talk about how mealtimes are at the moment (problem situation) and share ideas about how mealtimes should be in the future (solution situation).

It quickly becomes clear that the rituals stemming from the two original families could not be easily combined, but each side of the family was also unwilling to simply give them up. For the next session, they were all given a *self-reflection task:* Each member of the family had to decide which rituals were so important that they could not possibly give them up (see *also **Reflecting positions**, page 143*).

In the next session, each member of the family presented his or her wishes, and then the family considered together which rituals could be developed out of these. In the end, a mealtime routine was established that incorporated elements from the original families' routines as well as new, jointly created routines. As one of the twins appropriately put it: "That's us now!"

Thus, family rituals are turned into a point of discussion, and children and adults are asked which of the rituals are particularly important to them, why they are important, how these rituals developed in the family, and so on.

Disagreement about particular traditional family rituals, for example, what the family does over the Christmas holidays or how birthdays are celebrated, leads to more arguments, friction, and negative feelings than you might imagine, which is why it is worth probing and exploring the issue in detail.

TIPS. Combining rituals with other methods works really well, for example, with **Circular questioning** (see page 85): the family members are asked, in turn, which rituals are important to them and, for example, which of them should be retained in the new family constellation: *What would . . . say to that? What would he/she find important?*

Observation tasks and homework: Setting these tasks is particularly interesting with families, who are often convinced that they do not have any rituals or special routines.

The subsequent session is often revealing: After everyone has had time to reflect and observe, it is interesting to find out whether the family really has no routines or rituals, or whether there was in fact something to discover.

Other options include **Prescribing change**, as with the special techniques of drawing and painting together and timeline work (*see page 102*).

Rituals are very important during periods of transition or for marking transitions (e.g., starting kindergarten or school, puberty, graduation). Rituals can also play a role in cases of anxiety, bed-wetting, or other symptoms; they may even be contributing to the problem not going away, which is why it is important not only to ask about rituals but also to examine them closely.

INDICATION. Working with rituals is possible with all indications. Rituals work particularly well with families suffering from a lack of structure, ADHD, aggressive behavioral disorders, emotional problems such as anxiety and depression, lack of self-esteem, and issues surrounding divorce or separation.

Rituals and routines are particularly important for patchwork families and families dealing with separation or divorce! They also work well after the loss of a loved one or when there was no opportunity to say goodbye.

CONTRADICTIONS. Basically none.

Caution: Care should be taken when using with obsessive-compulsive behavior, as there is a danger of reinforcing the symptom.

SETTING. Individual therapy, family therapy, group therapy, couples therapy.

Breaking the pattern

IDEA. By breaking patterns, an attempt is made to break or change old and established behavioral patterns that have led to or contributed to the problem. This should lead to self-reflection, to a change of perspective, and ultimately to behavioral change. Breaking a pattern broadens the patient's perspective and changes his focus. When this is accomplished, the foundations for change have been laid.

Concentrating too hard on finding a direct solution to the problem is often counterproductive. The pattern-breaking approach is a more creative and roundabout way of reaching the desired goal.

All of the interventions in this book can help to break patterns. The intervention you choose depends on the problem.

METHOD. An unusual question, the setting of a task, or an ad hoc intervention in the conversation causes the client to pause and take stock; he has to reorient himself, reconsider his situation, and act accordingly. This reassessment process triggers change.

A case example: Couples therapy

An older married couple came to therapy because they could not break their habit of constant bickering. Sometimes he sparked off an argument; sometimes she did. The result was always the same: They ended up not speaking to each other for hours. This cycle was repeated several times a week. The groundwork for change had already been laid by both of them: neither of them wanted to carry on like this. The following intervention succeeded in breaking down the persistent pattern of arguing.

The woman was asked to think of a way of changing the pattern. After some thought, she decided on her secret hobby: When the next argument started she would sing an aria for three minutes and thirty seconds.

At the next session, two relaxed and smiling people came in and announced that they had not argued at all! The suspense and her hope of being able to sing had been so great, that there had been no room left for arguing! She had broken the pattern before it even began.

INDICATION. Any problematic constellation that follows a stereotypical pattern. If possible, there should be a strong basic trust between the people involved, accompanied by a willingness and desire to change the situation. If there is hostility or resentment, there is little chance of breaking the pattern. Breaking the pattern can also be used right at the start of a therapy or counseling session.

CONTRAINDICATION. Lack of humor and compliance.

SETTING. Family therapy, couples therapy.

Interventions for Home

Observation tasks

IDEA. An observation task is an effective way of changing a client's perspective. Without making it explicit, you invite the patient to look at his problematic situation from a positive point of view. The intervention is effective because it is almost always possible to find something positive! The client begins to see himself differently, suddenly seeing positive aspects where he had previously seen only negative ones. The client is invited to see "his other side" or the other side of the problem.

As a welcome side effect, the client is more motivated to continue with therapy, as therapy no longer seems threatening. It is no longer about dwelling on problems but about focusing on the positive. Children, in particular, like it when their parents also have to do "homework" (see **Therapeutic homework**, *page 110*).

METHOD. Observation tasks can be used for self-observation as well as for observing others. The classic self-observation task is: *Between now and our next session, observe when and where you were satisfied with what you did. And make a few notes so that in the next session we can discuss what you observed.*

This observation task can of course also be used to observe someone else: *Pay attention to what you liked about what your son did!*

TIPS. Observation tasks are *always* solution-oriented and resource-focused tasks; they never involve observing deficits.

Ask for permission to set homework!

INDICATION. Particularly suitable for deficit-oriented systems, and works in a variety of settings:

Individual therapy: What do you like about what you do? It is also good to get the client to observe the absence of a symptom: *Between now and next week, make a note of when you're not scared!*

Couples therapy: Parents and married couples who are at loggerheads can be given the task of observing each other and picking up on positive aspects of each other's behavior, for example, in relation to each other's parenting skills: *Mrs. X, between now and next week, please observe what you like about your husband in his role as a father.* And, of course, vice versa!

It is also possible to use an observation task to help couples without children: *Between now and next time, observe the things that you like about your partner. Don't talk about it with each other—you can talk about anything else, but not that.* Asking clients not to talk about it makes it more exciting and helps them stay more focused on the task. But there should not be too much time between sessions (a maximum of one to two weeks).

Family therapy: Observation tasks can also be very effective with families: Children enjoy observing their parents and checking whether or how they are doing their homework.

Parents who think they are lacking in parenting skills can be set the following task: *Please pay attention to when you are successful in asserting yourself with your children.*

In the next session the results of the observation are made "public," in connection with the question: *How did you do it?*

Group therapy: In group therapy, the intervention works well if the group members see each other between sessions (e.g., in a clinic setting), but not if they meet only during sessions (Caby, 2002).

CONTRAINDICATION. None to our knowledge. But proceed carefully with psychotic patients, who may have a different frame of reference!

SETTING. Individual therapy, family therapy, group therapy.

Prescribing the symptom (paradoxical intervention)

IDEA. It always comes as a surprise when the therapist prescribes the very symptom that the patient has come about. The symptom thereby either becomes less attractive (*I'm not going to do what he wants!*), or the symptom is implemented as part of the homework and loses its appeal.

The means with which patients make a negative impact on their environment (system) now become the goal of the therapy! The child or adolescent becomes an obedient model child because he does exactly the thing that he came to therapy for in the first place!

Another aspect is that patients have to consciously control something that they have done instinctively up to now. They learn to be impulsive in a controlled way and to handle their impulses in a cognitively different way. By having to act impulsively on demand, they gain control over their actions.

The other people involved in the problem system—the observers—have a task that suddenly turns the symptom that they previously suffered under into something desirable.

METHOD. Prescribe the patient his existing symptom. With this intervention, it is often important to assign an observer, who makes sure that the patient follows through with the task.

For example, a mother brings her child to therapy because of his constant lying. The task might be: *Are you prepared to do a rather unusual homework? Could you please lie at least five times a day before the next session? The lies should be so obvious that others are sure to guess them. Your parents have to work out when you are lying!*

For the therapist, this is a win-win task: If the patient completes the task, he has acted in accordance with the therapy; if he does not complete the task, the symptom has disappeared.

Retzlaff (2008) recommends explaining to the patient why such a paradoxical method makes sense: *In your situation it is very important to get to the root of the problem. That's why it is important to keep repeating it.*

As another example, a client comes to you with a very serious problem, and ideally you would like to refer him to a specialist right away. But as there is a long waiting list, something has to be done in the meantime. One possibility would be: *Your situation is so serious that I would strongly recommend that you don't change anything until you've seen a specialist. Until then, just carry on exactly as you are!*

TIPS. Your request will rarely be refused, but ask first if it is okay to set a rather strange task. The result: The task becomes more exciting, and the patient is happy to cooperate.

INDICATION. Defiant patients inadvertently act in accordance with the therapist, because by refusing to do what the therapist asks of them, they prove that they can in fact function without the symptom.

The intervention is also helpful with children who are notorious liars or reveal other provocative or disturbing behavior; children and adolescents who have tantrums: a controlled tantrum is no longer a tantrum. Children who have meltdowns are given the task of having a meltdown at particular times and, if possible, in between as well. The parents make a note of the meltdowns and report back in the next session.

Panic attacks and other sorts of attacks are special indications that patients say strike out of the blue. In this case it is important to get the patient to describe the situation from which the attack arises—there is often a precursor to a panic attack. This can also apply to meltdowns or loss of control. Get the patient to explain exactly how he knows that an attack is "on its way": *How does the attack begin?* and *How do you notice that you are about to get a panic attack?* If the patient is able to describe the feeling and/or localize where he feels it in his body, prescribe this feeling, say, three times a day. The patient should then try and cut short the emerging attack before it even begins. It is very important to practice this task together with the patient during the session. He has to concentrate on a feeling that has previously given rise to fear. If the patient does it in your presence the first time, he will not feel so alone. With the help of this task, patients gain a sense of security and feel less at the mercy of their fear. They are able to cut short the previously automatic transition from crisis to attack. The aura is uncoupled from the attack, and they can control the symptom.

CONTRAINDICATION. *Soiling* and other *unpleasant symptoms* that can jeopardize the compliance of the entire patient system if the homework is actually carried out—which is, after all, the aim of the exercise!

Under no circumstances should it be used with self-harming patients or those who are a danger to others, or with patients suffering from addiction.

A paradoxical intervention is a form of intervention that is usually embedded in a psychotherapeutic treatment, so it is only rarely used in everyday practice. That's why you should use it only if you feel very sure of what you are doing.

SETTING. Individual therapy, family therapy.

Prescribing change

IDEA. This task distracts the patient from the problem at hand, suggests that change is always possible, and shifts the observational focus to positive change. And it is fun, too!

The positive changes that everyone has noticed are then discussed in the next session. These "changes" are in fact often things that were working well but that were no longer obvious because they had become so familiar. The intended change is often lost in a sea of positive observations. But that is exactly what was intended!

METHOD. An exciting task for children and adults alike!

This intervention fits the bill if, during a conversation with a client and his system, you realize that it would do the system good to be shown what kind of effect change can have. But rather than explain it, you want everyone involved to appreciate the power of change for themselves.

For example, you ask a child to change something before the next session, about which everyone will say: "What a great change!" Of course, the child shouldn't tell a soul what he intends to change. The child writes down (if he can write already) or whispers in your ear what he wants to change, so that during the next session you can act as a referee to check whether everyone has done his or her job well.

The task of the parents, guardians, or siblings: *I want you to observe your son/ brother carefully between now and the next session and see if you can work out what has changed!* This is a classic win-win task: By the next session the parents will have discovered either the child's intended change or another positive development, the child is praised for his great work, and the parents for their excellent instincts.

Often the parents will have observed many positive things, just not the intended change: The child is praised for these positive things and is given the task of making the originally intended change even more obvious by the next session, so that it is easier for the observers to find out.

TIPS. The task works particularly well as an observation or homework task. It is often used with children but can also be used in couples therapy. Prescribing change should always be combined with self-observation or the observation of others.

For example, a mother comes with her child because he is suffering from tummy aches again, and she mentions that she and her husband regularly argue. The constant fighting is wearing her and her husband down, and she thinks that the tummy aches could have something to do with the arguing.

If this cycle of conflict really follows an almost stereotypical pattern, a good task might be: *As soon as you start arguing, do something differently. Start to sing or to hop! Or clap your hands! Think of something that will disconcert your husband!*

This task is also an example of **Breaking the pattern** (see page 97).

INDICATION. This task works well with any system that could benefit from change. It is indicated in the following settings.

Individual therapy: Change something and observe how it makes you feel! or *Change something and observe how the others react!*

Family therapy, couples therapy: Many couples would like something to change but can't put their finger on what. This task gives them a taste of all the possibilities.

Group therapy in a residential or semiresidential care setting: In a clinic, patients live in groups and observe each other constantly. These casual observations are usually focused on deficits. With this task you can change the focus of the group.

The many positive new aspects that come to light not only improve the atmosphere in the group but can also be integrated into the respective patient systems.

Group therapy in an ambulatory setting is less conducive because the members cannot usually observe one another between sessions.

CONTRAINDICATION. If the atmosphere in a family is dominated by animosity or hostility, this task will not work, at least not initially—the first task is to establish a more harmonious atmosphere.

SETTING. Individual therapy, family therapy, group therapy, couples therapy.

The change detective

IDEA. See **Prescribing change** (*page 102*).

METHOD. This method is similar to prescribing change, but now the children go in search of changes in their parents. This intervention works well when the mother's and father's parenting styles are out of sync or, for example, when a mother feels that she is doing all the parenting herself. If parents are suffering from something like parental burnout, this intervention reinvigorates their role as a "joint task force" and even adds a bit of fun to the situation.

Each parent has to think of (and write down) a change that he or she thinks the children, as well as the partner, would say is a good change.

TIPS. By getting the clients to write down the intended change, you know what they intend to do and whether the planned change is realistic or not. If it is not, discuss with the client if his or her plan is achievable.

For example, a father wanted to discuss the children with his wife *every day*, after she had complained that they never discussed the children together. When the therapist expressed doubt whether this was realistic, he initially limited his plan to the weekends.

INDICATION. See **Prescribing change** (*page 102*).

CONTRAINDICATION. None.

SETTING. Individual therapy, family therapy, group therapy (residential).

Prescribing what the patient is already doing well

IDEA. By prescribing something that the patient already does well, he is forced to consciously think about what he is doing and how he is doing it.

This method actually leads to the patient doing more of the same—with the result that there is a reduction in the symptomatic behavior. This is one form of paradoxical intervention.

METHOD. This type of intervention can take different forms:

Prescribing what he/she already does well: As the patient explains his problem, you realize that he is already on the right track: *From what you've told me, it seems that a lot of what you are doing is working well. Up to now you've been doing . . . for about one-and-a-half hours a day. Could you do it for three hours?* or *Look at what's working well for you, and do more of the same!*

Utilization: Based on Ericksonian hypnosis, Zeig (2006) uses the behavior he observes during a session to put his patient in a trance. This can be a very effective basis for therapeutic change.

For example, the patient is drumming on the table with his fingers. The therapist/counselor says: *Try drumming even faster with your fingers, and concentrate on the rhythm of your movements. If you concentrate on the rhythm of your movements, you'll notice that it changes. You'll notice that it slows down. Now breathe deeply. Relax . . .*

TIPS. Because of the unusual nature of the task, ask your patient for permission to use it. It is best to use this form of intervention only with clients that you know well. **Note:** It does not make any sense to explain that this is a paradoxical intervention.

INDICATION. As long as the problem you are presented with is not ethically objectionable or criminal, it is fine to use this intervention. But the patient must be in a position to understand why you are using this method.

There are no restrictions to prescribing what the patient already does. Ultimately you are simply picking up on something that the patient is doing himself and that is fundamentally okay.

CONTRAINDICATION. A paradoxical intervention is a form of intervention that is usually embedded in a psychotherapeutic treatment, so it is only rarely used in everyday practice. That's why you should use it only if you feel very sure of what you are doing.

SETTING. Individual therapy, family therapy, group therapy, couples therapy.

Prescribing problem-free times and rooms

IDEA. These tasks are also designed to give clients the feeling that they can influence the symptom and are no longer dominated by their problem.

Both problem-free times and problem-free rooms enable progress to be made. They also allow the patient to progress at his own pace, because he is in a position to decide on or negotiate the time or space in which he will forego his problem.

METHOD. Together with the client you work out *times* during which the problem is allowed to happen. It is a good idea to adapt these to the habits or system of the patient.

With an obsessive-compulsive disorder (see also **Compulsions and Tics**, *page 214*) the task might be:

When don't you have your compulsions?

What do you do during this time?

How long do you think you could go without succumbing to your compulsion?

If the answer is a few minutes, ask the patient to try and double the time.

If you manage to double the time, you can have your compulsions again.

Pay attention to how you feel during your compulsion-free times!

This task can be applied to *spaces* as well as time. A good way of going about this is to get the client to draw a rough plan of his house or apartment. The client chooses one of the rooms in which he intends not to have any compulsions. As soon as he finds himself in this room he has to stop his obsessive-compulsive behavior.

With this room version, it is a good idea to first ask the client in which room(s) he can imagine it working.

INDICATION. This intervention can be used for anxiety, behavioral problems such as nail-biting and thumb-sucking, obsessive-compulsive behavior, and conflicts and disharmony.

With families, couples, or other systems you can negotiate "conflict-free times" or stipulate rooms in which arguing is not allowed. It is advisable to appoint a referee who ensures that everyone sticks to the agreement!

For example, a new referee can be appointed each time, and his or her job is to make sure that the chosen times or rooms really are conflict free.

This could be augmented by stipulating times during which the clients *have* to argue! (see **Prescribing the symptom**, *page 100*).

Tips. For this task, as with **The forecast calendar** (*see page 108*), there should already be times when the problem is not present. It is difficult to stipulate symptom-free times or symptom-free rooms if the problem is omnipresent.

Once you are sure that there are exceptions to the problem, it is important to respect the speed at which the patient wants to progress. If he begins by establishing short symptom-free times, it is appropriate to continue the process in similarly small steps.

Contraindication. No other contraindications are known. It is important to have made a good diagnosis in advance, if, for example, you want to use the task with obsessive-compulsive disorders. The task can also work with tics, but tics are involuntary movements that cannot really be controlled.

Setting. Individual therapy, family therapy, couples therapy.

The forecast calendar

IDEA. Forecasting not only distracts from the problem (the focus is on the client's forecasting ability) but also takes away the negative pressure of the problem because, combined with the right forecast, it suddenly becomes associated with success.

Furthermore, the emotional aspect of the problem is removed, because it is reduced to an objective assessment of the correctness of the forecast. And last but not least, the patient realizes that he may in fact have some influence over his problem.

For the therapist or counselor, it is a win-win task, because either the forecasts are correct or the problem has abated.

Reports from families confirm that the task gave them some breathing space again and that they could care for their child "differently."

METHOD. For diagnostic reasons, keeping a calendar is a common practice with many clinical pictures. The purpose is usually to help the doctor or counselor clarify the frequency (e.g., soiling) or intensity (e.g., pain) of the problem.

A calendar can also be used therapeutically in combination with the forecasting task:

For example, a child is given the task of forecasting if his bed will be wet the following morning or not. He should write down his forecast in a calendar the evening before and the next morning write beside it whether his forecast was correct or not. *Can you carry on doing this until our next session? Because I would like to know if you are a good forecaster!*

In the next session, count up the number of correct forecasts or dry days. Your response should be based on whatever was most successful. If the patient's forecast was accurate, then you can show that you were impressed and explain that you are excited to see if it will be the same next time.

If a child has suddenly started wetting his bed less—which is usually the case—then you know that the child has become drier through the distraction of the forecasting. You should encourage the child to "keep it up!" and also discuss how this success was achieved.

TIPS. Please always check two things in advance:

- Does the child understand what is meant with a forecast? (You could give the weather forecast on the radio or TV as an example. Most children are familiar with this!)
- The intervention makes sense only if there are already exceptions to the problem. It will work only if there are already days when the problem does not arise. If a child always wets his bed, then forecasts make no

sense—if the weather was always good, we wouldn't need a weather forecast anymore!

Try not to explain anything! If you have to provide an explanation, tell the child that you want to find out how well he can forecast, not how well he can forecast his bed-wetting. It's about the forecasting, not the bed-wetting!

INDICATION. With all symptoms that take us by surprise, such as bed-wetting, soiling, panic attacks, syncope, insomnia, and nightmares.

CONTRAINDICATION. See Tips, above: This approach does not work if the patient does not know what a forecast is or the problem is omnipresent.

SETTING. Individual therapy, family therapy.

Therapeutic homework

IDEA. Associations with school can sometimes give the term *homework* a negative overtone, but in therapy and counseling, homework in fact offers a wealth of possibilities and can support the client's ability to bring about change in a wide variety of ways (Wendlandt, 2002).

Many different kinds of tasks can be given to the client to do between sessions, and they can have different functions, from self-observation and self-reflection, to managing symptoms, to psychoeducation and behavioral modifications (Ronan & Kazantzis, 2006; Fehm & Helbig-Lang, 2009).

Homework can also provide a taste of how solutions could be brought about, and it invites the client to continue experimenting with ideas as a matter of course outside of the consultation room. But there are two snags:

1. What do you do if the client does not do his homework? This question is perhaps the most difficult to answer. If the homework has not been done, it is best for the therapist to accept the responsibility, for example, *Then I probably gave you the wrong homework to do.* This applies as a general rule, but it is still worth asking the client why he did not do the homework: What, as a therapist, did you overlook, not register, or perhaps not check in advance?

2. The second problem arises if the therapist forgets that he set homework in the previous session. Ideally, the patient will remind the therapist of the homework, but in the worst-case scenario, homework will be regarded as something not particularly important.

In order to respond in more detail to these two problems, we have here summed up the main reasons for, and advantages of, setting homework:

- According to de Shazer (1989) the most important point of homework is to provide the client with opportunities to alter his perception and see situations from a different perspective.
- According to the motto "Therapy or counseling can be fun!" homework should also be enjoyable and contain the implicit invitation to move away from the problem.
- An important reason for doing homework is to bring about change without wanting to change anything: *Whatever you do, don't change anything!* This instruction automatically brings about change, because the client is so concentrated on what he is doing (the same) that he perceives it differently.
- Relaxation exercises can also be set as homework.

The Therapist's Treasure Chest

- Homework intensifies and supports the therapeutic process. Clients can try acting as if the miracle had occurred (see **The Miracle Question**, *page 87*), try something new, change their focus, and so on—what can be said against implementing wishes that one already has?
- Practicing something new activates and stabilizes new neurological networks: the problem behavior is gradually countered by the solution behavior, to the point where it is easier to call upon the latter.
- The new experiences happen in the client's own context and are therefore automatically adapted to this context, so that they can have an effect that would not have been possible for the therapist to foresee—which is a good thing. The point of homework is not to implement the therapist's plan but for the client to come up with his own ideas and for these to develop.
- The client is not the only one responsible for completing his homework. If the homework is positively designed, it improves the client's self-efficacy and supports the success of a therapy; unappealing homework, on the other hand, is often not done. It is the job of the therapist to make the homework exciting and context oriented.
- Clinical experience and initial studies suggest that therapies that include homework are more successful than therapies without homework (Fehm & Helbig-Lang, 2009).

METHOD. How do you determine if homework is useful or effective? A few criteria need to be considered:

- The homework must fit exactly to the client. It is therefore necessary to first discuss with the client if he can imagine doing a particular homework. *Act as if the miracle had already happened . . .* is unlikely to work with a family that is not creative.
- Homework must be doable and must be tailored to the stage of the respective stage of therapy/counseling.
- The therapist must feel absolutely sure that the patient is in a position to take on the responsibility for his own therapy. This, in turn, rests on the therapist's conviction that the most important therapy takes place between—and not during—therapy sessions.

The term *homework* often has negative connotations. This may be one of the main reasons why it is not done in many families. On the other hand, there is an attractive side to the word *homework*: Many children love the idea that their parents will also have to do homework and keep a close eye on their parents to make sure they actually do it!

Here are some other criteria for good homework:

- Before setting the homework, ensure that everyone involved considers the homework to be doable and that they are willing to take it on.
- Homework should be explained as precisely as possible and should be as closely related as possible to the therapy that has taken place during the session.
- Homework provides a link to the therapy process, which is why the therapist should ask about the homework in the next session or, if there is a long gap between sessions, call up to check how it is going.
- Written instructions with explanations can be very helpful in some circumstances. Some therapists or counselors even provide a report sheet for the client to fill in, to give the exercise more importance.
- All homework needs to be subsequently discussed and even become an integral part of the subsequent session.

Many of the exercises in this section are good "homework." Here are several ideas:

- Homework revolving around *asking about exceptions* (see **Asking about exceptions**, *page 79*) might be increasing the periods when the problem does not exist: *When is the symptom not there? What does the client do differently during these times?*
- Creating a *resources genogram* with the help of the whole family (see **The resources family tree**, *page 71*).
- Ask the client to try something new between sessions.
- With decision-making problems ask: *Which abilities speak in favor of which decisions?* (possibly in combination with **Resource memory**; *see page 74*).
- In couples therapy ask the clients to return to places that have been important in their relationship, for example, *Go back to the place where you met!*
- *Observation tasks* have many applications (see **Observation tasks**, *page 98*), for example,
    ° Have the client observe what is going well.
    ° Ask a family to reflect on a joint activity or endeavor (see *also* **Reflecting positions**, *page 143*).

○ Ask the client what he observes about himself that makes him realize he has made progress and that he has taken some small steps along his scale toward improvement.

○ Ask the client to observe what happens instead of the symptom.

• A popular homework is to get children to find out the meaning behind a saying like *You can really think outside the box* or *That seems to be the elephant in the room.*

• You can also set a very direct or confrontational homework, such as asking the patient to do exactly what he has set himself as a goal by the next session. For example, a boy who has a problem socializing with his peers could be set the task of making contact with other adolescents and making a note of how he manages this (i.e., solution activation).

The most important job of the therapist or counselor is to check the results of the homework in the next session. As an adolescent patient once succinctly put it: "It's a real turn-off if nobody cares how the homework went."

Clearly reviewing the homework with everyone involved works wonders!

TIPS. You can even make the setting of the homework seem more exciting: *I've got a task for you to do at home that could help you achieve your goal. Do you feel like giving it a go?*

As a therapist or counselor, you should not put yourself under pressure to succeed because this then puts the client under the same pressure.

Drawing solutions or writing letters are also forms of homework, as are **Observation tasks** (see *page 98*). And of course, you can also involve the client (system) in developing a homework: *What kind of homework do you think you would be good at?*

In the clinic where we work, we have a file in which we document homework and (if applicable) write down who the homework was set by and which objects the patient was given to take away with him.

INDICATION. Whenever the patient system needs to be motivated—particularly with anxieties, depression, ADHD.

CONTRAINDICATION. Whenever the patient system is absolutely unmotivated.

SETTING. Individual therapy, family therapy, couples therapy, group therapy, teams.

Letting fate decide

IDEA. There are patients who cannot control their behavior—one moment they behave one way; the next moment, another. They are unpredictable to themselves and those around them. In this case it makes sense to relieve them of the decision of how to behave. This is done by suggesting to them that fate will decide how they will behave on a given day.

For twice the effect, combine with **Observation tasks** (*see page 98*).

METHOD. If a patient feels that he is unable to control his own moods, it is important to give him a way of dealing with it—the *two-entity model* is helpful in this respect: *There seem to be two of you: the John who wants to be healthy, and the John who wants to stay ill. How do you decide when to be which one? Maybe it would be easier if you let fate decide which one you are going to be.*

You suggest an idea to the client: *I've got a coin, and it will decide which John you will be each day: one for heads and the other for tails. Every morning you should toss the coin in the presence of your parents, and depending which way it lands, you will know how you have to behave.*

And at the end of the day, I suggest that your brother and sister should try and work out which way the coin fell that morning.

A case example: "Good Aiden"

Aiden, a 12-year-old boy with Asperger's syndrome behaved appropriately around adults but extremely provocatively and unpredictably around his contemporaries. He had to change schools twice because there wasn't a single class that was able or willing to put up with him.

Aiden could not explain his behavior and was admitted to a clinic, where very soon he was displaying the same behavior and experiencing the same reactions: The other adolescents in the ward didn't want to have anything to do with him. He was almost at his wits' end, because he was beginning to think that the more he tried to do things properly, the worse things became. The nurses, on the other hand, reported positive changes in his behavior.

Because Aiden still did not know how he controlled his behavior, we decided together that every morning he would toss a coin in front of a nurse. In the evening the other nurses had to guess on which side the coin had landed that morning.

He did not find it difficult to be the "good Aiden"; it was more difficult to be the "other Aiden." As the "other Aiden" he had to exhibit his old behavioral patterns, which he wasn't able to do very effectively—the night-shift nurses usually thought that fate had chosen the "good Aiden."

TIPS. Instead of a coin, you can also use a die, which can make the exercise more varied. Since there are six possibilities, several scenarios are possible. With even numbers it is the turn of the "good side"; with the odd numbers, the "other side." Or from 1 to 4 it is the turn of the "good side"; with 5 or 6, the "other side." The weighting can be adjusted from session to session based on how well the client did. (*See also* **Dice: "Playing with possibilities,"** *page 182.*)

INDICATION. A good method to use with patients who seem unable to influence their behavior.

CONTRAINDICATION. To be avoided if the "other side" is prone to aggressive outbursts or harming himself or others.

SETTING. Individual therapy, family therapy, group therapy, couples therapy.

Acting-as-if tasks

IDEA. Sometimes it is important to simply *do* things instead of dwelling on the (supposedly) ideal circumstances needed for change. When patients are given the task of doing something, they get a taste of what it feels like to act in a certain way.

Many patients come to therapy thinking that they can change the way they act only after they have first changed their feelings and emotions. From a neuropsychological point of view, the opposite makes more sense—our brain learns by doing: "Doing is knowing" (Berg & de Shazer, 1998).

By prescribing change, you are inviting patients to behave differently so that they can literally experience the advantages of behaving that way—and it makes it easier to repeat this behavior later.

METHOD. This task works well in combination with, or as a continuation of, **The Miracle Question** (*see page 87*). It is also almost always combined with **Observation tasks** (*see page 98*).

The patient is set the following task: *I would like to make a suggestion: Every morning at breakfast, **act as if** . . . had occurred, and pay attention to what exactly you do and how you feel.*

It also works well in combination with **Scaling** (*see page 81*): ***Act as if** you were no longer at level 5, but at level 6!* (provided the client has a concrete idea of what he would do differently if he was at level 6 on the scale).

TIPS. This intervention can and should be used liberally, because ultimately you are "only" picking up on the ideas and wishes of the patient.

A variation of the acting-as-if task is *role play*, which works well with sibling rivalry, for example: *Act as if you are your brother, and he will act as if he is you!* This can also be set as a daily homework in combination with an observation task for the parents or the other siblings.

INDICATION. This is a popular form of intervention in family therapy. For example, following the Miracle Question, the children can be set the task of acting as if the miracle had occurred one day a week. The task of the parents it to work out which day it was.

The following week the roles are reversed. The parents act as if the miracle had occurred, and the children have to work out which day it was.

This intervention is also popular in couples therapy, and because it is a fun exercise, it is also often successful.

CONTRAINDICATION. None.

SETTING. Individual therapy, couples therapy, family therapy.

Reinforcing a positive mood

IDEA. By establishing a positive mood in the simplest sense, the patient often begins to believe in himself more and to implement his ideas with more confidence. From a neuropsychological perspective, the form described here serves to reinforce the patient's intentions with the aid of his own abilities (Renner, 2005).

METHOD. If a client is struggling or afraid of something he is trying to achieve, you can positively reinforce his intention.

Caution: This form of reinforcement should not be confused with the reinforcement of positive abilities used in trauma therapy or neurolinguistic programming, a form of psychotherapeutic intervention requires a lot of experience.

Ask the patient to think of a sentence that describes his intention, for example, "I can do it!" or "I am brave!" Then give the patient the task of writing this sentence as many times as it will fit on a piece of printer paper, but each time in a different color. Or ask the patient to write the sentence using his left hand (if he is right-handed). In this way his intention becomes linked with other areas of the brain and is stabilized.

This task can be carried out during the session or be set as homework. However, it is advisable for the patient to do it initially under observation.

TIPS. This task really works only when the patient is already in a "yes mood" (see **Creating a "yes" vibe**, *page 93*).

INDICATION. School phobia, social anxieties, shyness, depression.

CONTRAINDICATION. None.

SETTING. Individual therapy.

Special Techniques

Direct Interventions in Conversation

Glove puppets

IDEA. Dolls and toys are a popular medium for getting clients to answer (unpleasant) questions and to reveal things about themselves that might otherwise be difficult to formulate.

METHOD. Glove or finger puppets are a wonderful tool for getting a conversation started. Children and adolescents should be allowed to pick out a toy or puppet of their choice.

TIPS. Rooms for working with children or adolescents should always be equipped with a small selection of dolls, puppets, and other materials, for example, in a basket or box that is easily visible on the floor or a shelf.

Flea markets are a good place to find glove puppets or dolls for not much money.

Another variation is to work with the *child's favorite toy* (with **Circular questioning**; *see page 85*): *I see you've brought your teddy bear with you. Would it be okay if I asked him how he thinks you are doing?* or *I wonder if your doll has an idea what you could do next time you feel frightened?*

INDICATION. This method works as an icebreaker for establishing a therapist-client bond with mute children or children with disabilities.

It is a particularly good method for using with young children, but it can also be used with adolescents or adults who are unable to express their suffering—a doll often works.

In a clinic setting, it is often a good way of making initial contact with anorexic girls.

CONTRAINDICATION. None, although care should be taken with the choice of doll or puppet—it should not frighten the patient!

SETTING. Individual therapy, sometimes group therapy or family therapy.

Drawing together

Scribbling and doodling together

IDEA. Few words are required; the activity is enough of an invitation (Winnicott, 1971).

Even if a child and therapist have not yet had much contact with each other, this kind of shared activity is an effective way of establishing a relationship. And even if the therapist does not know anything about the child, the conversation usually provides interesting material that can be returned to later.

METHOD. Sit down together with the child with some pens and paper. Begin to draw little squiggles with your eyes closed, and then invite the child to continue the drawing in the same way.

Take turns scribbling and drawing, and talk about the picture as you draw.

TIPS. This technique functions well as a peripheral activity, for example, while simultaneously having a conversation with the parents.

This joint drawing activity can also be carried out on a nonverbal level, with the resulting picture talked about afterward.

INDICATION. A good way of starting a session, and always a good way of making initial contact, particularly with children who may initially be shy.

This method has also proven to be successful in family therapy, particularly with families who find it hard to talk to one another.

CONTRAINDICATION. If there is not enough time for a relaxed drawing session.

SETTING. Individual therapy, family therapy.

Ways of drawing together

- Scribbling and doodling together
- The self-portrait (resource-focused)
- The problem picture
- Working with the child's name
- Drawing with children and families
- Cartoon therapy
- Timeline work

The self-portrait (resource-focused)

IDEA. While drawing, it is possible to talk about the picture, to look for resources, and to ask about different situations or feelings. The picture also provides a good basis for further exploration in the diagnostic phase during the course of therapy.

METHOD. Invite the child to draw a picture of himself, either a portrait or a picture of his whole body, perhaps with his favorite animal or toy, or as an action picture in which he is doing something he likes.

Meanwhile, either talk with the parents, sit at your desk and do something completely different, or, if you ask for permission, sit nearby and watch the drawing process while asking questions: *I'm just wondering, how somebody who . . .* or *Can I ask you to explain what exactly you mean?*

TIPS. Girls often find it easier to draw; boys may need to be motivated first. It can be helpful to have a template with a cool frame, or in which the shape of the head has already been drawn, to make putting pen to paper less intimidating.

You can offer a paintbrush instead of a pen, as far as this is feasible in the rooms being used.

INDICATION. For the diagnostic phase and for delving deeper during the course of therapy; with children (and adolescents) with self-esteem problems and social phobias; also for portraying feelings (e.g., anger picture); with aggressive and oppositional behavior; also in the case of loss or separation.

CONTRAINDICATION. Children with *fine-motor-skill problems* might benefit more from other methods (e.g., **Glove puppets**, collages), depending on their age (see *page 118*).

SETTING. Individual therapy, family therapy, group therapy.

A case example: The story behind the picture

Michael, a ten-year-old boy, came to therapy with his parents because he was causing a lot of trouble on the afternoons when he had homework. He often needed several hours to do the work, far more time than his classmates. He had recently started junior high school, and he also needed much more time than was available during lessons to complete tasks. His father, a civil servant, often got into heated arguments with his son and in the first session emphasized how important it was for Michael to get the "right" grades so that he could follow a similar career path.

When Michael was asked to draw a picture of himself, he refused on the grounds that he was not a good drawer and asked instead if he could write something about himself (see Figure 7). In his text, Michael described the problem and the solution without it even being discussed in advance. His self-portrait or, rather, "self-description" served as a trigger to talk about each family member's goals and wishes for the future. Michael was able to express that he would really like to work as a craftsman, perhaps as a carpenter. After

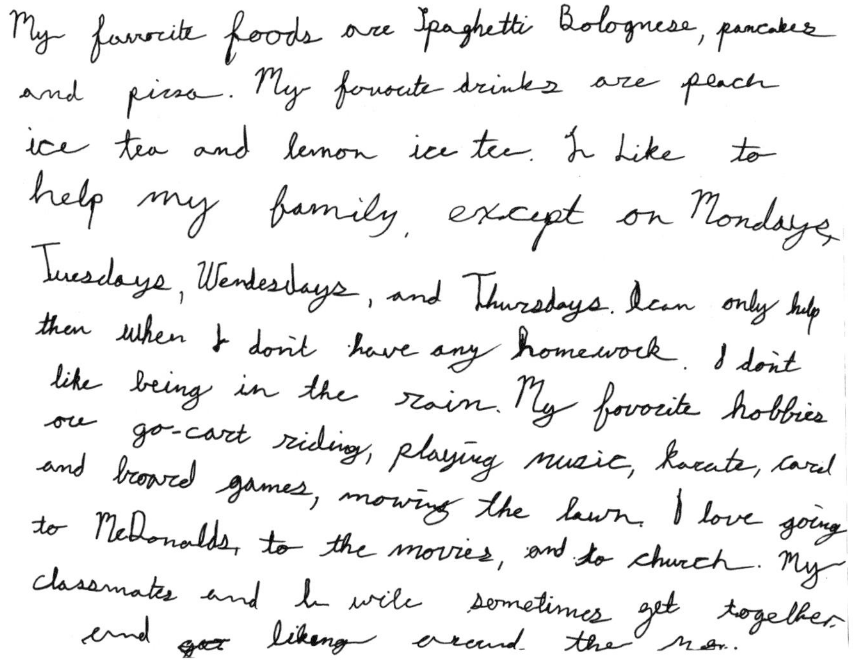

My favorite foods are Spaghetti Bolognese, pancakes and pizza. My favorite drinks are peach ice tea and lemon ice tea. I Like to help my family, except on Mondays, Tuesdays, Wendesdays, and Thursdays. I can only help then when I dont have any homework. I dont like being in the rain. My favorite hobbies are go-cart riding, playing music, karate, card and brownd games, mowing the lawn. I love going to McDonalds, to the movies, and to church. My classmates and I will sometimes get together and got liking around the mas.

Figure 7: Michael, 10 years old: How a self-portrait becomes a solution portrait

changing to a school with an emphasis on project and practical work, he blossomed and the problems at home were soon resolved.

The problem picture

IDEA. Some problems cannot be discussed, either because the client does not dare to or because the problem is so threatening or shameful that the client is overwhelmed by the mere idea of mentioning it. Some problems—for example, a generalized fear or pain—are not easy to describe.

In such situations, we have found that it often helps to give the client an opportunity to draw. A problem becomes a lot less threatening if it is visualized. Here, too, drawing can provide relief.

METHOD. The patient can be given the task of drawing a problem or symptom picture during the session or as homework.

The first option provides an opportunity to address the problem right away; the second option works well with adolescents and adults who need more time. You should discuss with the client when he should draw the picture.

But there are no limits to artistic creativity!

Tips. The problem picture is frequently used as the basis for further discussion. When talking about the picture, new aspects may become apparent that point toward a solution. This can be incorporated into a second picture, the so-called solution picture (Vogt-Hillmann & Burr, 2009a).

Indication. Fear, pain (see above).

Contraindication. None.

Setting. Individual therapy.

Working with the child's name

Idea. With this technique, the name of the patient is associated with particular abilities that he already has or that he wishes he had. Children in particular, but adults too, enjoy experimenting with their own name. Someone who does not like their name, for example, learns to see its attractive side.

Method. Ask the patient to draw, or write, his name in the middle of a big piece of paper (letter or legal). Then examine the name together and think of abilities that start with each letter, and write these abilities above the respective letters. This task can also be given to the patient to do alone—during the session or as homework—and discussed afterward.

The client may need some help getting started, for example: *Your name is S A R A H, so it begins with an "S." What strength or ability do you think "S" could stand for?* When the patient does not come up with ideas of her own, you can make suggestions: *Could the "S" perhaps mean strong? Or do you think "self-confident" would suit you better?*

The patient can then quickly develop her own ideas. For example, when she says that she would like to be more self-confident (thereby providing a topic for subsequent discussion: *What would you have to do to become more self-confident . . . ?*), she suddenly remembers that a school friend of hers once said that Sarah was "super sporty" (*Great! Two "S" words!*) and also a good "swimmer." Quickly Sarah thinks of abilities for the other letters and adds these to the picture, also writing down what she wishes for the future ("a horse to look after, so that I can go riding every day . . .") and proudly takes the picture home to hang over her bed ("Then I can look at it every night before I go to bed!").

Tips. You can also explore the name of the child in different ways; for example, you can ask if the child knows the meaning of his name and if he knows who chose this special name.

It is just as interesting to work with the first names of the parents, to discuss their origins and meanings and in some cases to look up the meaning together, as many names are associated with a special ability (e.g., Felix = the happy one).

The Therapist's Treasure Chest

With adolescents and young adults, this kind of work is very helpful when they are at the stage of choosing a career. The abilities that are discovered can be used in job applications. Young people usually do not have much of an idea which of their qualities and abilities would go down well in a job application, and therefore find this method especially helpful.

INDICATION. Particularly useful with children who are timid or lacking in confidence, adults with self-esteem problems, adolescents searching for their own identity.

CONTRAINDICATION. Care should be taken with adopted or foster children if you do not know how much the child knows about his roots. In this case you may want to limit the exercise to the first name.

SETTING. Individual therapy, family therapy, group therapy, couples therapy.

Drawing with children and families

IDEA. Getting a family to draw together provides an ideal opportunity to watch them interacting and to observe the relationships between the different family members. The completed picture can then be discussed, and the therapist can hone in on particular observations:

I was surprised that . . .

Can I ask why exactly you chose to draw this figure?

I'm amazed at how harmoniously you all worked together to create the picture!

METHOD. Getting a child to draw a self-portrait, a picture of another person, or his family as animals is a common method in individual therapy. However, when a child comes together with his or her family, other approaches are possible.

The adults in the family are usually surprised by the suggestion of drawing a picture together. The children are generally easier to convince but may, in turn, have to convince their parents (or siblings) to join in. There are frequently lengthy discussions about how to approach the task, but sometimes families find a solution surprisingly quickly; for example, they might decide to each draw their own picture.

Whichever way the drawing exercise proceeds, it is always interesting and always very unique. Every family develops its own dynamic, recognizes different challenges, and comes up with its own solutions.

TIPS. In most families, the children usually take the initiative and get things started; adults tend to be more reserved and less convinced of their abilities. But it is impressive to see how they are then supported and motivated by their children, how the roles are suddenly reversed and the children demonstrate all sorts of abilities—in the way they praise their parents, as well as in their drawing.

INDICATION. This method is a good introduction to the diagnostic phase, in order to understand the family dynamic better.

This is also useful during the course of therapy, to emphasize the resources of individual family members, to integrate each individual, and to shift the focus away from the client's "problem" and place him in a different context.

This technique works well with patchwork and separated families. Through the process of visualization, they can see the new or changed family structures from a different perspective.

ANOTHER TIP. It is important to get every member of the family involved in these tasks. Even small children, who cannot draw in the same way as their older siblings, should be allowed to join in and, indeed, be invited to do so.

Sometimes this can lead to surprising results.

A case example: "Finished!"

The Kendall family had four children; the youngest, Samuel, was three years old. According to his parents, Samuel was a particularly difficult child who whined a lot and quickly became aggressive if he was not constantly the center of attention or did not get his way. Even his siblings often did what he wanted in order to avoid constant pinching, scratching, and shrieking.

When the parents and the three older siblings were supposed to be drawing a family picture of their current situation, but weren't making much headway because they were so immersed in talking, nobody had noticed that Samuel had also begun to draw. While the others were loudly discussing why they did not want to be the first person to draw, or lamenting that they were bad at drawing, the youngest member of the family had already finished his picture.

He then picked it up from the floor where he had been sitting, went to the table where the other members of the family were still deciding what to draw, and placed it in the middle of the empty piece of paper (see Figure 8). Samuel looked at the little scrap of paper with his creation in the middle of the other piece of paper, and then looked challengingly at the rest of his family and said: "Finished!"

There was a short silence, followed by laughter, and the spell was broken.

CONTRAINDICATION. This technique is not usually powerful enough with extreme or acute conditions. It can lead to aggression and does not allow enough room for the family's actual problem to be discussed.

It is a good idea to ask the family if they would even like to draw together.

SETTING. Family therapy, group therapy.

Figure 8: The "Finished" picture by Samuel (3 years old)

Cartoon therapy

IDEA. This technique involves drawing in the style of cartoon whereby the client unconsciously taps into his own resources to develop a solution to his problem.

METHOD. The patient is asked to divide a piece of paper into six equally sized squares, similar to the way a cartoon or comic is divided up (Vogt-Hillmann et al., 1999).

1. In the first square, the patient is asked to draw his *problem,* for example, his fear.
2. In the next square he draws a *helper figure,* for example, an action hero that he knows from a book, film, or elsewhere, that he thinks would be a good helper. The helper figure could also be entirely imaginary. Whoever or whatever it is, the figure helps the patient to solve the problem.
3. In the third square, the patient draws how he and the helper figure decide on a *gift* to give the problem (for example, give "fear" a sled, so that it can quickly drive away).
4. In the next picture the problem is given the *gift.*
5. In the penultimate square, the problem is drawn again, but now how it looks *after* it has been given the *gift.*
6. In the last square, the patient draws himself and his helper figure in a different situation in which the problem might arise *again.*

At the end of the session, the picture can be taken home to hang on the wall—clients usually know immediately where they want to put it.

Adults may find this an odd-sounding task, but children are astonishingly creative and often create the most amazing cartoons. And even adults were children once . . . !

TIPS. It is important to be present while the client is drawing in order to watch the process and to express amazement at the abilities that are being revealed.

Around 20–30 minutes is needed for the drawing task, and it is important that it is carried out in a quiet atmosphere, without the constant interruption of a ringing phone, and so on—so perhaps at the end of the day or as part of a longer psychotherapy session.

INDICATION. Most suitable for school-age children, who often suffer from specific anxieties and are also happy to draw. Adolescents and even adults are also often happy to be set this task.

It is extremely helpful for dealing with fears and anxieties, such as fear of the dark, fear of going to sleep, separation anxiety, and fear of certain animals.

It is important to consider on a case-to-case basis whether this method is suited to the particular patient.

CONTRAINDICATION. None, except if the client has very obvious fine-motor-skill difficulties.

SETTING. Individual therapy.

Timeline work

IDEA. By drawing a timeline, particular important situations in a client's life can be viewed from different perspectives and discussed in a resource-focused way.

METHOD. This technique is suitable for children from school age onward, but is particularly good for adolescents, adults, and families.

Ask the client (or each member of the family) to choose symbols to represent significant events or stages in their life, or to write down these events on a card. These symbols can be personal objects or things in the consultation room. (Here, too, it is a good idea to have a dedicated "treasure chest" in the consultation room.)

Arrange the objects or cards in chronological order on the table or floor to create a biographical timeline from the past to the present. Some patients prefer a long roll of paper on which they can mark the stages of their life.

The advantage of laying out a timeline on the floor is that you can walk along it—from the present back to the past and vice versa, and even to the future:

Can you imagine how it would be if . . . ?

How would your life ideally be in 5 or 10 years' time?

What could you do to make this possible?

Which of your abilities could help you to achieve this?

You can also work with a rope, a cord or band, an imagined line, or an existing pattern that happens to be on the floor or carpet. The individual "stations" can be marked with objects that are in the room, for example, with glove puppets, soft toys, or postcards. Basically, it is possible to use anything the client would like.

Sometimes it is helpful to simply name the different situations and write them on a little piece of card (perhaps also with the date and year) or to draw a picture (with paper, colored cardboard, or rolls of wallpaper and a variety of pens).

Tips. You can be very creative with this task and use a wide variety of materials, for example, photos or collages.

This method also works with couples: here the focus could be on the shared "relationship path."

In some cases this task can be combined with other techniques, such as **Circular questioning** (see page 85), **Observation tasks** (see page 98), **Therapeutic homework** (see page 110), or **The Miracle Question** (see page 87).

Indication. For every kind of life crisis, particularly after the separation of parents, for puberty-related problems, for leave-taking processes, with issues like adopted or foster children, or with dissocial children or adolescents. In all cases, getting clients to walk along the timeline can be very revealing.

Contraindication. Unsuitable for severe depression or psychoses.

Caution: Special care should be taken with clients with suicidal tendencies—it is very important to ask for permission. Even in such cases, though, this method can be very effective.

Setting. Individual therapy, family therapy, couples therapy.

Biography work

IDEA. Those who do not grow up in their birth family often have unanswered questions regarding their biological parents, as well as about their early years, the pregnancy and birth, and their extended family.

In some cases, further information is available through contact persons or files; in other cases, there is no way of filling in the biological gaps.

Kindl-Beilfuß (2010) makes a case for turning a problem biography into a success biography, particularly with children and adolescents.

METHOD. Biographical work with children, adolescents, and adults can be an exciting but also an arduous and protracted undertaking. However, motivation can be increased by means of different creative approaches, changing perspectives, and opportunities for active involvement.

One approach—based on work with timelines (see **Timeline work**, *page 126*)—is to first of all address events from the client's life so far and to write these down on different pieces of card. These are then placed at intervals along a line (e.g., a ribbon in the client's favorite color, a rope, an available pattern on the wall or floor).

It is then up to the client and therapist to decide how to travel along this line—whether into the past or the future, or to a particular place or event.

If the client has had a very difficult or traumatic childhood, it is advisable to begin with a therapeutic story (see **Therapeutic stories and fairy tales**, *page 130*). The story provides the child or adolescent with helpful parallels to his own biography, as well as with another way of approaching and commenting on his personal issues.

For example, as nine-year-old Tabitha listened to such a story, she started to play with some plastic figures from a box in the room. It quickly became clear that she was not only portraying the scenes in the story but also creating her own vignettes. The story she was hearing began to take a back seat and she started to develop the ideas in her own way. As the session drew to a close, the therapist suggested that they could take a photo of the final scene she has set up with the figures, so that they can come back to it in the next session. Tabitha considered this suggestion for a while and finally answers: "No, you don't have to take a photo. I can photograph it with my eyes and have the picture in my head. But maybe next time I can also act out a different story?"

Metaphors (see *page 60*), *All about Me* books, painting/drawing, and **Glove puppets** (see *page 118*) lend themselves well, too. It is important to let the child or adolescent decide which method he would like to use. In some cases the same method is then continued in the next session; in other cases, it takes the client longer to find an approach that he thinks is right for him—which often makes the process more interesting and multifaceted.

The genogram (see **The resources family tree**, *page 71*) is another important method to use with older children and adolescents dealing with identity issues. Depending on the client's situation, the genogram can contain both his original family and his current living environment—ideally always combined with a resource-focused approach.

TIPS. These methods are particularly good for combining with **Dream your dream** (*see page 177*); working with resources is very important (see **Activating and working with resources**, *page 68*).

INDICATION. Adopted and foster children, family conflicts with difficult separation processes, posttraumatic stress disorder (following a stabilization period), psychosomatic disorders, and chronic physical illnesses.

CONTRAINDICATION. Biographical work is not very helpful in acute crisis situations.

SETTING. Individual therapy, family therapy, group therapy, couples therapy.

Therapeutic stories and fairy tales

IDEA. Fairy tales and stories are a great way of helping young children, in particular, develop their own problem-solving ideas in an imaginative way.

Fairy tales and stories can also help to relativize a child's own difficult situation so that they don't feel that they are carrying their burden alone.

Depending on their age and stage of development, the stories can be chosen to suit the child's individual situation.

Brett (1998) describes therapeutic stories as personified fairy tales. The child identifies with the main character/hero and experiences how there are other children his age with similar problems but closer to finding a solution. This gives him the confidence to use his own abilities to find a solution to his own problem.

METHOD. The child's parents or the therapist make up a story or fairy tale that incorporates elements that the child can identify with (e.g., same age as the main character/hero in the story, same favorite color, or a very similar problem). It is important to incorporate the abilities of the child into the story, that is, into the character of the hero, so that the child recognizes how he has contributed to the positive resolution.

Girls and boys alike are fascinated by stories in which little heroes overcome big problems. Sometimes older children, adolescents, or adult members of the family can also be inspired by these stories.

There are several ways of implementing this intervention:

- Read out or retell a classic fairy tale or story (Hans Christian Andersen, the Brothers Grimm), for example, the story of the ugly duckling who turns into a beautiful swan.
- Together with the child or family a story can be invented that integrates resources that are either already present or that the client wishes he had. The story can also be started by one member of the family and continued by each of the other family members in turn.
- The therapist starts to tell a story and the child thinks up possible resolutions, together with his family, reflecting on which resources might have played a role: *How did . . . manage to get out of that difficult situation again?* or *Which of his/her other abilities could he/she have also used?*

TIPS. Similarities between the child and the hero should be cleverly and not too obviously integrated into the story.

Families can guess fairy tales: Along the lines of guessing resources, (part of) a story is acted out in pantomime, and the others have to guess what it is, always with the strengths and abilities of the hero in mind.

As homework, older children can be given the task of finding and collecting heroic stories (e.g., from newspapers, the TV news, their neighborhood). Of course, these stories can also be drawn or written down.

For example, a four-and-a-half-year-old boy whose mother had been lying in a hospital for weeks with a life-threatening brain tumor came up with the idea of drawing some comic strips revolving around the family dog: "Max can help Mommy get well again." In the course of the therapy, the boy also motivated his mother to join in with the drawing. Later it was possible to turn back to these stories with the whole family, when the mother was healthy again but the whole family was still under a lot of strain.

Breaks in the story

Before continuing the story, it is sometimes also a good idea to ask the child whether he has an idea how the story might end or who could come and help the main character: *What do you think the boy did next?* or *Can you think of anybody who would be really good at helping him/her?* Sometimes children come up with wonderful solutions that the other members of the family didn't think of.

Even if the child does not come up with suggestions right away, it is still important to have asked. The client will usually continue to mull over the question and may come up with ideas later. In the meantime, you can continue to ask questions or continue telling the story.

Drawing the helper figure

Some children are inspired by the helper figure from the story, or come up with a helper figure that they are familiar with from another context. The client should be encouraged to draw this figure and hang up the resulting picture in a special place at home, for example, above his bed or desk, as a constant reminder of the message of the story. (*See also* **Cartoon therapy**, *page 125.*)

For example, Matthew, seven years old, had great difficulties getting up in the morning. When he visited his grandparents, though, he rarely had problems. The story he was told integrated his love of country life and reminded him of his grandparents' farm. In the subsequent drawing exercise, he quickly thought of and drew a helper figure, "Jack the rooster," who could help him get up in the morning.

INDICATION. Suitable for almost all problems, and particularly for children up to the age of 10.

Particularly suitable with anxious or depressive children, as well as clients with self-esteem problems.

Also helpful with enuresis, stomachaches, and headaches, as well as sleep disorders.

CONTRAINDICATION. The only limitation to this intervention is lack of imagination and motivation.

SETTING. Individual therapy, family therapy, group therapy.

Letters from the Fairy Kingdom

IDEA. An intervention based on Milton Erickson (Rosen, 2009): The fairy or another character from the Fairy Kingdom conveys the message that there is hope, that he is there to help, and that the child will manage to solve his problem.

METHOD. A case example works well here in place of a description:

The therapist—in the character of the fairy, or other character—wrote a letter to a girl and told her that she is a kind fairy and that she will be the girl's "seven-year-fairy" for as long as the little girl is seven years old. However, she herself is already grown up, has many eyes, and knows a lot about what the girl does. Her specialty is "Actually not wanting to steal (or lie)." She knows that the child also does not want to do this, and in order to make her wish come true, the fairy is going to help her get rid of her problem.

The girl invited the fairy to her eighth birthday party and in the invitation also wrote that she was able to get rid of her problem. The fairy replied that she unfortunately cannot attend, because she is only the seven-year-fairy. The girl will have to discuss any further wishes with the eight-year-fairy.

Before her eighth birthday, the girl sent the seven-year-fairy a farewell picture.

TIPS. This method works well in combination with **Glove puppets** (see page 118) or therapeutic stories (see *Therapeutic stories and fairy tales, page 130*).

INDICATION. Children with behavioral problems and who require outside control: snitching (tattling), stealing, lying, bullying, and so on.

CONTRAINDICATION. None.

SETTING. Individual therapy or group therapy.

Magic tricks

IDEA. Doing magic tricks with children, adolescents, adults, or whole families is always about bringing to light untapped resources and abilities. It involves wonder, surprise, the unexpected—things that we can usefully apply in problematic situations.

Sometimes the focus is on revealing different perspectives or approaches through simple tricks, inspiring a new way of thinking, and demonstrating, for example, "how the knot can actually easily be dissolved" (Neumeyer, 2000).

Magic tricks can be incorporated into a series of sessions, can lead a therapy toward a certain conclusion, or can provide some unexpected inspiration.

And of course, this method helps to cement the client-therapist relationship.

METHOD. It is possible to work with all kinds of magic tricks, from simple card tricks to more complicated disappearing tricks or knot-dissolving tricks. Here are a few suggestions.

Guessing the right card

This is a good way to kick-start a session. With this classic card trick, you "rediscover" a card that you have not seen before. The card, which somebody pulls out of the pack and shows only to the other members of the audience but not to the "magician," is slipped back into the pack and covered with other cards.

Unbeknown to the amazed audience, you easily find the card, having made a note of the card that is immediately below it when it is slipped back into the pack.

The knotted handkerchief trick

The question posed to the audience is whether it is possible to tie a knot in a handkerchief that you are holding in both hands without letting go.

To perform this trick you stand with your arms crossed, so that you are holding the handkerchief with both hands at diagonal ends. If you pull your arms apart, the handkerchief knots itself without you having to let go.

TIPS. With children and adolescents lacking in self-confidence, demonstrating a magic trick and then showing them how it is done can spark off the desire to learn it themselves. They learn a special new skill, which after some practice can be demonstrated to family members or school friends.

Very shy children, in particular, learn to overcome their insecurity or fearfulness. Performing magic tricks opens up new possibilities and increases self-confidence.

The fairy rocket

A. Neumeyer's fairy rocket, which is blasted off with the help of a tea bag, is an exciting intervention for making problems fly away. It can be integrated into a variety of methods and works as follows.

You show your client(s) a normal tea bag and ask whether it would be possible to make the tea bag fly. After you have removed the label, the thread, and finally the tea (perhaps as an evil witch, who wants to take away a stranded fairy's last escape route . . .), the remaining empty tea bag is stood upright on a plate and set alight at the upper edge—and suddenly starts to rise upward.

It is up to the client to decide whether it is the little fairy who has managed to escape the evil witch after all, or wishes that are rising up to the sky.

The magic glove

With unpleasant procedures like taking blood, this magic glove trick can be a helpful distraction with younger children (especially preschool and early elementary-school-age children).

While you are preparing the procedure, ask the child if he would like to try on the magic glove, which helps to lessen the pain of the needle being inserted and having blood taken.

Most children are curious and spontaneously agree. You then explain that this special glove is invisible and needs to be treated with special care. With pantomime-like exaggeration you take the magic item out of your desk, cupboard, or bag and begin to put it onto the child's arm with all sorts of explanations and plucking. The child is often so engrossed in "feeling" the glove that it is usually easy to take blood while chatting about the glove.

But don't forget to take the glove off at the end, because it is unique and will be needed again!

INDICATION. It never hurts, and it's fun!

CONTRAINDICATION. You should use this intervention only if you enjoy using it yourself. There is nothing worse than an agonizingly rehearsed magic trick that never seems to work!

But of course, you can also try a different trick with equally impressive results—after all, we can all discover new talents in ourselves, whether it is waggling our ears or doing number tricks.

Perhaps think back to your own childhood—you may very well remember a trick or talent that you'd forgotten about.

SETTING. Individual therapy, group therapy, family therapy.

Improvisation, movement, and more

IDEA. Improvisation and movement are key words in the context of resource- and solution-oriented approaches for opening up new, creative opportunities. The emphasis is on using simple means to develop new ideas; on changing perspective, positions, roles, and perhaps even rooms; on being spontaneous and flexible; on being carried away, daring to try new and unexpected things without lots of advance planning.

A case example: We could go for a walk . . .

Lisa was 13 years old and had ADHD and depressive tendencies, as well as a mentally ill father. She came regularly every few weeks for an individual meeting, including during a phase when the clinic building was undergoing extensive renovations.

During one of these meetings the construction noise was particularly loud, and both the girl and the therapist found it very annoying. Lisa became impatient and announced that she would rather go; it was impossible to hear a word that was being said.

So the therapist spontaneously suggested that they go outside and search for a solution together. They quickly found one: *How about having our meeting on the move rather than sitting down? We could go for a walk.* The girl agreed immediately and was relieved that there was now time for a longer chat.

The girl chose the route—along a little path that went past a cemetery and led to a residential neighborhood. And as the hour drew to an end, the girl spontaneously suggested that they do the same next time: "The noise is bound to be just as bad . . . "

From a therapeutic point of view, this approach was interesting because it provided alternative experiences. It was possible to set the pace of the conversation, as well as the pace at which they walked. If a sentence seemed very important, this could be clarified by abruptly stopping: *Hang on a moment, I think you need to explain that to me again.*

The power of the unexpected: Moving improvisations

IDEA. During a session, the focus of the clients can be (re)directed with the help of an unexpected approach along the lines of "let's do something different," "disruptions are good," or "a change of perspective helps."

Beaulieu (2010) uses the term "impact techniques" to describe interventions that "move" the client in a particular way. The therapist's message is visualized in a special way, among other things, in order to anchor the ideas. This stimulates and opens up new perspectives and creates new opportunities for development.

Sometimes clients are able to precisely describe a situation that might represent a possible solution in the future. At this point it can be a good idea to ask the client to act out this scene, to stand up, to get into this frame of mind, and to experience what this solution context feels like.

METHOD. During a group session, you can ask the clients to try something new and to change their positions—not in the sense of their outlook or attitude, but literally to change seats: *Could I ask you to now stand up and try something out?*

There are now a variety of ways to proceed. For example, you can ask the clients to swap seats and to try and adopt the other person's perspective in the ensuing conversation, or you can ask one of the clients to go to a corner of the room and to observe the rest of the group from there.

If I were to suggest an unusual experiment, could you imagine joining in?

In order to understand your situation even better, I would like to suggest the following . . .

I would like to . . . , so that I can get a clearer picture of the situation.

Supposing we would now . . . ?

TIPS. This intervention leaves plenty of room for creativity—you can give free rein to your ideas, as long as the clients show an interest in participating and feel comfortable and secure in the situation. It is also very important to ask the client(s) for permission.

Another variation can involve the client's pet; for example, you ask the child to tell his dog a story or to read to the cat from his diary.

INDICATION. All.

CONTRAINDICATION. None.

SETTING. Individual therapy, family therapy, couples therapy, group therapy, teams.

The rubber band

IDEA. Rubber bands can be completely limp, stretched to the point of almost breaking, or anywhere in between. With this method, the tension in a rubber band can be compared to the tension in a client (Beaulieu, 2010).

METHOD. The exercise starts as follows:

By stretching this rubber band between your fingers, can you show me the level of tension inside you at the moment?

How does it feel? Is it comfy?

Is there something that could increase this tension?

Is there something that could reduce this tension?

Move the rubber band until it feels more comfy.

Is there anything you can do so that the tension inside you matches the tension in the rubber band?

If you increase the tension now, how long will you be able to hold it like that?

If you reduce the tension again, how long will you be able to hold it, and what are you doing differently at this moment?

If I now try and increase the tension, can you put up some resistance?

TIPS. This can be a fun alternative to **Scaling** (*see page 81*).

INDICATION. Best used with children and adolescents; can also work with adults.

CONTRAINDICATION. None.

SETTING. Individual therapy, couples therapy, family therapy, group therapy.

Marking progress with colors and shapes

IDEA. Progress in therapy can be more firmly anchored by marking it in different ways, that is, not just by talking about it but in more creative ways, too. Ben Furman celebrates successes: By celebrating the achievement of concrete goals, the achievement becomes more meaningful (see Furman 2008a & b).

Steiner and Berg (2005) like to invite younger children to build "success towers" using colorful building blocks or other materials. The concrete representation of the client's success can increase self-confidence.

An achievement is a positive experience that can also be made tangible in other ways, for example, in a song, a **Certificate** (*see page 193*), or a figure out of modeling clay.

METHOD. At the beginning of the session, the child or adolescent—and his family, if they are present—tells the therapist what progress he has made since the last meeting. The therapist briefly outlines the concerns brought up in the last session, and initial successes are discussed. The described successes can be visualized with almost anything that happens to be available; for example, jelly beans or colored pens can be laid out in a colorful line. The important thing is to ask questions in very small steps, and to prompt further responses:

See if you can think of anything else? . . . And anything else?

And if you think about school, is there anything that you feel proud about?

The Therapist's Treasure Chest

As an alternative form of this intervention, the therapist or counselor can try to visualize what he has heard or understood so far, for example, by drawing a flower for each success. Children and adolescents usually like this kind of involvement of the therapist and can be asked to make suggestions of what to add to the picture or even how to finish it, *so that it's right.*

Tips. What-else questions (see *page 26*), **Circular questioning** (see *page 85*), and **Asking about exceptions** (see *page 79*) work well in combination with this approach. For example, *If your teacher were here now, what might he say impressed him most last week?*

This method can be further strengthened by repeating the "line of success" or tower-building exercise several times or getting the child/adolescent to explain what he has done.

Show me how high your tower is!

And what was that blue block for again?

If your tower is even higher next time, what extra thing will you have achieved?

The method can also be used with **Glove puppets**, dolls, and so on (see *page 118*): *Can you choose another doll/animal that best matches your success?*

Variations for children and adolescents

- The client draws different colored dots on each of his fingertips, to visualize and anchor successes.
- The client chooses a ribbon in his favorite color and adds a knot for every new achievement. In the next session it is important to ask the child if he remembers what the other knots stand for.
- The client has a little notebook, and a sticker is added for each achievement or step in the right direction. Advantage: The parents can also add stickers between sessions. Important: Establish exactly how you will recognize when progress has been made.

Variations for more than one person

- "Treasure chests" are very popular with groups of children. At the first meeting they can make the treasure chests together, for example, out of old shoeboxes. For each success, the children can add colorful stones, marbles, feathers, or chestnuts to their treasure chest.
- Group or family towers are a good way of visualizing therapeutic progress in group and family therapy.

Also, in recent years, building towers out of stones has become a popular method with adults. Big pebbles have a meditative quality, of course, but can also be used as discussed above.

INDICATION. Methods such as tower building are particularly effective with young children, but the visualization of therapeutic progress works with any age group. Be surprised by your own or your clients' creativity!

CONTRAINDICATION. None.

SETTING. Individual therapy, family therapy, group therapy, teams, couples therapy.

Marking progress with all the senses

IDEA. The use of sensory experiences when working with children and adolescents—such as, feeling different types of fabrics, surfaces, or temperatures, smelling and tasting exercises, or further linking these perceptions with sound— can be integrated into a variety of interventions (Oaklander, 1999), or used in combination with **Metaphors** (see page 60) or with **Relaxation and imagination** techniques (see page 154).

Using sensory qualities as a form of visualization is another way of defining goals and finding solutions (Steiner & Berg, 2005). Some clients have particular abilities connected to one or more senses, which can be usefully applied here.

METHOD. A sensory approach can be incorporated into a variety of methods, including therapeutic stories (see ***Therapeutic stories and fairy tales***, page 130) or working with **Glove puppets** (see page 118), as well as drawing, sculpting, and the activation of resources (see ***Activating and working with resources***, page 68).

> I would like to tell you about a girl who had a similar problem and who came up with the following idea as a solution . . . Which smell or sound would you associate with this, and how do you think it would feel?
>
> Supposing your strength had a sound or a color—what would these be?
>
> Imagine a helper figure: What do you think his/her favorite color would be and which music do you think would suit him/her best?

This results in a solution that can be drawn or summed up verbally: *What smell or sound and which color would you associate with your solution?*

TIPS.

- Patients can create or find little sensory talismans or objects that can be given to the client to take home to anchor the progress that has been made.

- Children particularly like to use modeling clay to create, for example, figures or other symbols like a heart.
- Therapy in motion/sensory exercises: Take an imaginary walk with the client, or use the time to literally go for a walk through nature (*see the case example* **We could go for a walk**, *page 136*).
- Ask the client to imagine a day on which everything is going smoothly: *Feel free to close your eyes: What can you smell? What can you feel? What music do you hear? What colors do you see?*

INDICATION. All.
CONTRAINDICATION. None.
SETTING. Individual therapy, group therapy.

Emotion cards and such

IDEA. The ability to self-regulate emotions, that is, to recognize and classify one's own or others' emotional state, as well as the ability to empathize with people's moods, is vital for interacting with others. This kind of empathy is an important foundation for social interaction from a very young age (Sarimski, 2005).

Even very young children are able to understand concepts like "sad," "funny," or "angry" and use them to describe certain states of mind or to react verbally to them.

In order to behave and react appropriately, children benefit from developing their emotional sensitivity and having an awareness of alternative ways of reacting in different everyday situations.

METHOD. In order for the client to understand emotions and reactions better, the therapist and client(s) think of and discuss different states of mind. These can also be written down or drawn on pieces of card. The way in which the client describes his interactions with his peers, parents, siblings, or other people in his environment can give some indication of whether his understanding of emotions and his reactions are age appropriate. Exaggerating emotions through body language, miming, or tone of voice can be an effective way of helping the client gain a deeper understanding of different emotions.

The memory method has proven to be very effective in our experience: On two pieces of card, write down or draw the same feeling or, alternatively, opposite pairs of feelings, for example, brave/fearful, sad/happy, and so on and use these to play Memory (*see also* **Resource memory**, *page 74*).

Younger children can try to describe the feelings with the help of examples from storybooks or fairy tales, by comparing them to their own experiences, or even drawing them.

With older children, adolescents, and adults the client can be asked to visualize people he knows in terms of emotions and to work with this picture. Translating a person's emotions and individual reactions into images can be an effective way of understanding them better.

Metaphors also serve this purpose well: *When mummy is angry with me, there is a big grey cloud in the room and sometimes also lightning (see page 60).*

An exciting method to use with children and families is to get them to guess emotions in a card or dice game.

Go Fish (for emotions): Groups of four cards with the same emotion are created and have to be collected by the players. However, in order to get a card from another player, the emotion cannot be named but has to be mimed and guessed by the others (or drawn, or created out of modeling clay!)

"Emotions dice": These can be created out of paper, or an old die can be remodeled. It is also possible to buy blank dice. Different emotions are then drawn or written on each of the six sides. The players take turns rolling the die, and depending on which emotion it lands on, they have to act it out or describe it, or incorporate it into a little story.

"Emotion masks": These can be created out of card or paper and used in a similar way to the dice and memory methods: Clients can practice emotions by putting on an "emotion mask" and acting out the emotion it represents.

Tips. With young children or mentally disabled people it is better to work with nonverbal approaches. We have found drawing emotions to be very effective. The client can also create visual pictures—drawn or using other creative means—of different people in his life. By "translating" emotions in this way it is often easier for the client to understand them and reflect on his own reactions to them.

These interventions can be difficult if there is a lack of compliance, for example, with adolescents. Certain music, films, or comics are "cooler" than games and can be a more effective way of tackling the issue of emotions—which due to puberty are often in a state of confusion anyway. One adolescent we worked with even used song titles and songs to depict his emotions in relation to a particular teacher.

Indication. For all types of social behavior disorders, interaction disorders, ADHD (particularly the hyperactive-impulsive type), and with adjustment and stress disorders, or with any other problem to help the client tap into his emotions.

Contraindication. None.

Setting. Individual therapy, group therapy, family therapy.

Reflecting positions

IDEA. The amazingly simple yet effective method of the reflecting team in family therapeutic and systemic approaches opens up an abundance of innovative opportunities (Andersen, 1990).

The process of reflection not only opens up new possibilities for the therapist and the team but also provides the client with different perspectives (in terms of self-perception as well as the way he perceives others), enabling him to see things in a fresh light and to openly "play with" reflecting positions during therapy sessions (Hargens, 2000):

How does my teacher/boss experience me? How do my friends/parents see me?

What do I contribute to this myself? What could I change? What could the others change?

METHOD. The basic idea behind the reflecting team method is to enrich a therapeutic or counseling process with newly gained perspectives. Besides the original constellation of client(s) plus therapist/counselor, this method requires another group of people who watch the session and reflect on what they have observed in a resource-focused way. The groups then trade places and the client and therapist listen—for about 5–10 minutes—to the reflecting team's observation's and their ideas and hypotheses (from von Schlippe & Schweitzer, 2009).

In a subsequent short session, the client team has another opportunity to comment on what they have heard and to discuss what they found of particular interest.

Because the reflecting method is so appealing, but the number of additional therapists/counselors or other staff members is generally small, the client system can also take on the role of the observer.

One option here is the *reflecting family*. Usually this works in an extended family constellation, but it can also be effective in a subsystem of a family (Caby, 2008; Caby, Vrdoljak, Hubert-Schnelle, & Caby, 2009), for example, with the parents on one team and the children on the other. Both teams are then asked to observe each other and subsequently comment on each other's observations.

In a "helpers' conference," the client and his immediate system (e.g., parents, grandparents, foster parents, or caregivers) can form one team, and the professional helpers (e.g., youth workers, teachers and school psychologists, or doctors) the other team. The child or adolescent can also first join his therapist as an observer and subsequently reflect on what he has seen and heard.

Many other variations are possible. For example, a client is invited to change his position and to take on an outsider's perspective in order to reflect on the conversation he has just had. In concrete terms, this might mean asking him to leave his seat and to stand or sit behind it to reflect out loud on the conversation he just had with the therapist/counselor.

If you are lucky enough to be able to carry out a family session with two therapists or counselors, it can be very helpful if the two therapists/counselors interrupt the discussion to reflect together in front of the family. Through a change of roles, the therapy team becomes the reflecting team and vice versa. The family members are free to comment on or add to what they have heard or to think on it after the session as homework.

TIPS. At the beginning of a session, it is a good idea to ask the clients for permission to use this intervention. The reason for wanting to use it might be based on what you have observed in previous sessions: the family/system is at a loss, many other solutions have already been tried without success, a conflict seems to be escalating, and so on.

This reflecting position has proven to be particularly effective when working with large teams.

INDICATION. All kinds of problems, particularly those that could benefit from the input of fresh ideas.

CONTRAINDICATION. None. It may have only limited success in crisis situations, but sometimes it is exactly the right way of finding a way out of a dead end.

SETTING. Individual therapy, group therapy, family therapy, teams.

Sculpture work: Understanding without words

IDEA. The family sculpture method, and variations on this, have proven to be effective not only in therapeutic work with clients and their systems but also in organizational consulting (from von Schlippe & Schweitzer, 2009).

This technique works particularly well with complex systems, as well as with families with hard-to-define problems. It gives each member of the system/family the opportunity to depict the situation and his own point of view and thereby to open up new perspectives for everyone involved.

METHOD. The members of the system are given the task of depicting their interrelationships by means of body language, facial expressions, and physical distance. You can ask the members of the system to work together to create this "sculpture," which in itself provides an indication of how the members of the system communicate with each other and how certain dynamics develop.

Alternatively, however, you can invite one person to be the sculptor and to arrange the others in a way that he thinks reflects the situation. Once the sculpture is complete, everyone is asked how they feel in their position.

The Therapist's Treasure Chest

The advantage of this technique is that it can be used at any time and without any need for special materials. However, it does require sufficient time or a subsequent session soon afterward to reflect on the outcome.

This intervention can be used to get the clients to depict their family relationships, or it can be used by the therapist/counselor to clarify something that has become apparent over the course of the conversation. *Can I quickly show you how I've understood the situation you've described?*

After the therapist has arranged the clients into a sculpture, the members of the group are given the opportunity to comment on and perhaps make changes to the arrangement.

TIPS. Children often like to depict family members with the help of stuffed animals, (glove) puppets, or other figures.

As the therapist/counselor, it is important to hold back and not try and develop solutions or interpretations too soon!

INDICATION. Works well with all issues involving family systems, from generational conflicts to separation and divorce to psychiatric clinical pictures such as eating disorders and ADHD.

This intervention is particularly interesting for adolescents who are in a conflict situation that they do not want to talk about.

CONTRAINDICATION. This technique is not always suitable in acute crises. This method seldom works as a way of de-escalating a situation, as it often has the effect of uncovering further issues.

SETTING. Individual therapy, family therapy, group therapy, couples therapy, teams.

A chair is (not) a chair, and more: Working with objects

IDEA. The use of chairs is very common in psychotherapy, and especially in systemic family therapy, particularly in combination with **Circular questioning** (see page 85) (Simon & Rech-Simon, 2001).

Beaulieu (2010) uses chairs in the context of her so-called impact techniques (interventions that should take the client by surprise and therefore make a greater impact) in a variety of creative ways and encourages therapists to adapt and develop these techniques.

In our work with clients and their systems we have successfully used chairs in combination with circular questioning, with the timeline technique (see **Timeline work**, page 126) and with family sculptures (see **Sculpture work: Understanding without words**, page 144), as well as with role reversals. Chairs or other objects can also be used to visually depict a problem (or solution) and also work well in combination with more unusual interventions. For example, with psychoeducation a chair can be used to depict an object to convey information to parents in an unusual and therefore memorable way.

METHOD.

Working with chairs (or similar objects)

- With "acting-as-if" interventions
- With circular questioning
- With timelines
- With family sculptures
- As an inner team
- In role reversals
- The "king's throne"
- To visualize a problem, solution, or obstacles
- With unusual interventions

Acting-as-if chair: Even with difficult decisions or **Acting-as-if tasks** (*see page 116*), the use of a chair can help to clarify the situation. Two or more different types of chairs can be used to depict the different options that the client has to decide between. The client sits in turn on each of the chairs, from where he discusses the alternative options: *Imagine you had taken this course of action—how is it for you? How does it feel?*

The client is asked to describe his feelings and to imagine how this situation might look. At the same time the client can be asked to describe the situation in a sensory way (see **Marking progress with all the senses**, *page 140*):

How does it smell, which colors can you see, how might it taste . . . ?

Imagine a miracle has occurred, and the problem is gone . . . And now imagine that the chair stands for the way things would be—sit down, and feel how things are now different.

Chairs with circular questioning: An empty chair is a classic prop for circular questioning: *If . . . was sitting on the chair next to you, what would he have to say to you on the matter?*

Sometimes it is effective if the therapist/counselor suddenly stands up during the conversation and asks the group if he can change the seating order. The therapist then gets the members of the group to move apart a bit and adds another empty chair to the circle. While everyone looks at it and wonders what or who it is, the therapist asks the above question.

Chairs or other objects with timeline work: Chairs or other objects can be helpful with timeline work, too—clients can give free rein to their imagination and creativity.

Compared with other objects in the room, a chair may seem particularly appropriate because of its size and because it can be seen as an obstacle that has to be overcome.

A chair can be deliberately placed at the start or end of a timeline as an invitation to the observer to sit down and take a good look at it. Here, too, it is possible to incorporate a look "back from the future": *Imagine you were to look back one day on your life so far. What would you remember most of all?*

Using chairs in family sculptures: A chair or other object can of course be used to compensate for the obvious absence of an important family member. Suggesting to the clients that they can use chairs and such to represent whatever or whoever they want often opens up new possibilities. For example, the clients might decide to incorporate other people who are just as important to the system but who may up to now have seemed out of reach.

Chairs as an inner team: In order to make even more of an impact with **The inner team** method (*see page 163*), you can use chairs to stand for different voices. You ask the client to choose a chair for each "team member" and to place these in the middle. When the client takes on the role of a particular person he sits in "his" seat, or he can reposition the chairs, turn them around, or do whatever seems appropriate to the situation. The names of the individual "team members" or voices can also be written on pieces of card and placed on the seats.

Role reversal with chairs: During the course of a conversation, it is almost always an option to invite the client to think himself into another person by actually swapping places with that person and taking on their perspective. *If you now sit in your husband's chair and take on his role in the conversation, what would you like to say?* At the same time the husband moves to his wife's seat and continues the conversation from her perspective.

Another role reversal: a child or adolescent takes on the role of a parent or teacher; the teacher could even be invited to the meeting in order to provide him with another perspective on his pupil. Sometimes it is enough to have simply discussed this idea. The teacher no longer needs to be invited.

The king's throne: Everyone is allowed to be king (or queen) once! The king's throne is a favorite variation of the role reversal method—and not only with children. A seat is given prominence in the room, for example, by covering it with a rug or decorating it with a flower or chain, or simply with a sheet of paper with the word "Throne" written on it. The person who sits on the throne is allowed to make decisions and to give orders to the others.

The others should give the king/queen a gift, either in the form of words or connected to a symbol. The aim of this exercise is to emphasize a new or special side of the king/queen in a resource-focused way.

For example, Linus, four-and-a-half years old, wanted to be the boss for once. After his mother, grandfather, and big sister tried out the chair and made their suggestions, he was burning to have a go. As soon as he sat down he immersed himself completely in this new role, first by getting the therapist to get the bowl of jelly beans from the waiting room. He then got his mother to lavish praise on him and finally got his sister to give him a glove puppet that he briefly looked at before laying it aside. He didn't want this game to stop. When it was his grandfather's go, he found it extremely hard to leave the throne.

Externalization with chairs: A chair can be placed in the corner of the room as "the problem," put in the cellar as an "unpleasant experience," or in an extreme case burnt. It can be wrapped in paper, covered in a sack, sawed through, and much more—all suggestions that clients have made [see **Externalization (narrative therapy)**, page 89].

With some of these options and ideas it is enough just to get them down on paper or to think about them; they do not actually have to be carried out. But in some cases, literally getting rid of the chair can have a lasting effect.

A different kind of argument: "What I've always wanted to tell you"! A discussion can be had on two chairs—back to back and without eye contact. After some ground rules have been established, each person is allowed to say exactly what he's wanted to say to the other person. But it is important that the conversation remain respectful and resource focused. It is also okay to express wishes and desires.

Afterward, the chairs can be turned around, and the clients can continue their conversation face to face. Now they should talk about how they found the "back-to-back" discussion, what they liked about it, what was new about it, and whether it helped them.

Obstacle course with chairs: Clients can explore different approaches to a goal, with chairs as obstacles.

A case example: A family overcomes obstacles— in very different ways

During their first meeting with the therapist, a patchwork family comprising two teenage daughters, a younger son, and two parents clearly revealed how their day-to-day life was increasingly overshadowed by arguments and discontent.

The two daughters from the mother's first marriage, 14 and 16 years old, had their own clear ideas about how things should work in the family, for example, how much housework they should do and when they should go to bed.

The mother's new partner, and father of the younger brother, tried in vain to assert himself as the head of the family, and tried to get the two girls to accept him and his rules. But his wishes were usually boycotted, sometimes he was ignored altogether, and discussions usually spiraled into arguments that ended with slamming doors and heated exchanges between him and his wife.

During the session they were invited to try the following exercise. Everybody present was told to pick out a particular point in the room that represented their goal and were then asked to move toward their respective goals as slowly as possible. This slow version was followed by a fast version, in which they had to head for their goals as quickly as possible. Other variations included going backward and with their eyes closed.

Then all of the chairs in the room were set up to create obstacles that blocked the way to their goals and that had to be overcome. Everyone was asked to pick their favorite variation and to try it again, that is, to head for their goal in the way that felt most appropriate to them.

The whole family clearly enjoyed the exercise and at the end of it recognized that each of them had their own way of reaching their goal: slow, fast, carefully, or deliberately with a couple of detours . . .

The two daughters were particularly thoughtful following this intervention. In a phone call a few days later, the mother reported that the situation at home had calmed down considerably and everyone was taking their own approach to things.

Role play with a chair: Imagine this chair is your teacher and you have a problem—how would you explain it to him?

TIPS. *When somebody can't decide*—This is a situation that most therapists/counselors have probably encountered in a discussion with a client. Chairs can be helpful here, too. By sitting on two different chairs, the different perspectives can be "experienced" before making a decision. To really clarify the situation, the chairs can be named, for example, the "Yes! chair" and the "No! chair."

How does it feel to be sitting on this chair?

Special Techniques

What would be different if you made a decision that went in this direction? What would be good about it? What might still be missing?

This method also works with individual or team coaching, particularly when a career move is being discussed, for example, if somebody from the team is about to move into a managerial role. To take this idea further, other members of the group could be asked to sit on one of the named chairs and to reflect on the way they experience each alternative.

INDICATION. Can be used with any kind of problem or concern.

CONTRAINDICATION. None—unless somebody cannot be motivated to actively participate.

Caution: Do not use this technique in crisis situations—a chair can also be used as a dangerous missile and should therefore not be presented as an option in the first place.

A case example: A chair becomes an unexpected focal point

A young family came with their three-year-old daughter to shed light on why her motor skills were not as advanced as those of most children her age. Pediatric-neurological tests had revealed nothing out of the ordinary, and in other areas of her development she was in no way backward.

During the conversation, the parents' anxiety became very apparent: they would jump up as soon as the child took something in her hands, headed toward something, or wanted to try something out.

Because of her parents' behavior, the girl had little freedom of movement, which obviously frustrated her. But on the positive side, she was clearly persistent—she was not easily discouraged and would cheerfully turn her attention to a new challenge.

This became particularly apparent when she discovered a chair and started to climb up it. The mother immediately jumped up to take her away from the chair and put her on her lap. But whenever possible the child escaped and headed back to the chair, with the clear aim of climbing up it, while her parents looked on, panic stricken.

After asking if he could make a suggestion, the therapist asked the parents if they could imagine their days without this constant anxiety. This developed into a discussion about why the parents were so excessively anxious and protective. After a short pause, during which both parents gathered their thoughts, they explained that their first child had died of sudden infant death syndrome at just a few months of age, and that since then they were plagued by feelings of guilt.

While they were talking, the little girl had managed to conquer the chair. Her beaming face caused her parents' anxious faces to break into smiles. After another session without the child, the parents decided to go to psycho-therapy together to deal with the death of their first child in more depth.

Perspective goggles

IDEA. Sometimes it is very helpful to look at a problem from different perspectives. Giving the client different pairs of "goggles" to try can make him more consciously aware of what he is doing.

METHOD. The client is invited to view the problem through a particular pair of goggles—a pair of goggles with special abilities. It might be a pair of resource goggles, through which you can see only a person's strengths and abilities, or opportunity goggles (in the sense of **Reframing**; see page 84), which show you only the positive side of a difficult or problematic situation: *What is good about the fact that you feel as if you've reached a dead end?*

A father who was completely at a loss about how to improve his conflict-ridden relationship with his son answered this question as follows: "I feel like I really need to explore all my options again, to search every corner, every nook and cranny of this dead end for opportunities and for ways of escape."

You can also ask the client to sit comfortably and, if desired, close his eyes. After getting the client to put on the imaginary or actual goggles or glasses, you can ask him to explain his feelings:

How do the goggles feel—are they light or are they uncomfortable anywhere? What color are the frames, and what color is the glass?

What can you see through these goggles? Are you suddenly aware of more things, or only of certain things?

This exploration can be associated with different sensory perceptions—you can ask about the smell or particular sounds, or simply stay focused on visual impressions (see **Marking progress with all the senses**, page 140).

Together with the client you can consider other possible types of goggles—but every option should incorporate a solution-oriented or resource-focused perspective.

A stressed mother was immediately taken by the idea of putting on a pair of relaxation goggles. She complained incessantly about the chaotic situation at home, the frequent resistance of her children, and the lack of support from her husband. With the help of these "special goggles," she managed to observe her day-to-day life from a certain distance and with some serenity and calmness. She liked the idea of keeping these imaginary goggles in her bag as a form of support and putting them on when she felt she needed them.

The goggles can also be a magnifying glass or a glass ball in which you can see into other times or places. Seen from above or from a completely unexpected angle, the change of perspective is especially clear.

For example, Simon, a boy with Asperger's syndrome, took on the role of a scientist, looking at his world through a microscope. This allowed him to analyze certain problems he was having at school in minute detail and to judge them differently from how he had before. Finally he hit on an idea of how he could come into less conflict with other pupils and teachers.

TIPS. The goggles can also be drawn on a piece of paper or cut out of a magazine or brochure. Children like to decorate them with colorful stickers, feathers, and so on.

In a family or group therapy session, some glasses frames picked up at a flea market or a pair of cardboard 3D movie glasses can be passed around the group. Whenever a person puts them on, he can assign them with whatever magic qualities he would like them to have.

INDICATION. Whenever it seems as if a new perspective would help the client progress.

CONTRAINDICATION. None. Try it out and see what happens. It may turn out not to be the right intervention for the client in question, but that shouldn't stop you from giving it a go.

SETTING. Individual therapy, family therapy, group therapy, couples therapy.

Relaxation and imagination

IDEA. Stress is an everyday part of many people's lives. Children, adolescents, families, couples, singles, and seniors can all be affected by stress to a greater or lesser extent, consciously as well as unconsciously. Even kindergarten-age children are subject to periods of stress; when they start school, the majority of children experience regular stress. It is important to establish strategies for dealing with stress in the family, particularly when it is affecting a person's health (Thyen, Szczepanski, Krötz, & Kuske, 2009).

Children or adolescents suffering from stress are usually unable to learn well and are at a greater risk of developing an aversion to school and developing physical symptoms (Krowatschek & Hengst, 2006).

It is not unusual for a person's body language or tone of voice or the atmosphere within a group to provide an indication of the stress levels of the persons present.

Sometimes the subject of stress or stress factors provides a good way into a conversation, particularly when the client's problem revolves around everyday stress and lack of support.

Imagination exercises can be a useful strategy for dealing with cases of extreme stress, for example, if the client has suffered abuse or other traumatic experiences.

METHOD. Systemic-hypnotherapeutic techniques can be used with all age groups and in all settings alongside classic relaxation exercises such as progressive muscle relaxation or autogenic training. Methods already mentioned include **Metaphors** (see page 60), **Scaling** (see page 81), **Externalization** (see page 89), and different forms of questioning (see **The Art of Questioning,** page 23).

Metaphors can provide a way in to talking about an issue—based on the client's body language, you can ask him to express his feelings more strongly; at the same time, you can get him to focus on his different senses:

Can I describe how I am experiencing you today? It seems to me as if you were carrying a very heavy load.

If you were to sit down on this chair, what would your posture be like?

What might you smell or hear? Which color or smell would you prefer to experience?

A more physically focused intervention would be to try to get rid of the heavy load: *If you wanted to stand up now, how would you get rid of the load? Why don't you give it a try!—How does it feel?*

You can also use scaling questions to find out how the client perceives his stress levels. *If you had to rate your current stress level on a scale of . . . to . . . in fact, how high or low would the scale have to go to reflect your personal stress level? Up to 100, or even 1000? Or would it have to go into minus numbers?* (As a father once suggested.)

You can ask the client to stand up and show the scale in relation to the room: *So if 0 was here by the door and 100 was by the window, where would you position yourself today?*

To finish off, you can prescribe relaxation homework: *Please find five minutes every day to do absolutely nothing!*

Imagination exercises: With imagination exercises to deal with traumatic experiences, you ask the client to imagine a safe room or place (in the form of an externalization), in which the negative memories or fears can be locked away as a way of taking away the burden. This could be, for example, a cave, a desert island, or a vault ("Vault exercise," see Pfeiffer, 2008).

Tips. "Inner pictures" are a good way of anchoring positive situations and successes that the client has experienced.

Krowatschek and Hengst (2006) recommend the use of rituals as a way of integrating relaxation methods in children's daily routines.

Children, but also adolescents, are wonderful at using their imaginations to go on "relaxation journeys." For example, 10-year-old Tammy used a combination of relaxation and drawing to deal with her regularly occurring headaches and stomachaches. During a one-on-one session, she decided to put her feelings onto paper and remembered a tortoise that she used to have as a pet: "He could always pull in his head and go into his house. It must have been really quiet and cozy inside." From then on, Tammy's drawing of her tortoise hung over her desk. "The great thing about a tortoise is that it can use its neck to stick out its head very, very carefully to see if everything is okay again." In subsequent sessions, Elsa the tortoise became an imaginary companion whom she sometimes invited to her house or rode on to go and meet a friend to play!

Relaxation exercise: 5-4-3-2-1

IDEA. The self-hypnosis technique invented by Betty Erickson and further developed by Yvonne Dolan is often used in the context of trauma therapy. However, it also works as a relaxation technique and sleeping aid with children, adolescents, and adults.

This hyperconcentration technique functions by concentrating on different sensory perceptions: hearing, feeling, mental pictures. With sleep disorders, for example, worries and concerns are blocked out, and thoughts are concretely steered in a less threatening direction—a bit like with counting sheep. Unsurprisingly, this technique is an effective stabilizing intervention in the context of trauma therapy.

METHOD. When they go to bed, clients should breathe slowly and deeply until they feel relaxed. Then in their heads they should tell themselves what they hear, feel, and imagine. This works as follows:

Five things that you hear . . .

Five things that you feel . . .

Five things that you imagine in the dark . . .

Continuing with four things, three things, and so on

Hearing: Lying in bed, the client concentrates on everything that he hears, for example, a car driving past outside. In his head, he says to himself: "I can hear a car driving past." Then he concentrates on the next sound, for example, the ticking of the clock, and says to himself: "I can hear the clock ticking." In the first round he repeats the same with three other sounds . . .

Feeling: The client then concentrates on his body and focuses on exactly what his body is feeling: "I can feel the pillow in my neck," "I can feel my heart beating," "I can feel how my legs are crossed," and so on. In the first round, he thinks of two other sensations . . .

Mental pictures: The client lies in the dark in his bed imagining where things are in the room, and says to himself: "I imagine I can see my shoes. They are at the end of my bed next to the chair." This is followed by four more mental pictures.

TIPS. This exercise is carried out with closed eyes.

It is advisable to test it out with the client during a session—on a couch or simply sitting on a chair.

Sometimes it is difficult to hear five different things. It is also okay to concentrate twice on the same sound or the same sensation. It is also fine if you forget something while doing this exercise. The only thing that is really important is not to let your mind wander off, because then the worries preventing sleep often start looming up again. So if the thread breaks, it is fine to swap from feeling to hearing, or vice versa, to maintain your concentration.

INDICATION. This exercise is useful for fear of exams and testing, for sleep disorders, and in the context of trauma therapy. If clients dissociate, as is often the case when dealing with a trauma, this exercise is a way of stabilizing them in the here and now.

CONTRAINDICATION. Acute conditions such as psychotic agitation or panic attacks. The patient must be able to concentrate on himself.

SETTING. Individual therapy, group therapy.

Family coat of arms

IDEA. The symbols in a family's coat of arms can say a lot about the family. All symbols in heraldry have a meaning that can be looked up in books or on websites. Some coats of arms have just one symbol; others have many symbols, either whole or in part, that are linked to each, for example, in different colored sections.

Many families have inherited family myths that survive from generation to generation (see also **Mottos, mantras, and myths,** page 171). Only very few families actually have a coat of arms, which is why creating a family coat of arms is an excellent way of anchoring these mythical resources. All family members can then literally see these resources and can turn to the family coat of arms whenever they are looking for a new solution.

METHOD. In order to kindle a family's interest in the subject, you can introduce the subject of family coats of arms with some visual examples. Children have often seen coats of arms in museums or on buildings and remember certain shapes, symbols, or figures. You can start by getting clients to guess what typical heraldic animals like horses, bears, or lions might stand for, before starting to reflect on the family's own special qualities in terms of resources.

With the therapist's help, the clients can go on to compile a list of symbols, figures, or words that are or could be of significance in their family.

To really reinforce this method, it is a good idea to invite the clients to design the coat of arms together and to draw it on a piece of paper. A couple of big pieces of paper, or simply a roll of wallpaper, that can be spread on a table or pinned to the wall are all that is needed. So the clients can really let their imaginations run wild, you can also provide thick felt-tip pens, stickers, pages out of old magazines or newspapers, feathers, fall leaves, colorful stamps, and so on.

Usually there is one member of the family who is best at drawing, another one is a very accurate cutter, another may have a good sense of color or design . . . getting the whole family to work together provides a good opportunity for the therapist to watch them together in action and can raise further issues to discuss afterward: *Watching you all work together just now, I was really impressed by how well you all listened to each other.*

This method also works well in combination with a genogram (see **The resources family tree,** page 71).

TIPS. This method can be used in an individual setting, for example, with a child or adolescent. In this case you can work in a future-oriented way: *Supposing that one day you would have your own coat of arms—what would it look like? What symbols or what words would be really important for you to have on it?*

You can also invite the child or adolescent to show his draft for a new family coat of arms to the rest of the family and perhaps to get some further ideas and inspiration from the others.

INDICATION. Can always be used.

CONTRAINDICATION. None.

SETTING. Individual therapy, family therapy, group therapy, couples therapy, teams.

Redesigning the past

IDEA. Just as Furman (2008a & b) argues that it is never too late to have a happy childhood, so it is also never too late to have had a nice past and to still actively contribute to it.

However awful and traumatic this past may have been, and however important it is to acknowledge and respect the patient's suffering, there is always another side to the story. Behind the worst trauma, there are abilities that made it possible for the person to survive the experience.

Inviting a client to see the past from another perspective should be done on the understanding that in a therapeutic context it is not necessary to reexperience a trauma in order to overcome it. However, the speed at which you help the client to "redesign" his past should be determined by the client.

METHOD. Redesigning the past is achieved through questioning:

Is there anything positive that you can take away from your past?

What helped you to survive your past?

How did you manage to overcome all of that?

How did you manage to prevent it turning out much worse than it did?

What aspects of your past might you still need to find a new solution today? What worked even at the time? (see **Coping questions**, page 27)

TIPS. Of course, the client does not have just to talk—he may find it more helpful to draw or redesign his past in another way. *If you had to draw the good side of your past, what would it look like? Would you like to have a go at drawing it?*

INDICATION. It goes without saying that this intervention should be used in individual therapy. But it would be equally plausible to use a genogram, which focuses not just on the resources of individual family members but also on the coping strategies of whole generations, so that their pasts are also given a new coat of paint. This would also provide an opportunity to come up with a family myth—which in turn could be turned into a **Family coat of arms** (see page 158).

CONTRAINDICATION. None.

SETTING. Individual therapy, family therapy, in certain cases couples therapy.

Playing with hypotheses

IDEA. Asking why a client behaves in a certain way is generally unhelpful—usually he does not know himself. Nonetheless, the patient should be invited to reflect on his own actions. An effective approach in this situation is to present a variety of hypotheses about the client's behavior and to discuss with the client how each one fits.

Hargens (2000) refers to a "hypothetical solution field" or "possibility space"; together with the client, the therapist searches for possible solutions and describes these.

METHOD. This method is best described by the example of Frank.

A case example: Frank

Frank, 18 years old, is in a negative state of mind, and with each intervention he expresses his doubt that it will be of any help.

When the therapist asks the next question, he does not even respond—he is silent. Rather than asking him the reason for his silence, the therapist responds as follows: *I've just realized that you have not answered my last question. I have a couple of ideas why—can I share them with you?*

Frank nods. The therapist continues: *My previous experiences with silences have taught me that there are several possibilities. I'm wondering if your silence means that you won't answer any questions that put you in an active role, whether you're just not in the mood to answer any more questions, or if you're afraid that your answer would force you to noticeably change something . . . ? What do you think most applies to you?*

Hypotheses should always enable a change of perspective—all three hypotheses describe the client in an active role, and the final question, which of the three best applies to his situation, initiates the new perspective.

TIPS. The hypotheses can also be very contrary, for example,

- *Today you're obviously not in the mood . . .*
- *Every time you're supposed to decide something, you clam up.*
- *You obviously need more time to answer the question.*
- *You have not understood the question.*

When developing these hypotheses, you can of course present your own idea as one possible hypothesis!

Special Techniques 161

INDICATION. There are hardly any situations that cannot be hypothesized about.

CONTRAINDICATION. None.

SETTING. Individual therapy, family therapy, couples therapy, group therapy, teams.

The inner team

IDEA. Schulz von Thun (1998) developed the inner team model as a way of reconciling the need to express oneself clearly and effectively to the outside world with the need to listen to one's many inner voices—often experienced as inner turmoil: "Should I or shouldn't I? Am I allowed to do that, or would it better to . . . ? Or maybe something completely different?"

In order to untangle the often very contradictory and usually manifold inner voices that arise in every form of communication and in almost all everyday situations, it helps to imagine an internal team with a team leader and an inner conflict management system.

The model of the inner team enables the client to better accept inner conflicts and even to use this plurality as a resource instead of experiencing it as a burden. Providing this special team with an inner forum enables every voice to speak up and for creative and helpful (inner) dialogues to take place.

METHOD. A step-by-step approach should be taken when working with the inner team. First of all, it is important to establish which voices—or team members—are talking and what their respective messages are. The process is made easier by giving each of the separate voices names.

Next, each of the individual voices has its say: each for about the same amount of time and without interruption. Further steps include an open discussion moderated by the team leader. Finally the team leader sums up the different strands of the discussion and suggests a solution.

A case example: The complainer

With the help of the team model, a young man was able to resolve his relationship issues, which had been tormenting him for some time. He was torn between whether to start a family with his partner sooner rather than later, or whether to make a new career start, if necessary somewhere completely new and without his girlfriend.

Within his team he identified

The "complainer" who always had something to gripe about
The "optimist or hopeful one" who was able to see the positive sides of
    the possible changes in his life
The "jittery one" who was anxious and unsure
The "traditionalist," who didn't want anything to change

Sometimes he thought he also heard the voice of a "mummy's boy," who wanted him to stay living close to his parents—but eventually he rejected this voice.

During the discussion the young man discovered yet another team member, who stormed onto the field quite suddenly—the "adventurer seeker."

He eventually opted for pursuing his career and to ask his girlfriend to come with him as an indication of his commitment to a shared future.

TIPS. An important aspect of this model is its versatility, especially in a resource-focused context. For example, you can ask the client to concentrate on the abilities and strengths of his inner team:

Which of your team members do you think is especially helpful?

What is good about somebody who can also doubt things?

Which voice do you wish was sometimes louder (or quieter)?

Who might do your team some good—and where/how could you find him?

You can also play through other scenarios and possibilities with hypothetical questions, for example, by sending one of the voices off on vacation.

Some patients and clients find it helpful to write down or draw the individual voices, or team members, on pieces of card, to shape them out of modeling clay, or to use symbols, buttons, postcards, and so on, to represent them. Again, there are no limits to what is possible, and the client usually comes up with good suggestions.

When working through traumatic experiences, it can be important to confront the "inner child," the "trauma child," both during the initial stabilization phase and when looking back at the situation with more distance later on (Pfeiffer, 2008).

In this context, Beushausen (2010) describes stabilization exercises that involve imagining the "inner helper or hero." This helper or hero can take on a variety of forms, for example, the inner doctor, the inner observer, or the co-adviser.

If all else fails and the inner team cannot come to an agreement, it can still be turned into a reflecting team (see **Reflecting positions**, page 143) with the purpose of finding out which of the other team members' thoughts would be worth pursuing.

INDICATION. The technique is best suited to people who are able to see things from a variety of perspectives. Therefore, in the case of children, usually only from elementary school age onward.

The inner team method can help with decision-making processes in particular; it works best in an individual setting.

CONTRAINDICATION. Not suitable for patients in psychological crisis situations or generally with people who chronically experience their thoughts as oppressively plural, engulfing, or confusing.

Can be difficult if there is a lack of compliance, but it can also provide an opportunity to try something completely new or to structure the intervention completely differently.

SETTING. Individual therapy, family therapy, group therapy, couples therapy.

The pocket helper

IDEA. The pocket helper is a classic example of how the therapist or counselor can extend and secure therapeutic progress beyond the session. The pocket helper serves as a constant reminder to the client to develop the newly acquired ideas or knowledge or to continue the strategies that were discussed during therapy. (*See also* **Compliments, praise, and such**, *page 168, and* **Talismans, courage stones, and other helpers**, *page 186.*)

From a neurological perspective, this process can be described to the client as the emergence of a new neurological network that goes into battle with the old, very strong problem network. And because learning processes are most effectively anchored through constant repetition, it is important to practice them. But of course it is always difficult to remember that you want to bring about change, which is why the pocket helper can serve as a useful reminder.

METHOD. It is important that the client applies what he has learned in the session in his everyday life. To help jog the client's memory, the therapist can give him an object to carry with him in his pocket or bag. Whenever the patient feels or sees it, he will be reminded of what was talked about in the session.

Typical objects include a small stone (but not a smooth pebble), a piece of wood, an old chess figure, a scrunched up piece of paper (which doesn't have to have anything written on it, but can), a little ball (which can roll away, so must be looked after), or any other little object that happens to be at hand. But the object should be big enough that it cannot be ignored.

Ideally, the patient should decide—based on his own habits and lifestyle—what kind of object would work best and is less likely to get lost. Some clients are quick to come up with their own ideas and make concrete suggestions. An object with an unusual shape or size is more likely not to be ignored.

Children are usually very imaginative—let yourself be surprised!

TIPS. This is a good intervention if the patient—or therapist—has doubts about being able to do something, or about compliance:

This method also works well with groups—you can reinforce the group identity by giving the same object to every member of the group.

Sometimes it is a good idea to write on the object . . .

For example, a borderline psychotic young man, 18 years old, wanted to achieve a C grade in physics class, but in order to manage this he had to sort out the chaos in his physics folder. His problem was that he was able to complete only clearly structured homework; he did not have the self-discipline to learn by himself, for example, to revise material for an exam. He was finally able to make progress after he had broken the work down into small steps with the help of the therapist and reinforced his intentions with a pocket helper—a little figure with a "C" on its chest.

INDICATION. Whenever an additional boost is required to implement change in everyday life, for example; also with chronic illnesses.

CONTRAINDICATION. None.

SETTING. Individual therapy, group therapy.

A case example: A touch of glass

An adolescent with congenital lung disease was sent to a psychotherapist by his lung specialist following another prolonged stay in a clinic. He was suffering from the fact that he had to take a lot of medication and do regular breathing exercises. He was negative about his future but motivated in the therapy—and he remarked that he wished that everything would work this well at home. When he was at home he never managed to get anything done and was constantly arguing with his parents.

After discussing the situation with his doctor, it became clear that he was having problems breaking away from his overprotective mother, and family therapy was suggested. But for the next session, the therapist set the patient the following task: *You're able to cooperate really well here in therapy, but you seem to have more of a problem at home. I'm going to give you this colorful shard of glass that I found on the beach, and I want you to carry it around with you as a reminder of how much you should value yourself.*

If you're familiar with this kind of smooth glass found washed up on shore, you'll know that it took years of being filed down by the waves to lose its sharpness: It can therefore symbolize how it often takes time for things to get to the point where they are ready to be used.

The adolescent kept the shard of glass in his trouser pocket where he could always touch it. He really did feel reminded of his task and made progress.

Compliments, praise, and such

IDEA. According to de Shazer and Dolan (2008), validation and compliments are one of the most important aspects of solution-oriented therapy and counseling. Showing appreciation for what the client has already achieved to resolve his problem can stimulate further attempts at change.

At the beginning of a therapy session, as well as during and at the end, it is a good idea to briefly sum up the points of discussion and to comment on them in an appreciative and resource-focused way. This approach increases rapport, makes the client feel validated, and encourages him to pursue his solution strategies:

Today I have learned that you are somebody who already knows yourself very well! Thank you very much for being so open. I really appreciate this quality in you.

You have just shown me that as a family (team) you are full of ideas and focused on the same positive goal.

METHOD. Interesting things will always jump out at you if you observe the client(s) carefully. When this happens it is a good idea to politely interrupt your observation with a compliment: *Could I briefly interrupt? I noticed that you all managed to . . . ! That's very impressive.*

Something similar can be asked of the clients: *Mr. Meyer, supposing your daughter deserved some extra praise for her achievements last week—what aspects of her behavior would you want to emphasize?*

TIPS. Like with **Certificates** that can be used to mark successes or to consolidate progress (see *page 193*), courage stones to remind clients of particular abilities or tasks (see *Talismans, courage stones, and other helpers, page 186*), or **The pocket helper** to extend and secure therapeutic progress (see *page 166*), you can give out "compliment stones" to help clients focus on their positive attributes (Caby, Hubert-Schnelle, & Caby, 2005).

Anything can be used that has some kind of special quality to it, for example, because it was collected somewhere (shells, feathers, pine cones), because it is pretty and colorful (marbles, glass stones) or particularly tactile (pebbles, horse chestnuts), because of its ideal pocket size, or because there is a nice story behind the object that can be told when handing it over.

I've got something special here for you that you can take with you. There's an interesting story as to how this came into my possession . . .

I would like this pretty piece of glass to remind you of my compliment—I want it to remind and encourage you to be as thoughtful as you have been up to now, even when you find yourself in situations that are hard to navigate.

With groups (see below) you can incorporate compliment stones into leaving rituals, for example, to wish a departing member of the group all the best for the future.

Tips. This intervention should be carefully dosed, so that this special "currency" does not suffer from inflation.

It is ideal as a parting gift at the end of a therapy.

Indication. All.

Contraindication. None.

Setting. Individual therapy, family therapy, couples therapy, group therapy (if the members know each other well and spend time together outside of the session), teams.

Concentration?! "How can I learn to concentrate?"

IDEA. There are numerous tricks that children and adults can use to remind themselves to concentrate. Some people tell themselves off, others talk with themselves, others read aloud the task that lies in front of them—sometimes several times. This is also a good approach when something doesn't sink in: When you read it aloud, the meaning often becomes clear. These experiences have also been incorporated into various aspects of Marburger Concentration Training (Krowatschek et al., 2007a & b).

METHOD. If a client has concentration problems, you can go through the following steps with him during the session:

1. What exactly is the task? Either the patient brings one along or the therapist presents him with one.

2. The therapist asks the client to read out his task and then to write it down or repeat it in some way in order to positively anchor it.

3. The client completes the task and provides his own commentary—to himself or out loud—by listing the order in which he has to do something.

4. The client is invited to praise himself for his successful concentration, and his praise is corroborated by the therapist.

TIPS. To further aid concentration, you can suggest that the client underline the written text in various colors or quietly sing the task to himself. Some people know from experience the best way of getting through to themselves.

Consolidating a task with movement is another good way of anchoring it. Here, too, clients often have their own ideas of how to do this and how to incorporate it into the learning process. Children tend to use "movement breaks" for homework, studying, or learning at school—it is better for these necessary physical breaks to take place wherever the learning is happening. Those who put too much distance between themselves and their work—for example, by going outside—are in danger of breaking their flow of concentration. Doing little exercises directly at the desk works well, for example, with balloons or pieces of cloth (so that nothing gets broken), with little balls that are, for example, tipped from one cup into another, or with feathers or balls of cotton wool that can be blown along the floor into a "goal" and picked up again.

Once again, the possibilities are endless, as long as the method suits the client and his environment.

INDICATION. All situations in which it is necessary to concentrate, such as patients with AD(H)D, adolescents with exam-related anxiety, or in preparation for job interviews.

CONTRAINDICATION. None.

SETTING. Individual therapy, group therapy.

Mottos, mantras, and myths

IDEA. Conversations with families often reveal certain shared attitudes, values, or value systems. In many cases there are beliefs that have been passed down the generations that have a special significance for the entire family system or at least for certain family members: "This family has always found a way out of difficult situations" or "We stick together in our family." (*See also* **The resources family tree**, *page 71, and* **Family coat of arms**, *page 158.*)

Such beliefs, attitudes, or even mottos can, on the one hand, bind a family together, on the other can set a (too) narrow framework, therefore leading to potential conflict. When problematic situations arise, they may prevent the family or system from seeking outside help, because "we've always managed to solve our problems on our own."

These (verbally or nonverbally) anchored aspects of a family can be picked up on in therapy, as long as they already have positive connotations. But many beliefs or ritually repeated phrases have negative connotations—from "It isn't worth the effort" to "Don't even try, you won't manage it anyway!" Adolescents, in particular, experience these kinds of casual remarks heard during arguments or at school, almost like a mantra and turn off right away: "Oh no, not that again" or "I really can't be dealing with those stupid comments."

Carefully approaching this subject in family therapy often triggers confusion or even consternation to begin with—often clients will claim that they had never thought about it in that way, that it's just a common phrase and shouldn't be taken so seriously.

In this case it can be helpful to think up new positive and solution-oriented standard phrases for the family, to develop a completely new motto, or to reframe it (see **Reframing**, *page 84*).

Exploring family myths works in the same way: A myth is in fact a story that has been passed down from generation to generation that usually has something magical about it. Most myths have positive connotations and are therefore good to use in a therapeutic context. A myth can also be scrutinized more closely and if necessary dismantled, should it have negative connotations.

METHOD. It is important for the therapist or counselor to listen carefully and if necessary to ask for permission to analyze such a phrase or motto:

> *I've heard you use exactly this phrase several times. I would be interested to find out where it comes from and since when you have used it in your family. It occurs to me that it could also be formulated as follows: . . .*

The "invention" of a family myth is therapeutically very significant: *Let's imagine that a myth already existed in your family 10 generations ago, which, however, got lost over time. What might it have been?*

This kind of task fascinates parents and children alike and leaves room for creative elaboration—as a story, picture, or family coat of arms—and frequently it leads to an astonishing turnaround in the therapeutic process.

Another exciting approach is to develop a motto based on the family's current situation: *What could your new family motto be? What would be the most important elements of this motto?*

Parents can use such myths or mottos to help them in their daily interaction with their children. In this case, humor should also play an important role.

An example: "Pulled through a hedge!"

During a discussion about family mottos, a father suddenly remembered the very funny and memorable sayings of his grandmother. She had actually had quite a reserved and quiet character, but on occasion she would come out with some very memorable sayings, like "You look like you've been pulled through a hedge backward!" After being initially irritated, the family found it impossible not to laugh—and the mood lightened.

Using a genogram, the family members then began thinking about who else in the family had had similar abilities and discovered other surprising sides to (past) family members' characters, besides the humor "gene" . . .

The family was also given the task of observing within the family when and in what form these grandmotherly phrases still cropped up. Astonishingly, they were still being used, but sometimes just in a modified or "modernized" form.

Tips. Exploring mottos and myths works well not just with family systems; shared attitudes and commonly cited phrases are found in work situations, too. Here it is also worth examining such a phrase, perhaps reformulating it or working together to create a new motto:

- *Music—2—3!* Music and films can be helpful in this context, especially very catchy songs that you can't get out of your head and that have a positive, resource-focused message, for example, "Hakuna Matata," well known from *The Lion King* but originally a Swahili saying from East Africa meaning "There are no problems," or "Don't worry—be happy!" Due to the popularity of the film song, one immediately associates it with a particular rhythm.

- Searching for an appropriate motto in this way can be combined with homework, for example, **Observation tasks** (*see page 98*) or a mission for clever detectives for children (*see **The change detective**, page 104*). Book titles work well, too. This kind of homework could also involve sending the family to the movies or the library—a task that often has the welcome side effect of getting the family out of the house and providing a relaxing break.

INDICATION. Perfect for using in family therapy (and also with teams).
CONTRAINDICATION. None.
SETTING. Family therapy, couples therapy, teams, individual therapy, group therapy.

Systemic and creative psychoeducation

IDEA. Ludewig (2002) has suggested that systemic therapists and counselors may spend too little time on explaining diagnoses and illnesses. He advocates using systemic approaches to convey disorder-specific knowledge about illnesses and to provide the client with explanatory models and treatment options. He also describes the possibilities and limitations of this knowledge-based approach for the therapist.

Psychoeducation refers to the attempt to convey knowledge regarding an illness or disorder to a patient or his next of kin, and thereby to support the processes of coping with the illness. By clearly and simply explaining the clinical picture and the conditions in which the illness comes about, as well as therapeutic approaches, the patient has the chance to learn how to deal with the disorder responsibly and autonomously.

Psychoeducation is already an established method in individual and group settings in the treatment of psychiatric clinical pictures, and it is increasingly being integrated in the treatment of chronically ill children and adolescents. Yet knowledge about the illness and suggestions of how to deal with it are usually shared only with the parents (Walter & Schmid, 2009).

Pfeiffer (2008) refers to psychoeducation as part of the therapeutic process in the treatment of traumatized children and adolescents. Together with their parents, the clients are offered a factual explanatory model with which they can face their uncertainty, worries, and fears.

Experience has also shown that children and adolescents benefit enormously from being part of these discussions about their disorder and how to deal with it, as long as the information is conveyed in an age-appropriate and inspiring way. The rule of thumb here is not to talk *about* the child/adolescent, but to talk *with* him.

For example, 10-year-old George suffered from ADD and was considerably overweight. School was difficult for him; he was often ostracized and did not have any friends. So far he had dealt with his problem by being the wise guy; in conversations he was often loud and obnoxious. It was difficult to convince him to take medication. When prompted, George would say, "I don't know why I'm like this. I don't really notice it, but everyone else seems to." With the help of psychoeducation, George began to change and the first signs of progress became apparent. He was particularly fascinated by the picture of a brain and its many different processes, and was motivated to ask questions.

By increasing the client's knowledge of the disorder (and the solution), the aim is to improve understanding of the illness and to activate further resources in order to support coping strategies and self-regulation.

METHOD. Systemic techniques, as well as creative methods, can facilitate a psychoeducational approach.

While finding out and discussing the client's existing knowledge of his illness, systemic questions can be used to invite the client to try new perspectives, for example,

- Using **Circular questioning**: *What do you think your mother/father already knows or has learned about the illness? What else do you think they would like to know about it?* (see page 85)
- **Scaling** to illustrate the client's existing knowledge or understanding of an illness (see *page 81*)
- **Externalization** to look at the illness from a distanced perspective (see *page 89*)
- **Observation tasks** (see *page 98*) and **Therapeutic homework** (see *page 110*) work well in this kind of situation, including **The change detective** (see *page 104*): *Please find out what . . . !*

Drawing and sketching works well not only with younger children. Here it is necessary to decide who will even pick up the pen: the therapist, to illustrate his version of what is going on, for example, in the brain or stomach, or the child, to show what he already knows or understands about the illness.

You can also invite the child/adolescent, perhaps together with his parents, to draw the illness in order to clarify what they already know.

Often one person starts the picture, which is then added to and developed with the input of the others. The accompanying discussions are revealing not just for the therapist; they are also helpful for establishing a shared understanding of the client's situation and his environment.

TIPS. With younger children, a glove puppet can be used to do the asking and/or explaining. At the beginning or end of a discussion it can check what was understood and what still needs to be discussed: *What else would it be good to know?*

Children and adolescents sometimes enjoy showing off their knowledge of a clinical picture in the context of a quiz. The clients and/or family members can be asked to formulate the questions themselves, which then need to be answered by the others.

To begin with, everyone can rate themselves on an "expertise scale"—and at end they can see how much extra knowledge they gained through the quiz.

The questions and answers can be written down, for example, on pieces of card and used again or added to a few months later.

A group of children—or family—can create a book or wall newspaper that explains the clinical picture, for example, depression, to other affected children. Each member of the group can create a page, and everyone can decide together which information is important and in what form it should be conveyed.

And you can ask the question: *And how would you have to explain your illness so that your classmates could understand what is happening inside your body?*

INDICATION. Particularly good with chronic disease processes and with the children of mentally or physically ill parents.

CONTRAINDICATION. None.

SETTING. Individual therapy, family therapy, group therapy.

Dream your dream

IDEA. Nightmares are often the reason that children and adolescents, as well as adults, come to therapy. Often the horrible dream also dominates their waking hours. And often they go to bed with the premonition that the dream will return tonight!

Many clients would also like to know what the dream might mean, because nowadays nearly everyone is familiar with the originally Freudian concept of interpreting dreams.

Because our dreams are always the product of our own minds, we actually have a far greater influence on them than we might think. Why should we not try to use this influence? By discussing and shaping the content of dreams, they can become less disturbing and can even be actively influenced.

Milton Erickson frequently wrote about his experiences with dreams and, among other things, describes how patients can use their dreams to successfully conclude the work begun during the therapy sessions (Rosen, 2009). He explains that therapy stimulates the unconscious to utilize all of the insights gained during therapy, so that it is even possible to dream the solution to a problem.

METHOD. *First,* if the client would like to know what the dream might mean, it is advisable to follow up one's own hypotheses with questions about the dream. As a therapist or counselor, you can only glean the meaning from your own context, but you do not know whether your own context fits that of the client. Although there are many dream symbols that supposedly have this or that meaning, these meanings have a generic value at most and do not tell us much about its particular significance for the client.

What do you think might be the significance of this dream for you?

Imagine you knew what the significance of this dream was for you—what would it change for you?

Second, if somebody suffers on account of a particular dream, and this dream always ends at the same point—as is usually the case with nightmares—the dream exercise could be: *Practice another end to your dream!*

A case example: Dream your dream

During therapy sessions, Josh told of a recurring dream: he was being pursued and forced to the edge of a cliff. The pursuers would come closer, and one of them would stretch out his arm and push him. At that moment the dream would always end, and Josh would wake up.

After describing his dream, the therapist explained to Josh that the dream was acted out in his mind: *Our brain often does things to us that we cannot completely comprehend. Sometimes we also have to give our brain a bit of a "leg up," so that it does what we want, and not vice versa. The dream always ends at the same point, and you think: "If I had carried on dreaming, I would have fallen off the cliff"—which of course is not possible, because you are lying in bed. Your brain knows that too . . . which is why the dream does not continue.*

The therapist went on: *"If the dream was going to continue, what do you think would happen?* "I would fall off!" Josh replied.

Who says that? "It couldn't happen any other way."

Perhaps, but if you could determine how the dream was to continue, would you fall off the cliff? "No, of course not!" *What would happen?* "I would be able to break the fall."

Fantastic! How exactly would you break the fall? "I would fall onto a tree. And then I would climb back up." *Great! And what would you do then?* "Feel happy to be alive!"

TIPS. Children can draw or create (with figures or modeling clay) the actual and the desired end to a dream.

Sometimes adolescents and even adults like to be creative on this front. You can suggest the different alternatives, and they can decide if they would be interested in trying any of them out. Writing a story with a "new" ending to a dream is one of the more commonly used methods.

These methods can also be incorporated into homework to be completed by the following session, for example, to draw an alternative ending to a current dream.

The combination of helper figures (see **Cartoon therapy,** *page 125*) works well, particularly with children; for example, a "dream dragon" could positively influence the ending of a dream.

INDICATION. Particularly with nightmares, fear of going to sleep, general anxieties, and self-esteem problems.

CONTRAINDICATION. Posttraumatic stress syndrome, suicidal tendencies.

SETTING. Individual therapy; in groups, the other members of the group can help the affected person decide how the dream could continue—in the form of hypotheses that can be used or rejected.

Exaggeration

IDEA. "There's no need to exaggerate" is a commonly used phrase and is typically heard when someone takes on a suggestion and implements it in an over-the-top way. But an exaggerated response to a suggestion can sometimes be used therapeutically.

Exaggeration is an effective way of making things clear, of breaking out of a rut, or opening up new perspectives. **Prescribing the symptom** (see page 100) also often involves an exaggeration of the symptoms described by the client.

In combination with **Scaling** (see page 81), it is often possible to brighten up a gloomy picture.

For example, Jack, a 17-year-old suffering from depression, rated himself as 1 on a scale of 1 to 10 on the two scales "confidence" and "mental state." The therapist reacted to this by saying, *That sounds to me like you're close to suicide!* To which Jack replied: "Well, it's not that bad!" So the therapist asked: *So what makes life worth living?* Suddenly the patient's focus completely changed, and he provided convincing arguments for why he should carry on. At the end of the session he had moved himself up to a 3 on both of the scales.

As another example, the parents of an obese child described how every morning they made sandwiches for their son's school lunch—in quantities that certainly wouldn't be helping their son's obesity problem. The therapist commented, *Excuse me, but I don't quite understand: Are you making sandwiches for the whole class?*

METHOD. With exaggeration you always go one step further than the client. In a slightly exaggerated way, you validate the client's condition and "accidentally" present it in an overblown form so that the client reacts differently from the way he did before. For example, someone with depression feels the need to defend himself against the doom and gloom depicted by the therapist and automatically adopts a resource-focused approach. He even provides arguments why it isn't actually that bad and claims that the therapist must have misunderstood him.

It also works the other way around—with humor, you can take up the situation described by the client and spin it out in a very extreme way. Depending on how provocative the intervention is, you may need to ask for permission to use it in advance.

TIPS. You can also instruct the client to exaggerate. For example, you can ask the client to exaggerate his symptoms the next day and to closely observe how the people around him react.

INDICATION. Whenever you feel that it would suit the current situation/client. It is a good idea to ask the client's permission. Basic requirements for using this intervention are respect and confidence that the client system has the necessary resources to react to the exaggeration in the right way.

CONTRAINDICATION. None.

SETTING. Individual therapy, family therapy, couples therapy, group therapy.

Rewind → Reset

IDEA. With this intervention, the client is invited to revisit a problem situation or a recent conflict that is still bothering him, to look at it from a new perspective, and then to formulate a reply to the other person or people involved (Reichelt-Nauseef & Heidbreder, 2009).

Besides this concrete approach, the client can also draw on his experiences to equip himself for future situations. By reflecting on solution scenarios, he can prevent future conflicts.

METHOD. The client is asked to act out an unpleasant or unsatisfactory experience again. The therapist or counselor takes on the role of the other person, and the encounter is wound back to the beginning and reset. The client describes the way he originally experienced the encounter and his feelings at the time, in order to then formulate the way he wished he'd responded.

1. He tries to describe the way he experienced the situation emotionally, how he felt, and so on.
2. The client responds to the person in a positive way and, for example, praises a reaction or quality of his imaginary adversary.
3. He describes the way he would like similar situations to play out in the future, and makes concrete suggestions as to how this could be achieved in a solution-oriented and resourced-focused way.

At the next available opportunity, the client can talk about the situation again with his "adversary" and suggest a new solution.

TIPS. Younger children often like it when an imaginary "reset" button is pressed before discussing or acting out alternative scenarios. You can also ask the child where exactly this button is situated and in which situations it might be a good idea to use it to avoid the situation playing out again in the old way.

Teams can also use this intervention to solve conflicts among themselves in a resource-focused way.

INDICATION. Basically in connection with any "conflict" issues.

CONTRAINDICATION. Avoid when the patient is cognitively unable to reflect on his past experiences and to "reset" it for the future, and with clients under severe emotional strain.

SETTING. Individual therapy, couples therapy, family therapy, group therapy, teams.

Dice: "Playing with possibilities"

IDEA. Decisions, decisions . . . Many therapy and counseling sessions revolve around decision making: Should I start therapy or not? Should the child welfare services continue to provide support? Should we include the teacher in the next session? Would it be better for this or that adolescent to be admitted into a clinic?

Dice are often helpful in stalemate situations, when a decision has to be made between two alternatives. And a die has six sides, which enables a more nuanced decision, or "dosage" in some circumstances (see *also* **Letting fate decide**, *page 114*).

METHOD. If a child or adolescent is frequently skipping school, for example, it is advisable to begin with a very low dosage: The client only needs to go to school if he rolls one of the six possible numbers, for example, a 6. If he rolls one of the other numbers he should not go to school that day. After this "dosage" has been applied successfully for two or three weeks, the pressure is increased: He has to go to school if he rolls a 6 or one other number, for example, 1.

However, this intervention is based on the premise that the adolescent (child), as well as the parents and the school want him to go back to school, and that everybody sees it as a mark of progress when he manages to go to school. Not going to school is then no longer a problem but a consequence of the rules of the game. It is also important to have established in advance whether there are serious reasons why the pupil does not want to go to school.

Sometimes clients describe the way they behave in one way one day, and differently the next day—without knowing why (see the case example **A toss of the dice**, below). If a client has a problem deciding how to behave on a particular day, the decision can be taken out of his hands. He can delegate the decision to another person or "thing." But first he has to agree to accept that decision!

The least complicated delegates are dice or coins. The only way they differ from one another is the number of options they offer. A coin has two sides, a die has six! Some dice even have six blank sides so that the client (and his system) can decide what the six different options will be.

A case example: A toss of the dice

Luke, seven years old, was on his second round of therapy. Sometimes he felt like cooperating, and sometimes he didn't. In the latter case he would sit down and demonstrate the reason that his parents decided to seek help: He would go on strike and refuse to do anything. The same thing was happening at school, and the principal had warned that he might have to repeat the year. So far he had made no apparent progress in therapy. Neither the teacher, nor the parents, nor Luke were able to explain why he behaved in this way.

The Therapist's Treasure Chest

The dice intervention was the breakthrough. At the beginning of every meeting, Luke was asked to decide how he would behave with the help of a die: 1, 2, and 3 meant "Cooperate!"; 4, 5, and 6 meant "Refuse to cooperate!"

Beforehand, the therapist had drawn up a contact with Luke, in which he agreed to stick to the rules. If he fulfilled his side of the contract, he would get a reward.

Luke really enjoyed the game to start with, but after a while he began to dislike the forced noncooperation. He came up with the idea of increasing the chances he had to cooperate: the 4 now also meant "Cooperate!"

His parents decided to use the same intervention for school, whereby Luke secretly achieved his goal: He had the feeling that his parents were now interested in what he did at school.

TIPS. *Rule dice:* When talking with families it often emerges that the different members of the family have different takes on the issue of rules. When asked if they have rules at home, parents usually spontaneously answer in the affirmative, but with a little more probing they often find it difficult to define what these rules are.

But if it becomes apparent that all members of the family see the sense of rules and are theoretically happy to work with them, a die can be a useful means of helping to implement them.

The first step is to define the rules that will be implemented and to write these down for everyone to see, for example, on a big piece of paper. If the family/system cannot decide which rules to introduce first (*see also* **The rule of the month,** *page 192*), they can be narrowed down to the three most important ones. These three rules can now be assigned to numbers on the die:

1 and 2 = Meals will be eaten at the table

3 and 4 = Nobody interrupts when another person is talking

5 and 6 = Everyone tidies up their own mess

Then the family decides when the die will be rolled. For example, they might decide to roll it every Sunday and in this way determine which rule they will especially focus on in the coming week.

INDICATION. All concerns and processes that offer so many options that the client finds it difficult to make a decision.

CONTRAINDICATION. None, unless there is no consensus regarding what a decision means and the expectations connected to it.

SETTING. Individual therapy, family therapy, couples therapy, group therapy, teams.

Interventions for Home

Signed and sealed: Contracts with clients

IDEA. To increase the binding nature of agreements with patients or clients, the agreement can be put into written form. Just as **Certificates** are used to consolidate achievements by writing them down (*see page 193*), this method of carefully formulating a contract together helps the client to more clearly define his next and future goals.

METHOD. The "nonsuicide contract" is the classic among written agreements made with clients about the further course of therapy. In resource-focused terminology this is called a "life contract."

But it can also work like this: Thirteen-year-old Martin has a mild intellectual disability and is often very provocative and offensive toward weaker children, who then react very strongly. When the boy extended this behavior to new members of staff and interns in his residential unit, he was admitted as an inpatient to a child and adolescent psychiatric clinic. At the end of his treatment the following contract was drawn up between Martin and his doctor: "I hereby agree not to bother my housemates, and in return Dr. . . . agrees to be less strict."

The contract was signed, and with a shake of the hands they both agreed to check that the other kept his side of the bargain.

For most young patients this will be the first contract they ever sign, and they often take it very seriously because they feel that they themselves are being taken seriously as a "contract partner."

TIPS. With young children, in particular, creatively drafted "written" contracts are a way of increasing motivation, as well as cooperation, in the therapy process. Adolescents as well as children feel they are being taken seriously, as it is usually the first time in their lives that they are being asked to sign a document.

An additional question could be: *What will be your personal contribution to making our contract work? What else could I do?*

INDICATION. Running away, trust-building issues, all persistent symptoms, suicidal tendencies, lack of compliance, skipping school.

CONTRAINDICATION. There is little point to such a contract if compliance is very bad or if there is absolutely no willingness to cooperate.

SETTING. Individual therapy, family therapy, group therapy, couples therapy.

Keeping minutes for a meeting

IDEA. Adolescents and young adults with borderline disorders may make considerable progress during a session but subsequently struggle to implement what they have learned—not because they don't want to, but because they are used to being given instructions by others and not having to rely on themselves. This led to the idea of giving them minutes to take away with them that briefly sum up the main points of the session.

METHOD. The client writes down the main points of the discussion, especially what the client intends to do. Signing the document can strengthen the effect.

INDICATION. Early stages of a disorder, borderline personality disorders, forgetfulness, and so on.

CONTRAINDICATION. None.

SETTING. Individual therapy.

Talismans, courage stones, and other helpers

IDEA. The items that the clients are given to take home with them should remind them of a particular ability or task and reinforce a therapeutic message that they can fall back on in crisis situations. (*See also* **The pocket helper**, *page 166, and* **Compliments, praise, and such**, *page 168.*)

METHOD. Anybody who works with patients—of any age—should have a treasure chest of such objects on hand.

Talismans and courage stones can be collected on country walks or on vacation (pebbles and shells at the beach, chestnuts, feathers, leaves, etc.), bought (small gifts/freebies, e.g., marbles, beads, small animal figures), or made (felt balls, figures out of salt dough, key rings).

For specific therapeutic tasks, a small stone, a little doll, and so on, can be given to the patient to take home as a reminder of their task (like a knot in a handkerchief).

For example, when the solution-oriented therapist Yvonne Dolan came to our clinic a few years ago, she gave a live demonstration with a highly traumatized young man. At the end of the session she started to rummage around in her bag and took out a little angel figure, which she gave to her patient with the following message: *This angel expresses my admiration for you and will always remind you of our talk and give you courage.* The patient still carries the angel around with him . . .

TIPS. If you are in a shared practice, it is worth reserving a (treasure) chest or special drawer to keep such objects and have them ready to hand out.

It is a good idea to have a fixed place for your "treasures," as children love these rituals and will make a mental note of it.

At the start of a new group therapy, we let the participating patients build a box for exactly these kinds of treasures. As therapists, we are constantly surprised how well the patients remember—at a much later date—what each of the objects represented.

At the end of every group session it is a ritual for patients to choose a talisman to take home as a reminder.

INDICATION. This method is generally for reinforcement (see **Reinforcing a positive mood**, *page 117*) and is particularly good with fears (e.g., fear of separation or of school, fear of sleeping, fear of homework, or exams).

It is also helpful in psychotherapeutic work with mentally disabled patients; talismans, or lucky charms also work well and strengthen the patient-client bond.

It can never hurt! With these little objects, you also ensure that the therapy works beyond the session.

CONTRAINDICATION. None really. However, it works well only once a good relationship has been established with the patient.

It's always a nice gesture that the patient remembers!

SETTING. Individual therapy, couples therapy, family therapy, group therapy.

Dream catchers and worry dolls

IDEA. These objects function as protectors or anchors. For example, they help a therapeutic story told to a child make a lasting impression, or serve as a reminder of the ritual of when the object was handed over.

It is also a simple method to reinforce externalization (the helper, who supports you). (See also **The pocket helper**, *page 166, and* **Talismans, courage stones, and other helpers**, *page 186.*)

METHOD. These kinds of materials are most commonly found in fair-trade stores or at arts and crafts markets, and so on.

You may also find them on vacation, at school bazaars or similar charitable events.

We have found that items like dream catchers are often hand-made by children in kindergartens and schools or at home—this is, of course, a great idea.

And we never cease to be amazed by how creative parents can be!

An example: The "travel dream catcher"

The father of five-year-old Phillip told us that the dream catcher had been a great help during a prolonged period when he was afraid of the dark and couldn't get to sleep—particularly because he was fascinated by Native Americans.

However, one vacation they forget to take the dream catcher that hung above Phillip's bedroom door, so on the first evening in the hotel there was a big crisis. In despair, the father unpacked the invisible "travel dream catcher" and fastened it with pantomime-like exaggeration to the hotel room door, after which Phillip fell peacefully asleep.

For some time afterward, this version of the dream catcher was an indispensable part of the family's vacation luggage, and the boy himself would always remind them not to forget this invisible helper.

INDICATION. Ideal for children who have difficulties falling asleep, or who suffer from nightmares or wake up in the night.

The dream catcher can be wonderfully combined with **Therapeutic stories and fairy tales** (*see page 130*) and works with adults as well as children. It also reinforces the therapeutic relationship!

CONTRAINDICATION. None that are known.

SETTING. Individual therapy, family therapy.

The anti-anxiety thread

IDEA. Establishing trust and security.

METHOD. Patient and parent(s) are given the task of finding a nice piece of thread, ribbon, or string at home that is long enough to reach from the child's bed to his parent's. Together they should attach the thread/ribbon to both beds, so that the child can easily reach out and touch it at night.

By pulling on the thread, the child can also assure himself that there is someone at the other end of the line.

The thread becomes a visible bridge. For example, the child can also feel his way along the thread with closed eyes to his parent's bed.

To take it a step further, the thread can be tied to the wrist of one of the parents and to the child's. This creates an even closer sense of proximity and sometimes leads to funny little games. One father even attached the thread to his big toe!

TIPS. The thread or ribbon could be in the child's favorite color, and the child might want to attach a little note to the thread. The child may also want to hold the thread while he is going to sleep.

INDICATION. For children who have problems falling asleep or are scared of going to sleep alone.

CONTRAINDICATION. None.

SETTING. Individual therapy, family therapy.

Traffic-light cards

IDEA. Like traffic lights, these cards provide children with a clear signal. The method provides parents with a fast way of reacting and leaves no room for discussion! And with the help of the results table, children learn to control their behavior.

METHOD. The family is given the task of introducing a traffic-light card system at home, that is, to make three cards: red, green, and yellow. When typical problematic situations arise, the cards can be put to use:

The *yellow card* (yellow = WATCH OUT) is given as a warning. The child at whom the card is directed knows that if he is not careful or does not stop, he will get a red card.

The *red card* (red = STOP) is shown when the child does not change his behavior and leads to the *consequences* he was warned of, for example, being sent out of the room.

The *green card* (green = OK) signals a return to normality—*everything is OK*, let's try again. The green card can, of course, also be used when something has worked really well or to acknowledge certain achievements, to counterbalance red cards.

At the end of the day the family can add up the score, although at the start of the intervention the family needs to decide whether the green cards cancel out the red cards.

The family can also create a balance sheet:

3 green cards or more means . . .

2 green cards means . . .

1 green card means . . .

An even score means . . .

1 red card means . . .

2 red cards mean . . .

TIPS. This intervention is often combined with a discussion about whether the family already has rules that everybody is supposed to stick to (see **The rule of the month**, page 192). This often leads to the realization that the family does not have many rules and that now would be a good time to start. However, before using the cards, it must be made very clear what the positive and negative consequences will be.

INDICATION. Problematic, disruptive behavior of any kind. It is particularly suitable for families who tend to discuss everything at length without coming up with concrete solutions, and for parents who have difficulties asserting their authority.

CONTRAINDICATION. It works only if everyone has understood the system and is willing to go along with it.

SETTING. Family therapy.

The rule of the month

IDEA. For this idea to work, and to increase motivation to take further steps, it is often important to start with a fairly small rule that is easy to stick to. This way there is always a clear objective, and the task or approach is doable.

Some parents have a long list of rules in their heads that they would like to introduce. Here, too, initial small steps can help build up confidence to take the next, bigger steps.

METHOD. With a rule of the month or, to start with, just a rule of the week, you can work together with the client, step by step, on one specific problem. In some families it many even work best to have a rule of the day.

TIPS. In addition to discussing the selected rule, the family can also write down (or draw) the rule on a piece of paper as a reminder and hang it in a prominent position at home; individual family members usually immediately come up with some creative suggestions.

And not to forget: The rule applies to everyone!

INDICATION. Useful with disorders such as ADHD, oppositional behavior or lack of motivation, and parental inconsistency.

CONTRAINDICATION. None.

SETTING. The rule of the month is usually used in family therapy, but with the right motivation can also work well in individual therapy. The patient can impose a rule upon himself and try to adhere to it over a set amount of time.

The Therapist's Treasure Chest

Certificates

IDEA. The client's achievements are highlighted, acknowledged, and made a focal point at home. By hanging the certificate, for example, above the child's desk or bed, it also serves as a positive reminder.

METHOD. Certificates can convey a number of messages:

We're proud of you!
Great work!
Over the last week you've managed to . . . !
I'm so pleased that you've managed to . . . !
We always knew you could do it!

Many other ideas can be immortalized on a certificate in order to remind the child (or adolescent) of what he has done to solve his problem.

It is important that the message is formulated in a solution-oriented and resource-focused way, for example, instead of *You're not wetting your bed anymore!* it is better to say: *You've done it! Your bed is dry in the mornings!*

The certificate can be ceremoniously handed over at a special moment, either in the presence of the child's family (ask the child first) or in front of the clinical staff at your practice, and can be combined with a talisman or courage stone (see **Talismans, courage stones, and other helpers**, *page 186*), which is given to the child at the same time: *So that you can carry on the great work!*

Important: parents sometimes deserve a certificate too!

TIPS. Very effective and quick and easy to make with some colored pens, stickers, and stamps. You can also keep a few colorful templates in your drawer, to which you need only to add the client's name and information about his achievement—it is easy to whip up a certificate in no time!

INDICATION. Suitable, for example, to mark the end of a therapy or whenever a problem clearly improves. Works with a variety of problems, including enuresis, lying, aggressive behavior, and refusal to do homework.

CONTRAINDICATION. None: Praise never hurts if it is sincere!

SETTING. Individual therapy, family therapy, group therapy.

Part 3

Indications: What Works Best When?

Introduction

This section presents suggestions for the best interventions to use with particular disorders or behavioral problems.

It should be emphasized that all of the recommended approaches can be used either at the start of a consultation or after a diagnosis has been made, and also if the client has already been through therapy.

It goes without saying that in the case of severe symptoms, chronicities, or disturbances or psychological stress, a specialist diagnosis is necessary. It is also necessary if the suggested "tips and tricks" don't bring about any improvement and the hoped-for results are not achieved.

In the case of all indications, the reader should feel free to try other techniques apart from the ones we suggest. We do not claim that our suggestions are the only effective interventions.

The tabular overviews outline approaches that have proven to be effective in our or our colleagues' experiences working with clients or patients in a variety of settings. In many cases these are complemented by helpful case examples and frequently asked questions.

With every indication, a resource-focused approach is key. Having a resource-focused "attitude" can in itself create a special framework and can help the client move away from the problem toward a solution. A resource-focused conversation can be structured around the following questions:

Which of your resources do you think you could use to solve problem X?

When would you use these resources?

Which other resources do you need?

If you had these resources, what would you do differently?

Which resources that exist in your family/environment do you think could help you now?

If you had these resources, what would change in the way you deal with problem X?

Aggressive Behavior

When it comes to aggressive and violent behavior, Petermann and Petermann (2007) stress the importance of an enhanced behavioral repertoire—meaning that the therapist should try, as much as possible, to make the client aware of, and encourage him to try, alternative patterns of behavior—as well as reinforcing the child's and the family's resources.

In order to find the right therapeutic approach, it is necessary to explore whether the patient has himself been subjected to violent behavior, in order to eliminate the possibility that he is using violence as a protective strategy.

Alongside approaches incorporating relaxation techniques, the development of social skills and self-assertiveness, and self-control exercises in behavioral group therapy for children and in family therapy, the following interventions can improve conversation situations, reinforce initial successes, and provide parents with additional ideas for daily use:

Asking about exceptions (see page 79)

Externalization (see page 89)

Circular questioning (see page 85)

Observation tasks (see page 98)

Acting-as-if tasks (see page 116)

Externalization works well with the two entities model; that is, one part of the client is the aggressive, angry part, and the other part is the person the child or adult would like to be, and who is already present to an extent. For example:

I have the impression there are two of you—the one is aggressive, and the other is the kind one, who I see here today . . .

Imagine, if you were to divide up a pie, how big would the slice of the "bad" you be, and how big would the slice of the "nice" you be?

What would have to happen for the "nice slice" to be bigger? or How would you notice that your nice side has the upper hand? What would you be doing differently?

Careful: Prescribing the symptom and other paradoxical interventions are **contraindicated** because of the potential risk to others.

A creative and multimodal approach is often the only solution with clients diagnosed with behavioral or oppositional defiant disorders, often in combination with ADHD.

A case example: Marvin

Marvin, who was nine years old, had been treated as an outpatient for some time because of frequent aggressive behavior toward his classmates, as well as his mother and younger sister. After being diagnosed with a hyperkinetic conduct disorder, he was treated with a variety of drugs and underwent behavioral therapy at the child/family/school level with only limited success. A breakthrough occurred with the following approach.

Marvin's sister and his parents were set a joint *observation task* combined with a *prescription for change*, packaged in a detective game that was particularly appealing to children. The task was as follows:

> *I want each of you to think of a change that the rest of the family would find good, and to carry it out without letting on what it is to anybody else. Between now and the next session, try and work out what the others have changed!*

To reinforce this approach, at the end of the session all four were asked to write down their "change" on a piece of paper, which would remain with the counselor/therapist. Nobody was allowed to show or tell anybody else what he or she had written down.

At the next session, four weeks later, the family members arrived in high spirits and reported a particularly good phase without any significant problems. They were bursting to reveal what they had guessed about the others, each of them convinced that they had guessed the others' changes.

First the parents were asked to report on the changes they thought they had detected in their children. This led to the mother and father starting a lengthy discussion about who had made what observations and what they had experienced, with the result that the children became more and more immersed in listening and were more and more amazed at the positive developments their parents had noticed.

After the children had also reported their observations, the intended changes were revealed—it turned out that nobody had recognized the changes that the family members had written on the slips of paper, but they had noticed many other positive behavioral developments. For example, Marvin had made the concrete promise "not to hit my sister anymore," and while this change had gone unnoticed, his parents as well as his sister had discovered many positive sides to him—it was only after the intended changes were revealed that it occurred to everyone that Marvin had not hit his sister.

Anxiety Disorders

Anxiety disorders, such as fear of school, separation anxiety, and fear of exams, should always be taken seriously, as it serves an important protective function (Görlitz, 2005). Therapy with children and adolescents with anxiety disorders usually focuses on cognitive behavioral therapy, treatments involving confronting the object of fear, and pharmacotherapy (Schneider, 2004).

In contrast to this, a purely psychotherapeutic approach—solution oriented and resource focused—works just as well or can be used to complement other forms of treatment. Similar approaches are used for treating anxiety disorders in adults, and the methods suggested below can be used with clients of all ages.

- **Asking about exceptions** (see page 79): *Can you give an example of when you managed to conquer your anxiety?* or *What did you do differently when you didn't feel any anxiety?*
- **Externalization** (see page 89):
  ° *Draw the anxiety, blow it away, or lock it up . . .*
  ° Establish boundaries for the anxiety: The anxiety is only allowed to "come out" at certain times or in particular rooms.
- **Cartoon therapy** (see page 125)
- **Prescribing problem-free times and rooms** (see page 106)
- **Activating resources** (see page 69): *How did you manage to conquer your anxiety?* or *What have you tried that worked well?*
- **The anti-anxiety thread** (see page 189)
- Reinforcement
- Other questions: *Does anxiety have its advantages?* or *Can you draw something positive out of your anxiety?*
- Boost body consciousness (massage techniques, "body map")

A particularly fast and effective intervention with young children is the *anti-anxiety thread*, as well as *externalization*, for example, blowing away the anxiety.

With children it can be a good idea to ask them which methods they think might help them conquer their anxieties.

The creative ideas that children come up with never cease to amaze—and approaches that integrate the children's suggestions are usually the ones that work best.

Some examples: Addressing anxiety disorders

Different types of externalization plus questions: A five-year-old boy had the idea of burying his fear in the garden. He drew a picture depicting his fear, locked the picture up in a little box, and buried it at the far end of the garden. He chose the place where his fear was to disappear: *I'm going to bury it in a spot that I can see from my bedroom window. That way I always know where it is.* This was followed by a discussion about why it was good that the fear was now buried there:

> *Why is it good . . . ?*
>
> *How do you know that you feel better?*
>
> *What else could you do if the fear came back again?*

Asking about exceptions and prescribing symptom-free time: A young woman with social phobia was asked if there were times when she did not experience her anxiety. She said there were. She was then asked to consider how long these periods lasted, and then: *Could you imagine extending these times? If yes, by how many minutes?*

Attention Deficit Hyperactivity Disorder (ADHD)

In recent years, a wide range of interventions based on multimodal, individually adaptable approaches has become established in the treatment of ADHD in children and adolescents as well as in adults. Depending on the age group and intensity of the problem, several methods can be used in combination with a drug-based treatment. These include patient-centered interventions, parent- and/or family-centered interventions, and school- or context-centered interventions, with techniques ranging from psychoeducation and cognitive therapy to parental training and targeted approaches in schools (including kindergarten) and other contexts (Döpfner et al., 2008).

Possible complementary interventions

- Supporting questions to further reinforce the success of the above measures:
  - ° **Scaling** questions (*see page 81*)
  - ° Asking about changes and positively acknowledging these (perhaps in combination with **The Miracle Question**; *see page 87*):
    - * *Who do you think will notice the changes first?*
    - * *Do you think the change might have brought some advantages?*
- **Reframing** (*see page 84*)
- Strengthening the family system is another method, particularly with ADHD families (resource work; *see* **Activating and working with resources**, *page 68*).
  - ° Getting to know the child and parents:
    - * *What do you like doing?*
    - * *During an average day, are there times when you function well as a family?*
    - * *What has always worked well for you and how did you do it?*
  - ° Positive experiences and shared achievements
- Additional interventions, depending on the client's level of motivation:
  - ° **Observation tasks** (*see page 98*), which might begin with the classic task of getting the client to observe what has gone well between the current and next session (child/client or parent/partner)

- * Did your ADHD prevent some of your strengths from coming to the fore?
- * What should stay the way it is?
- ° In the following session, particular methods can be enlarged on:
  - * Asking about changes
  - * "What's going well?" diary
  - * Has the sibling constellation changed? Have new perspectives been opened up?
  - * Is another child suddenly the main focus of attention?
  - * What benefits does ADHD have? (see **The what's-it-good-for question**, page 28)
  - * Intervention: Do more of what is already working! (see **Prescribing what the patient is already doing well**, page 105)

Careful: *Many ADHD families have gone through a lot of suffering. It is important and beneficial for the therapeutic relationship, and for compliance, if the therapist acknowledges what the family has been through and shows an interest in how they have coped with the situation (Selekman, 1997).*

ADHD 2.0: Focus on Adolescents and Medication

ADHD is one of the most common disorders affecting children and adolescents, and it is becoming increasingly common among adults (Barkley, Murphy, & Fischer, 2008).

Adolescents and young adults with ADHD are often also struggling with the transition into teenhood or adulthood, and the taking of medication can present a considerable challenge.

Focus: Adolescents

When dealing with young people on the threshold of adolescence or adulthood, aspects such as transparency, authenticity, and respect play an important role. Therapists or counselors play a particularly important role with clients with ADHD, as they frequently need to support them at crucial stages in their lives, such as starting a new job or their first long-term relationships—periods that can be potentially explosive. Here, too, the ability to connect with the client is crucial—it determines the therapeutic relationship to a large extent.

Some approaches have proven to be particularly helpful for working with adolescents, and for working with adults, too:

- Take on the role of "coach"—develop coping strategies with the client
- Help the client remember and focus on stress-free periods in his life
- Encourage parental presence and patience, and parental coaching if necessary: Practice resource-oriented language, for example, instead of "You always do . . . ," "You've never done . . . ," encourage more positive formulations like *It would be great if you could . . .*
- Activate support systems
- Relaxation, peace and quiet, serenity, time for each other, cooperation
- Realistic pedagogical assessment of what the adolescent already understands/can decide for himself

The solution-oriented approach is an important step in working with ADHD-affected adolescents and opens up many new possibilities and perspectives (Bauer & Hegemann, 2010).

Issues such as self-efficacy and autonomy play an important role in the process of identity formation and require adequate support. Many clients have not been given enough opportunity to develop coping strategies during their childhood and are now suddenly grown up.

Focus: Medication

Psychoeducation and psychotherapeutic measures play an important role in the treatment of ADHD and its common concomitant disorders, and in some cases medication is additionally indicated (Döpfner et al., 2008). If a decision is made to use medication, this aspect of the treatment can of course also be dealt with during therapy or counseling.

Note: The decision to prescribe medication can of course be a team decision, depending on the treatment situation, but the responsibility of overseeing the treatment ultimately lies with the patient's doctor. Nonetheless, it is important for everyone involved in the patient's counseling and therapy process to provide backup and interdisciplinary support. This multiprofessional approach can only benefit the patient and his system.

Some examples of questions to work with:

- *Why do you think that it has got to the stage that people think you should take medication?*
- *How could you convince everyone that you don't need medication?*
- *What abilities would you need for this?*
- *When have you managed to successfully use this/these ability/abilities?*
- *What did you do differently?*

- *What did the others have to do differently?*
- *What else could you contribute yourself?*

At the end of such a resource-activating program, clients can still decide against taking medication. In this case, the following is necessary:

- Clarify *all* possible options if the client does not want to take his medication
- Show understanding for the client's decision and confidence in his ability to act responsibly
- At the beginning of a session ask: *How can you help the medication to help you?*
- At the end of a later session: *How can the medication help you to manage without the medication?*

During pharmacotherapy for ADHD, it can also be helpful to reinforce the role of the observer—not just with adolescents.

Who are the observers? Ideally, the observers should include everybody in the patient's everyday life: family, school teachers, perhaps friends; in a clinic setting, of course, also the staff. The observations are classically focused on the core symptoms of concentration, impulsivity, and hyperactivity, as well as possible side effects.

But the observation should also incorporate questions like:

- *Which resources have suddenly become apparent?*
- *Which resources are suddenly more noticeable than before?*
- *How do others react to these changes?*

In this way the system becomes involved in the client's treatment, with the added benefit that the system's reaction to the changes can be registered and provide helpful pointers for the therapist or counselor.

At the next meeting it is worth spending some time discussing the observations, because the focus of these observations is usually positive and may have nothing to do with the medication, yet still be important for the patient's progress.

Approaches for ADHD

- Resource activation (see **Activating and working with resources,** *page 68*): *Which of your strengths do you value in particular?*

- **Relaxation and imagination** (see *page 154*)
- Psychoeducation (see ***Systemic and creative psychoeducation,** page 174*)
- **Metaphors** (see *page 60*)
- **Family coat of arms** (see *page 158*)
- **Rewind** → **Reset** (see *page 181*)
- **Signed and sealed: Contracts with clients** (see *page 184*)
- Marking progress (see ***Improvisation, movement, and more**, page 136*): "What have I achieved so far?"
- **Reflecting positions** (see *page 143*): *With ADHD families in particular, an outside perspective often helps the family to rethink deep-seated behavioral patterns within the system and to change them.*
- Timeline with families (see ***Timeline work,** page 126*)
- **Mottos, mantras, and myths** (see *page 171*)
- **Asking about exceptions** (see *page 79*)
- **The rule of the month** (see *page 192*)
- **Therapeutic homework** (see *page 110*), for example, the client writes himself a letter from the future or writes a letter to the illness.
- Genogram work (see ***The resources family tree**, page 71*): *Who in your family could be a role model because he also had ADD/ADHD? What would he advise you to do?*
- **Drawing together** (see *page 119*): Adolescents and young adults only rarely agree to the suggestion of drawing something (together). They are usually much more open to the idea of creating a collage out of torn-out magazine photos. **Tip:** As homework you can also get the client to portray his current family situation on video. Adolescent clients usually respond enthusiastically to the suggestion of adding their favorite music to the video.
- **Circular questioning** (see *page 85*)
- **Scaling** (see *page 81*)

Autistic Behavior

For children and adolescents with autism spectrum disorders accompanied by aggressive and/or impulsive behavior, a variety of methods can have a positive influence.

From our work with residential and semiresidential patients, we know that some interventions work particularly well with children and adolescents, but also with adults with autistic tendencies.

Interventions for autism

- **Letting fate decide** (see page 114): Autistic people need clear instructions and are often very systematic about following them. By helping them make decisions, they are saved from a decision-making crisis while also learning to control their behavior.
- **Traffic-light cards** (see page 190) are helpful for patients with autistic tendencies.
- **Reframing** (see page 84): Autistic patients often have very structured daily routines and are very good tacticians. There are striking similarities with a game of chess.
- **Glove puppets** (see page 118): Children can, for example, talk with the puppet rather than with the therapist.
- Allow children to bring along their favorite toy.
- **Breaking the pattern** (see page 97)
- Drawing something, for example, do something new with the child's name, by emphasizing letters and developing words out of them that stand for particular abilities (see **Working with the child's name**, page 122).

A case example: Zac

Zac, a 17-year-old high-school student with Asperger's syndrome, had two kinds of attack that corresponded perfectly with the dynamics of his divorced parents: The panic attacks were observed only by his mother; the psychomotoric attacks, only by his father.

Both parents accused each other of ignorance, because each never confirmed what the other one said. They continued to argue about who was responsible for their son's disorder.

Zac was a good chess player. In the context of therapy, we redefined his clinical picture as a game of chess, and it soon became clear to him that his father was the castle and his mother the knight. He saw himself as the queen. The king was missing. Confronted with this fact, it occurred to him that the king must be the family that no longer existed.

Thus, the game lost its objective. He reflected on the fact that he was 17 and nearly grown-up, and stopped having attacks.

Biting

Biting—or pinching or scratching—other living beings is particularly prevalent among preschool children and children with mental disabilities. In most cases it is only a phase, but sometimes the behavior lasts over a longer period of time.

Interventions for biting

- Resource activation (see **Activating and working with resources**, *page 68*)
- **Relaxation and imagination** (see *page 154*)
- **A chair is (not) a chair** (see *page 145*): *King's throne and role reversal*
- **Compliments, praise, and such** (see *page 168*)
- **Rewind → Reset** (see *page 181*): *What could you contribute yourself next time?*
- Marking progress (see **Improvisation, movement, and more**, *page 136*)
- **Metaphors** (see *page 60*)
- **The pocket helper** (see *page 166*)
- **Externalization** (see *page 89*)
- **Asking about exceptions** (see *page 79*)
- **Therapeutic stories and fairy tales** (see *page 130*)
- **Talismans, courage stones, and other helpers** (see *page 186*)
- **The forecast calendar** (see *page 108*)
- **Traffic-light cards** (see *page 190*)
- **Breaking the pattern** (see *page 97*)
- **Glove puppets** (see *page 118*): With younger children, conversations with glove puppets can initiate or accompany behavioral changes. They also help to get to the root of the feelings of the victim: *Do you know how Max felt after he was bitten?*

A case example: "Victor the biter"

The mother of four-year-old Victor, herself an experienced teacher, was at the end of her rope. Since starting kindergarten a year before, Victor had been biting other children. This happened above all when he was angry and did not know how to defend himself.

His mother reported that Victor had begun biting as a baby when he was just nine months old. At the time, his biting had been directed especially at the family dog and his big brother. At the age of two-and-a-half he had gone through a particularly intensive phase, when he was not yet as advanced in his speech as other children his age. In this way he quickly got everybody's attention, even if the reactions were negative. For his parents, it was as if a switch was suddenly flipped in Victor, and out of despair he felt there was no other option apart from biting.

The teachers in his kindergarten had tried everything—from time out, to having him collected by his parents, to explaining his unwanted behavior to him—but so far without any success. Meanwhile, the mothers were already calling him "Victor the biter," as were the other children, who would run away from him but also show that at some level they respected and admired him.

Victor really liked the idea of a having an imaginary "mini-pincher" as his pocket helper, whose job it was to stop Victor from biting. The mini-pincher would give him a quick, imaginary pinch, which would cause Victor to hop a few times. These sudden jumps, in combination with the invisible pinching figure, earned him the respect of his friends who were curious and also found the new Victor funny. The biting gradually came to a stop.

Chronic Physical Conditions

The most common chronic conditions in children and adolescents include allergies, neurodermatitis, scoliosis, and cramp attacks (Bode, 2009b). In adulthood these are joined by mental conditions such as depression, which is extremely widespread, as well as chronic backache and cardiovascular conditions. In industrialized nations it is estimated that up to 20 percent of all children are affected by chronic physical conditions, which have significant repercussions not only for the child but also for the child's whole system (Günter, 2004). Continuing to support chronically ill adolescents as they make the transition to adulthood presents a particular challenge. A successful transition is an important prerequisite for quality of life, as well as for the acquisition of suitable strategies for dealing with specific stress situations.

Complex chronic health problems and disease processes accompanied by mental development problems are collectively referred to as "new morbidities" (Thyen et al., 2009).

Chronic illnesses, of course, require medical intervention in the classic sense, but the patient also has to come to terms with the increasing psychosocial strain and, consequently, with aspects such as coping with and accepting the illness, as well as cooperation (compliance and adherence). In addition, the family and environment of the chronically ill child or adolescent play a pivotal role in how and whether the difficult situation is dealt with.

Compliance problems are common among adolescent patients, particularly at the stage when they are breaking away from the family and seeking greater autonomy. But associated mental disorders, acute crises, and the overall strain on the family, including possible coping patterns and resources, must equally be taken into account.

Chronically ill children and adolescents, for example, with a congenital heart defect, cystic fibrosis, kidney problems, rheumatic diseases, or metabolic disorders, are usually treated by pediatricians, general practitioners, or specialist doctors. The care provided by a multidisciplinary team, on the other hand, can make a considerable contribution to improved physiosocial care, particularly with problem constellations. For example, it is no longer enough to provide children and adolescents suffering from diabetes with ongoing self-management training; it is necessary to provide social and psychotherapeutic help for the whole family (Lange, 2011).

Interventions to address chronic physical conditions

- Psychoeducation (see **Systemic and creative psychoeducation,** *page 174*): With adolescents, in particular, it is often astonishing how little they know about their illness, even when they are expected to deal with it autonomously, which is why it is always worth asking: *Can I ask to what extent you are already an expert in your illness? And what else would you have to know in order to feel really in control of your illness?* Questions do not have to be asked as a way of gleaning information; they can also be a way of providing information: *I would like to know if you would be interested in finding out more about this clinical picture? The facts can also be described as follows . . .*

- Resource activation (see **Activating and working with resources,** *page 68*): *Which of your strengths do you value in particular?* and *Of the things that you can do well, which do you like best?*

- **Relaxation and imagination** (see *page 154*)

- **Mottos, mantras, and myths** (see *page 171*)

- **Metaphors** (see *page 60*): The type of image used to deal with the illness can vary greatly from patient to patient, but it can considerably ease the way in which certain issues are dealt with and verbalized (e.g., "my suitcase," the "monster," or "Lisa's secret").

- **The inner team** (see *page 163*): The method of the inner team can help the client, for example, send his "coughing" or "ill" self on holiday.

- **The pocket helper** (see *page 166*): This intervention is particularly effective for problems along the lines of "I always forget to take my medication/to do my exercises" or "I ought to keep a pain diary but I always forget."

- **Signed and sealed: Contracts with clients** (see *page 184*)

- Collage work/creating own videos and films with self-portraits

- **Asking about exceptions** (see *page 79*)

- **Circular questioning** (see *page 85*)

- **Scaling** (see *page 81*)

- **Externalization** (see *page 89*): *If your body could talk, what would it say?*

- **Therapeutic homework** (see *page 110*), for example, the client writes himself a letter from the future.

- **Timeline work** (see page 126): How might your life look in the future with or despite your illness? Your career? Your family?
- **Prescribing problem-free times and rooms** (see page 106): Whenever you are with your best friend you can leave your illness behind.

General suggestions and ideas:

- Taking stock: What have you achieved so far?
- Setting realistic goals for the future: What could work—and what couldn't?
- Favorite films, pieces of music, friends, dreams . . .
- Joining a self-help group or Internet forum
- Diary in the form of a "dialogue with the illness"
- Asking family, friends, or those who are affected for further suggestions: What do you think might also help?

Compulsions and Tics

Compulsions and tics are not the same thing, but because the symptoms are very similar, a diagnosis can be difficult.

Basically, compulsions differ from tics in that the obsessive-compulsive patient becomes edgy if he can't pursue his compulsion or if he is prevented from doing so.

The danger of tics is that they sometimes disappear, only to reappear at a later date. Because it is difficult to distinguish between tics and compulsions, the diagnosis should be made by a child and adolescent psychiatrist.

With *compulsions* the important thing is for the patient to learn to control his compulsions rather than the other way around.

Interventions to address compulsions and tics

- **Prescribing problem-free times and rooms** (see *page 106*): The patient can also be asked how long he thinks he could survive without acting compulsively. Once he has decided on the length of time, you can negotiate about extending these problem-free periods—but only in small steps!
- **Forced compulsions** (based on Nardone, 2003): The therapist/counselor, together with the client, determines a time and a room in which all of the compulsions have to be acted out—every day at the same time, and timed using a watch or clock. During this period, the client should think those thoughts that he usually suppresses with the compulsions. The rest of the day should be as normal as possible. The prerequisite is a *trusting* relationship between client and therapist.
- Questions: *How will you notice that you have managed to live with the compulsion?* or *What are the benefits of having these compulsions?*
- **The forecast calendar** (see *page 108*): If the compulsion is not constant, then this method can be very effective.
- **Reframing** (see *page 84*), for example, *The compulsion provides structure* or *The compulsion helps you not to be too fast.* With a tic it is about acceptance, but also about trying to control the tic: *Can you suppress the tic? For how long? Would you be able to suppress it for another minute?*

Coughing and Such:
Psychogenic Breathing Problems

Respiratory disorders are one of the most common disorders in children, and coughing is the most common symptom (Rieger, Hardt, Sennhauser, Wahn, & Zach, 1999). Pediatricians deal with children with coughs on a daily basis. Coughing, and its milder form, clearing the throat, are the most common types of naturally forced exhalation and extremely important for clearing the respiratory tract. Coughing has various practical functions and can be stimulated in a number of ways, for example, by a mechanical irritation (breathing in dust, cigarette smoke, or particles such as bits of peanut) or by a respiratory infection (Taussig & Landau, 1999). Coughing can be *acute*, for example, in the case of a respiratory infection or a foreign body aspiration, particularly in young children, or *chronic* (according to the World Health Organization, lasting longer than three weeks).

Psychogenic causes also play a role. A cough that does not occur while sleeping may be a psychogenic cough, a habitual cough, or a coughing/throat-clearing tic. Here Taussig and Landau (1999) emphasize the importance of looking into the patient's social and family case history, for example, to find out possible conflict situations at school or in the family. In addition, possible causes such as exposure to tobacco smoke or an allergy to animal hair can be uncovered (Banner, 1986).

A more extensive diagnosis of a cough is required if it lasts longer than three weeks or if coughing episodes occur more than four times a year (Rieger et al., 1999). An early referral to a lung specialist is indicated here in order to eliminate somatic causes (Nicolai & Griese, 2011).

Besides psychogenic coughing, there are other types of respiratory abnormality that, for example, affect breathing frequency or depth of breathing. Particularly noisy sighing, snoring, or the feeling of having a "lump in the throat" with or without respiratory problems (globus sensation) can also be psychogenic or have primarily physical causes. Non-organically caused respiratory problems can usually be discerned by the fact that they do not have typical triggers, they are very erratic, the patient is less irritated than his environment, and they usually do not occur at night.

Here, too, a comprehensive diagnosis should take into account possible psychogenic causes. Systemic, solution-oriented approaches that have proven to be effective in everyday practice are ones that consolidate a changed approach to the problem (e.g., the pocket helper), that take the client's focus away from the problem (e.g., exceptions to the problem) or that emphasize it in a provocative way (e.g., prescribing the symptom).

Interventions to address psychogenic breathing problems

- **Relaxation and imagination** (see *page 154*): Techniques for coping with stress are important in this context and can be creatively supported with imagination and relaxation exercises (depending on the client's age and level of interest).
- **The pocket helper** (see *page 166*): This is a good way of helping the patient remember what he wanted to do differently, for example, smile or give the figure in his pocket a firm squeeze to prevent the symptom from arising.
- Marking progress (see *Improvisation, movement, and more, page 136*)
- **The inner team** (see *page 163*): The inner team method can help the client to, for example, send his "coughing" or "ill" self on holiday.
- **Metaphors** (see *page 60*)
- Sculpture work (see *Improvisation, movement, and more, page 136*)
- Psychoeducation (see *Systemic and creative psychoeducation, page 174*): Information about how the respiratory tract works, the important function of coughing, and possible solutions can be creatively explained—if desired, in conjunction with drawing, modeling, or telling **Therapeutic stories**.
- Resource activation (see *Activating and working with resources, page 68*): Coming up with an appropriate American Indian name, for example, "The-child-that-did-not-have-to-cough-anymore," can emphasize a success in a special way and be used as a source of strength.
- **Prescribing problem-free times and rooms** (see *page 106*)
  - ° *Take note of how you feel when you're not coughing! How long do you think these periods last?*
  - ° *Can I ask you to turn 5 minutes without breathing problems into 10 minutes?*
  - ° *Could you manage not to clear your throat in the living room? In other words, to leave your problem outside the door . . . ?*
- **Externalization** (see *page 89*): *If your cough could talk, what would it have to say?*
- **Prescribing the symptom** (see *page 100*)
- **Drawing together** (see *page 119*)

- **Therapeutic stories and fairy tales** (see *page 130*)
- **Asking about exceptions** (see *page 79*)
- **Scaling** (see *page 81*)

TIPS. Sometimes simple breathing exercises can be used to back up psychotherapeutic interventions: *Take the time to count to 10 when inhaling. And do the same when you exhale! Especially then when you feel the cough coming on!*

Depression

Perhaps the most important thing when treating a depressive patient is to make him aware of his own goals and not be distracted by the goals of others (Johnson, 2001).

A depressive client poses a challenge to a solution-oriented approach because he is unable to focus on or imagine the future. Nonetheless, you can—cautiously—begin to change his outlook.

Interventions to address depression

- **Questions:**
    - ° *What goals do you think you can achieve in your current condition?*
    - ° *Do you think there are other ways of achieving these goals?*
    - ° *What have you done to try and stop it getting any worse?*
    - ° *How did you find the energy to make this appointment and to stick to it?*
- **Scaling** (see page 81): Scaling usually involves asking the client to make a self-evaluation. It is important to compare the client's own scaling with circular scaling: *How would you rate your mental state on a scale of 0 to 10? If I were to ask your partner, what would she say?* Usually there is a difference between the two answers, which gives rise to further questions: *Could it be that your partner sees some things differently than you? What does she see that you don't see?* The client can then be given the task of trying to move one level up the scale.
- **Reframing** (see page 84)
- **Externalization** (see page 89)
    - ° *If you could talk with your depression, what would it tell you? And what would you tell your depression?*
    - ° *What can your depression do for you?*
- Drawing is also a good method of externalization for creative people. By drawing the problem, it is usually easier to objectify the problem (see **Externalization**, page 89).

Eating and Feeding Disorders

Unusual behavior related to eating can range from a mother's concern about her thriving child's appetite to anorexia and bulimia.

From babyhood onward, it is important, on the one hand, to prioritize regular mealtimes but, on the other hand, not to make too much fuss about the subject of eating. Even very young children soon realize how important this topic is for their parents, grandparents, or other caregivers; for older children and adolescents, mealtimes can therefore become a battleground for more deep-seated issues.

In relation to this kind of everyday situation, the "How?" question is the most important: *Can you describe one of your family mealtimes?* This is accompanied by lots of further questioning along the lines of *What else?* and *What do you do then?* and *How should I picture that?* and *Why is he allowed to do that?*

It is permissible and, indeed, desirable, to show surprise, but it is also important to show acknowledgment and respect if a situation has, or had to be, endured over a longer time period.

Some families, of their own accord, bring a video recording of the problematic situation, which is often very revealing.

In some cases it is worth asking about the dinner table rules at home, as we did with 12-year-old Anna, the eldest of three siblings. The girl had to think for a long time: Rules? No, they didn't have any. The parents vehemently disagreed but, after some more questions, admitted that they had probably never discussed them in concrete terms. Of course there were certain rules, but perhaps it was important to go through these again with the children.

Interventions to address eating and feeding disorders

- **Asking about exceptions** (see *page* 79): *Do you sometimes have mealtimes that go smoothly? Are there times when he/she doesn't have any problems with eating?*
- **Prescribing problem-free times and rooms** (see *page* 106)
- **Activating resources** (see *page* 69): *Can you give me an example of how you once managed to sit down to eat without it being an issue?* and *What have you already tried that worked well?*
- Reinforcement
- **Drawing together** or sketching the mealtime situation (see *page* 119): This approach is particularly useful during the diagnosis stage, because it provides a lot of information about the family's

"mealtime culture" and what it looks like, for example, who sits where. It also provides a good basis for further questions: *Does everyone always sit in the same place? Who lays/clears up the table?*

- **Rituals** (*see page 94*): Mealtimes, in particular, benefit from certain rituals and routines with set times.

- **Breaking the pattern** (*see page 97*) can alleviate the rigidity of strict rules, for example, if on the weekend the family is allowed to eat in front of the TV as a special treat.

- **The rule of the month** (*see page 192*): If there is any disagreement about the rules, or if they have to be introduced first, it is a good idea to introduce them one by one and to try a particular rule over a set amount of time, so that it is grasped by everybody involved. This can be something basic like:
  - ° *Everyone stays seated until everybody at the table has finished eating.*
  - ° *Everyone takes his own plate to the sink/dishwasher.*
  - ° *This week we are all going to try and eat a portion of vegetable/fruit at each meal.*

Enuresis

When working with a child who wets himself (particularly at night), the most important thing is to promote the child's autonomy (Mrochen, 1997).

The therapist should work directly with the child or adolescent, rather than just talk about the situation with the parents while the key person simply sits passively, perhaps not even listening properly.

It is extremely important to listen to the solution ideas of the person who is (or should be) the center of attention.

And experience has shown that it is always important to ask about the circumstances in which enuresis occurs, for example:

- *Does the child still wear a diaper because of this problem?*
- *Who knows about the problem? School? Relatives?*
- *What exactly happens when his pants are wet? Who does what?*
- *How much is the child suffering?*
- *Does anybody benefit from the child wetting himself?*

Interventions to address enuresis

- Rules and **Rituals** (see page 94): Ensure regularity and set times. It might also be a good idea to create a bathroom plan so that the client is made to go to the bathroom regularly (e.g., every three hours to start with).
- **The resources family tree** (see page 71): It often emerges that other family members had the same problem as a child. In this case it is important to ask:
  - ° *How did he (e.g., uncle, grandfather) manage to solve the problem?*
  - ° *What particular abilities did they use?*
  - ° *Could it be that you also have these abilities?*
  - ° *How would you notice that you have these abilities?*
- Asking about circumstances: *How do you "do" the problem?* (see **What Makes a Good Question?**, page 23)
- **Asking about exceptions** (see page 79): *Is the child's bed sometimes dry in the morning?* This is very important in order to show that there are days/nights when it works!
- **The forecast calendar** (see page 108): With enuresis, this calendar, based on the popular method of the "sunny and rainy (or

cloudy) days," is an exciting method enjoyed by children and parents alike.

- Praising, and no pressure on the client! (See **Compliments, praise, and such,** page 168.)
- **Certificates** (see page 193): *You've stayed dry for three weeks!*
- **Therapeutic stories and fairy tales** (see page 130)
- Promoting autonomy: Increase the child's autonomy after he has wet himself, by getting the child to remove the wet sheets and perhaps even put on fresh ones.

Note: Interventions like reducing the amount the child drinks in the evening, waking the child in the night, or putting on diapers are not usually very helpful.

Family Constellations with Adopted or Foster Children

Families that adopt children or foster them in the short or long term are faced with specific challenges, depending on the child's age at the time of adoption/fostering and the child's background. They may also be faced with potential developmental problems and health risks—attachment and interaction disorders, trauma and posttraumatic stress disorder, compulsions, depression, concentration problems, and learning and concentration disorders are just a few of the possible disorders that can arise from a child or adolescent with a difficult past.

Adoptive and foster families encompass a range of different family setups and come with diverse concerns. A frequently recurring issue is biological roots, which may not have been addressed by the child or adolescent for a long time, or may even have been avoided completely up to this point. It can suddenly erupt, and when it does, it needs immediate time, space, and patience.

Another important issue can be the child's or adolescent's relationship with his siblings—his biological ones as well as his adoptive brothers or sisters. Issues to do with family interaction, proximity and distance, jealousy and power struggles, or their standing in the family (which are problems encountered in other familial systems, too) frequently need to be addressed. Other behavioral patterns or issues can include very low frustration tolerance, aggressive outbreaks, crises revolving around self-pity or self-doubt, withdrawal tendencies with phases of being unable to react at all to instructions or questions, regressive behavior with babyish traits, or dissocial tendencies, such as running away, lying or stealing, among other things (see also **Lying**, page 243, and **Stealing, playing with fire, running away**, page 278).

It is not unusual to experience these children or adolescents as "migrants between two worlds"—a metaphor once used by a science-fiction-obsessed adolescent client—particularly if contact with the birth family, and everything this involves, continues to play an important role.

Transitions and leave-takings are issues that regularly affect families and children—whether planned or not—from taking a child in, to handing him back over to his birth parents, to the sudden decision that it is not possible to carry on together. Separation anxieties and fear of the future, insecurity, and similar problems sometimes suddenly require meaningful and creative action to be taken and courageous decisions to be made.

For example, Jenny was seven years old but looked no older than five and had been in full-time foster care for two years. Once a week she saw her biological parents who lived a 70-minute train ride away. She was accompanied on these visits by staff from the local youth welfare office, and the visits usually lasted for about two hours. At the first meeting, the foster mother reported that the child came back from these visits a changed person, slept badly, and became increasingly aggressive. She could not concentrate properly at school and was unfocused and whiney. This behavior always lasted a few days and then died down before flaring up again after the next visit. In addition, Jenny was permanently listless, lacking in appetite, and showed no interest in playing. Psychotherapeutic board games were used intensively with Jenny and her foster family in subsequent sessions, and Jenny frequently took up the offer of drawing. This was accompanied by a review of her case, which led to a change in the visiting arrangements.

Interventions to address issues with adopted and foster children

- **Biography work** (see page 128)
- Resource activation (see **Activating and working with resources**, page 68)
- **Emotion cards and such** (see page 141)
- **Mottos, mantras, and myths** (see page 171)
- **Redesigning the past** (see page 160): Is there anything good that you can take with you from your past?
- Sculpture work (see **Improvisation, movement, and more**, page 136)
- **Observation tasks** (see page 98)
- **The change detective** (see page 104)
- **The forecast calendar** (see page 108)
- **Rituals** (see page 94)
- **Timeline work** (see page 126) with families
- **Traffic-light cards** (see page 190)
- **Talismans, courage stones, and other helpers** (see page 186)

Gifted and Talented

A special gift does not always involve academic or career success (Bode, 2009a). Often, people with an IQ of 130 or above are afflicted by specific problems that develop out of their giftedness.

Problems can include fluctuating performance, lack of motivation, or playing the clown due to being permanently underchallenged, as well as aggression or psychosomatic disorders due to social isolation. These and other behavioral problems can also be due to accompanying disorders such as ADHD or developmental disorders like Asperger's syndrome.

Normally, a first important step is to establish the particular nature of the giftedness through an adequate diagnosis. It is important to explain the client's condition to him before subsequently exploring his personal interests, environmental factors, and options for developing his abilities.

A case example: Julie

Julie is 17 years old when her mother requests a consultation. The mother comes to the first meeting without her daughter, because she has not spoken to her daughter yet about her concerns from a parental perspective.

For some time, she has been concerned about her daughter's well-being, because Julie has always been different from other children, always far advanced developmentally, and often interested in completely different things from her peers. Julie has many interests and abilities but does not like to show them and is always rather reserved. Right now, getting good grades at school is particularly important in order to achieve the necessary grade point average to get into college. But put under pressure by her mother and teachers, Julie has gone in the opposite direction and is getting only bad grades. This is unusual, because up to now things have always gone relatively smoothly: Her three children—Julie and her two brothers—have coped well over the many years growing up with a single mom; the children have had no contact with their father for years.

Julie's mother goes on to explain that her daughter had had a psychological assessment about 10 years ago, which revealed that Julie had an IQ of 149. Asked whether her daughter had inquired about the result, she replied that she had never told Julie the result, as she had been afraid of unsettling her.

Working with **Reflecting positions** and **Mottos, mantras, and myths** relieved the strain of the situation considerably and led to more mutual understanding, as a result of which the family situation relaxed and Julie was able to explore new perspectives. With the help of various **Therapeutic home-work** tasks, which she fulfilled meticulously, she experimented with further solutions and managed to improve her grades—not enough to get into college right away, but giving her the opportunity to take a year out to travel. Subsequently, the situation between Julie and her mother improved greatly, and Julie still has the **Resource memory** cards.

Interventions to address issues with gifted and talented children

- **Reflecting positions** (see page 143)
- **Perspective goggles** (see page 152)
- **Relaxation and imagination** (see page 154)
- Resource activation (see *Activating and working with resources, page 68*)
- **Playing with hypotheses** (see page 161)
- **The power of the unexpected** (see page 136)
- Psychoeducation (see *Systemic and creative psychoeducation, page 174*)
- **Metaphors** (see page 60)
- **Mottos, mantras, and myths** (see page 171)
- **Timeline work** (see page 126)
- **Asking about exceptions** (see page 79)
- Improving self-esteem (see *Activating and working with resources, page 68*)
- **The forecast calendar** (see page 108)
- **Therapeutic homework** (see page 110), for example, the client writes himself a letter from the future.
- **Letting fate decide** (see page 114)
- **Circular questioning** (see page 85) and **Playing with hypotheses** (see page 161): Highly gifted people also like very simple solutions, such as *Imagine you could see yourself from an eagle's perspective. What would you notice? What advice would you give yourself from up there?*

Grief and Mourning

Sometimes grief can last a long time and paralyze daily routines. The younger the affected person is, the more unspecific the symptoms can be, and the less correlation there can be between the symptoms and the event that triggered them.

Some people have not come to terms with the death of a family member even many years later. In these cases several interventions can be helpful.

Interventions to address grief and mourning

- **Circular questioning** (see page 85): *If your grandmother were in the room now and we could ask her, what do you think she would say you should do?*
- **Therapeutic homework** (see page 110): *If your father were to write you a letter explaining what he would do in this situation, what might the letter say?* or *If your grandmother were to remember your strongest ability, what would she remember?*
- Further questions:
  - *Which special qualities did your grandmother have, and which of them have you inherited? How do you know?*
  - *Which of her special qualities would you like to rekindle?*
  - *What do you think Uncle . . . would want you to do, so that he could finally come to rest 10 years after his death?*
  - *I almost get the impression that this tyrant is still around, although he has been dead for many years. How would he know that he no longer has any power over you?*
- **Drawing together** (see page 119): Draw "nice-things-from-my-life," and as a group compile these into a "collage of hope or re-membrance."
- Collect pictures, photos, stories, souvenirs, and so on, in a home-made, decorated book: "Don't-Be-Sad-Book," "(Name of the child)-Book," or "Book of Remembrance" (Hobday & Ollier, 2001).
- Goodbye **Rituals** (see page 94): On the subject of "letting go," letters or pictures could be sent off in the following ways:
  - Tie a letter to a helium balloon
  - Turn a picture into a paper boat or put it into a bottle and allow it to drift off down the river
  - Leave mementos on the grave of the deceased

Head Banging and Other Repetitive Behaviors

Banging with or against one's own head is one of the most common forms of self-harming, along with scratching or biting oneself, gouging or picking various body parts, and hair pulling, and often occurs among children and adolescents with mental disabilities (Petermann & Winkel, 2009).

In such cases, the specific behavior occurs almost daily and almost automatically, and usually over a long period of time. Factors that need to be taken into account include self-regulation, communication, and over- or understimulation.

The spectrum of treatment possibilities encompasses behavior therapy and psychodynamic measures, as well as psychotropic drugs. Depending on the underlying clinical picture, or which stress factors play a role in a given case, several interventions can also be used.

Interventions to address harmful repetitive behaviors

- Resource activation (see **Activating and working with resources,** page 68)
- **Relaxation and imagination** (see page 154)
- Marking progress (see **Improvisation, movement, and more,** page 136)
- **Therapeutic homework** (see page 110): The tasks for the client to complete between sessions should be based on his individual complaint and can include, for example, observation, relaxation, or structuring techniques. These in turn can be used to support successful behavioral strategies.
- **Emotion cards and such** (see page 141)
- Psychoeducation (see **Systemic and creative psychoeducation,** page 174)
- **Signed and sealed: Contracts with clients** (see page 184)
- **Glove puppets** (see page 118)
- **Scaling** (see page 81)
- **Asking about exceptions** (see page 79)

Headaches and Migraines

Headaches tend to increase as children get older. Around 10–20 percent of all preschool children complain of headaches or migraines; by the end of elementary school, 80 percent of children have already had headaches, of which 60 percent are tension headaches and 12 percent migraines. And this percentage rises during adolescence (Lee, von Stülpnagel, & Heinen, 2006).

As well as seeking medical advice, it is also important to record the symptoms together with the client's case history, for which the following points are helpful:

- Does the patient keep a headache diary?
- What aspects of therapy have been useful so far? What has helped?
- Precise description of the pain
- Does the patient take painkillers on a regular basis?
- Has there been a consultation about/an elucidation of the diagnosis (psychoeducation)?
- Was a trigger found? Were any connections established? (Diet? Lifestyle? Particular stress situations?)

Interventions to address headaches and migraines

- **Externalization** (*see page 89*): Aim for a new perspective on the pain: *Put the pain in a box, put it away, send the pain away . . .*
- **The problem picture** (*see page 121*): Drawing the pain is an important intervention from a diagnostic as well as a therapeutic point of view. In some cases, the problem picture becomes a "solution picture." The picture can provide information about the "character" of the pain, possible solutions to the problem, or possible helper figures
- **The forecast calendar** (*see page 108*)
- Trying new relaxation rituals (see **Rituals**, *page 94*), besides ones that the client may already know, for example, withdrawing to a darkened room, peace and quiet, massage and acupuncture, rubbing essential oils on the forehead or neck, or—very important: *What might help before the pain even starts?*
- Reinforcing existing resources (see **Activating and working with resources**, *page 68*): *Concentrating on something you can do well to distract yourself from the pain*, for example, "It helps me if I then . . ." and "It always helps me to get fresh air and exercise and . . . "

- **Prescribing the symptom** (see page 100): Headaches are often accompanied by an "aura," or the headache is preceded by a slight pain, nausea, or a "funny feeling." The patient/client should try and consciously induce this feeling by concentrating on it, and—initially with the help of the therapist—try to intercept it. If he can do this, the client is given the task of repeating this exercise three times a day. He thereby gets the feeling that he is able to intercept an attack without being overcome by pain. He learns to stop the pain before it even starts. **Tip:** This feeling can be reinforced with a talisman—a tactile object like a marble, horse chestnut, or pebble (see *Talismans, courage stones, and other helpers,* page 186).

- **Certificates** (see page 193): For trying to consciously control the pain, for making lifestyle changes (avoiding stress and other triggers), for regular relaxation exercises, successful externalization, and so on.

Headaches 2.0: Pain Here and There

Between early childhood and adulthood, headaches in a variety of forms and of varying intensity tend to become more frequent. Many children are affected by stomachaches, in many cases acute or chronically recurring, but these tend to lessen during adolescence and adulthood, while back pain and joint pains become more prevalent. Getting the patient to keep a pain diary, working out potential triggers such as stress or certain food, and finding out about previously successful treatment approaches are all important.

A physical examination and a diagnostic clarification are of primary importance, but if there appear to be possible psychogenic aspects to the complaint, several interventions can also be helpful.

Other interventions to address headaches and migraines

- Resource activation (see *Activating and working with resources,* page 68)
- Marking progress (see *Improvisation, movement, and more,* page 136)
- **Perspective goggles** (see page 152)
- **Relaxation and imagination** (see page 154)
- **The inner team** (see page 163): "Today I am definitely going to take the 'hero' from my team with me, and I'm going to leave the

'pain expert' at home" (a quote by an adolescent with an inflammatory bowel disease and recurring stomachaches before an interview while looking for his first job).

- Inspirational fairy tales (see *Therapeutic stories and fairy tales*, *page 130*) work well, particularly with younger children, if the (head)aches seem to dominate the client's life. Fairy tales can be used to present problem-free times and solutions in a way that is not possible in the context of a regular conversation (see, e.g., *Prescribing problem-free times and rooms*, *page 106*).
- Psychoeducation (see *Systemic and creative psychoeducation*, *page 174*)
- **The forecast calendar** (*see page 108*)
- **Drawing together** (*see page 119*)
- **Asking about exceptions** (*see page 79*)
- **Externalization** (*see page 89*)
- **Prescribing problem-free times and rooms** (*see page 106*)
- **Therapeutic homework** (*see page 110*): Writing a "letter to the illness" has a strong impact with adolescents and adults in particular—it invites them to see their own situation from a new perspective.

Intellectual Disabilities

Children, adolescents, and adults with an intellectual disability can develop problems that present challenges to their entire (family) system. These include hyperactivity and aggression, as well as social withdrawal or depression (Sarimski & Steinhausen, 2008).

Because people with intellectual disabilities cannot take on certain responsibilities themselves, it is the job of the therapist or counselor to do so. This also applies to working out solutions—the client won't always be able to come up with his own solution ideas. Sometimes, however, the system is available to help: With intellectual disabilities, as with other problems, it should be the system's and not the therapist's ideas that determine the course of the therapy.

This constant balancing act in the therapeutic process is what Färber (1983) describes as the "specific adventure of psychotherapy with disabled patients."

It is impossible to generalize about the psychotherapeutic care of people with intellectual disabilities because these disabilities can take so many forms. Factors that play a role include the person's actual intellectual ability, his psychosocial environment, his stage of development, and his emotional state.

This requires a high degree of rapport and creativity from systemic and solution-oriented therapists. Experience has shown the effectiveness of typical methods such as resource orientation, scaling, pattern breaking, observation tasks, or asking for an explanation (Sickinger, 2000).

Interventions to address intellectual disabilities

- Resource activation!!! (see **Activating and working with resources**, page 68): *What are you particularly good at?*
- **Relaxation and imagination** (see page 154): Coping with stress is another factor that should not be underestimated.
- **The power of the unexpected** (see page 136)
- Marking progress (see **Improvisation, movement, and more**, page 136)
- **The pocket helper** (see page 166)
- **Compliments, praise, and such** (see page 168)
- **Signed and sealed: Contracts with clients** (see page 184)
- **Metaphors** (see page 60)
- **Emotion cards and such** (see page 141)
- **Glove puppets** (see page 118)
- **The rule of the month** (see page 192)

- **Asking about exceptions** (*see page 79*): Other systemic solution-oriented techniques can be used, depending on the abilities of the client, and these can also be creatively adapted: **Scaling**, **Therapeutic homework**, **Observation tasks**, **Prescribing change**, **Prescribing the symptom**, **Breaking the pattern**, and so on
- **Letting fate decide** (*see page 114*)
- **The change detective** (*see page 104*)

A case example: A metaphor as an intervention

The son of a close-knit family made a real effort in therapy to make quick progress despite his weak intellect. In this context, a family is described as close-knit when the relational structures binding the family members together are very strong and there is little outside influence on the family. He conformed to the ambitious expectations of his parents, who also expected that the problem would be dealt with swiftly. The mother, in particular, was very skeptical about what her son had to say, while the father was very understanding of his son, including of his repeated failures. The idea of quickly finding a solution suited the whole family: The son had a reason to be constantly motivated, the mother could feel justified in her skepticism, and the father could yet again show understanding and empathy when the "quick solution" failed.

The therapist in this meeting, which happened to take place in winter, presented the family with the metaphor of a train journey, which brought a smile to the face of every member of the family: Sudden snowfall had caused many train connections to be disrupted. Surprisingly, it was the faster intercity express trains from west to east that were stuck in the snowdrifts; the slower regional train had managed to make it from one station to the next. It had needed more time but had reliably reached its destination, while the other trains remained stranded.

The whole family understood and accepted the metaphor of the regional train that is not deterred and makes slow progress—and it led to some urgently needed relief. The boy was under less pressure, the mother could give up her skepticism by imagining the reliable regional train, and the father could refer to the robustness of this simple solution to express his confidence in his son.

A metaphor is a visual description of feelings, of an emotional state, or of certain behaviors. The similarities between the metaphor and the symbolic state of affairs are very obvious and memorable. The image becomes etched in one's memory and can be called upon whenever it is needed. Metaphors connect memories, current issues, and symbols.

TIP: When words fall flat. People with an intellectual disability are often overtaxed with words. Therapists are often confronted with a lack of understanding. Sketches, symbols, and simple activity games can be very effective in this situation!

Interaction and Regulation Disorders

The term *interaction disorders* covers a variety of problems and disabilities in the area of interpersonal relations. A classic personality disorder is when there is a clear discrepancy between how a person perceives himself and how others perceive him, while a social interaction disorder is when a person finds it hard to interact with other people and displays behavior ranging from shyness to severe inhibition.

Feeding problems, excessive crying, and disruptions in the sleep/wake rhythm in babies and toddlers are collectively referred to as regulation disorders. Usually a variety of risk factors play a role, for example, psychosocial stress, or if the parents suffer from mental or physical illnesses, substance abuse, or experienced childhood traumas themselves.

But regardless of how they are classified, these disorders are usually characterized by obvious or suspected communication difficulties that can occur in the context of different problem situations.

Kriz (2008) describes from a systemic perspective how distinct communication patterns can form and stabilize in partner relationships or families. When working with parents of a young child, who now have to reconfigure the family system, the search for solutions revolves around the careful modification of established patterns.

The following interventions are recommended to help the participants (usually parents, children, and other caregivers) move from feeling insecure and helpless toward feeling confident and capable.

Interventions to address interaction and regulation disorders

- Resource activation (see ***Activating and working with resources,*** *page 68*): *Which of your strengths as parents do you value in particular?*
- **Reflecting positions** (see page 143)
- **A chair is (not) a chair** (see page 145)
- **Rewind → Reset** (see page 181)
- **Relaxation and imagination** (see page 154)
- Sculpture work (see ***Improvisation, movement, and more,*** page 136)
- **Perspective goggles** (see page 152)
- **Metaphors** (see page 60)

- Marking progress (see *Improvisation, movement, and more*, page 136): *What have you achieved so far?* and *What else could you achieve?*
- **Asking about exceptions** (see *page 79*)
- **Timeline work** (see *page 126*)
- **Prescribing change** (see *page 102*)
- **Prescribing problem-free times and rooms** (see *page 106*)
- **Circular questioning** (see *page 85*) and **Scaling** (see *page 81*)
- **Therapeutic homework** (see *page 110*), for example, the client writes himself a letter from the future.
- **Letting fate decide** (see *page 114*): Sometimes the situation is so stressful for parents that it is advisable to take turns. The parent who is currently not responsible observes the other parent in terms of what he is doing well. A die can be rolled to decide whose turn it is to take on particular responsibilities.

Lack of Motivation

Trapmann and Rotthaus (2003) speak of children's unwillingness to exert themselves or make an effort. This lack of motivation is either general or specific; that is, either the child is generally uncooperative and unmotivated, or he is unmotivated only in certain environments, such as school, or perhaps only during certain activities, for example, ones that require fine motor skills.

There are many reasons for this kind of behavior, and usually a number of factors come together in varying degrees: the child being spoiled, cognitive limitations, obesity, lack of self-confidence or role models, ongoing stress caused by early traumas or mentally ill parents, among many others.

A major factor that should not be ignored is a fear of change: "I would rather come across as 'cool' than change anything."

The therapist or counselor first needs to carry out a thorough diagnosis of the problem, for example, look into the client's case history, previous and existing illnesses, and stress factors in the client's environment. The client needs to be carefully observed, and it is important to show respect and understanding.

Circular questioning can be a good way in: *Why do you think that others think you should make more effort?*

On the other hand, rewarding unmotivated behavior is a *paradoxical intervention* (see **Prescribing the symptom**, *page 100*). A provocation might be: *Some people think that you're afraid of changing something!* (see **Provoking**, *page 91*).

Interventions to address lack of motivation

- **The power of the unexpected** (see *page 136*)
- **Reflecting positions** (see *page 143*)
- Resource activation (see **Activating and working with resources**, *page 68*)
- **Relaxation and imagination** (see *page 154*)
- **Rewind → Reset** (see *page 181*)
- **The inner team** (see *page 163*): *Could you imagine leaving the unmotivated part of yourself at home today?* or *How would it be if you were to send the listless side of yourself on vacation for a while? How would things be different?*
- **Mottos, mantras, and myths** (see *page 171*)
- Marking progress (see **Improvisation, movement, and more**, *page 136*)
- **Biography work** (see *page 128*)

- **Metaphors** (see page 60)
- **Asking about exceptions** (see page 79)
- **Observation tasks** (see page 98)
- **The change detective** (see page 104)
- **Therapeutic stories and fairy tales** (see page 130) and helper figures (see **Cartoon therapy,** page 125)
- **The forecast calendar** (see page 108)
- **Traffic-light cards** (see page 190)
- **Prescribing the symptom** (see page 100)
- **Scaling** (see page 81)

A case example: Motivation

An 11-year-old boy was at first unwilling to talk at all about his concentration and learning issues. For some time he had been doing badly at school and often barely managed to scrape through tests and homework. When the parents helped him at home, he achieved a lot, and he used this fact as an argument for why he did not have to make any more effort—he could concentrate if he had to, and that was enough.

He was helped by a soccer metaphor that can be described in a few words: *What would you say if your favorite team only ever scored goals when they were training and never in actual matches?*

Learning Disabilities and Developmental Disorders

Learning problems are widespread among children, adolescents, and young adults, and are more prevalent among boys than girls, as well as among immigrants and people from socially deprived backgrounds (Lauth, Grünke, & Brumstein, 2004). In some cases the problems remain undiscovered into adulthood and become a life-long burden.

Learning disabilities include, above all, developmental disorders relating to academic ability: partial performance disorders, such as reading and spelling disorders or a weakness in arithmetic, as well as combined forms and general learning difficulties or disabilities. Developmental disorders also include problems with language and speaking, as well as motor skill deficits.

Besides diagnostics, supportive measures include establishing learning structures and strategies and promoting concentration, memory retention, and other specific competencies such as motivation. Several techniques have also proven to be effective. (Profound developmental disabilities such as early childhood autism or Asperger's syndrome are not addressed here—see **Autistic Behavior**, page 207.)

Interventions to address issues with learning disabilities and developmental disorders

- Resource activation (see **Activating and working with resources**, *page 68*): *Which of your abilities could really help you in this situation?*
- Marking progress (see **Improvisation, movement, and more**, *page 136*)
- **Relaxation and imagination** (*see page 154*)
- **Relaxation exercise: 5-4-3-2-1** (*see page 156*), for example, for coping with exam stress
- Concentration exercises (see **Concentration?! . . .**, *page 170*)
- **Signed and sealed: Contracts with clients** (*see page 184*): Behavior contracts can be very helpful when working with people with developmental disorders, learning difficulties, or even a clear intellectual disability. First of all, the therapist and client come to an agreement about what exactly the contract will include, for example, "I hereby confirm that I will practice . . . twice a day over the next four weeks."

- **Emotion cards and such** (see page 141)
- Psychoeducation (see **Systemic and creative psychoeducation**, page 174): *What exactly is wrong with me? Why do I feel like this?*
- **The pocket helper** (see page 166) serves as a reminder to do concentration/relaxation exercises and so on.
- **Glove puppets** (see page 118)
- **Scaling** (see page 81)
- **Asking about exceptions** (see page 79)
- **Observation tasks** (see page 98)
- **The change detective** (see page 104)
- **The rule of the month** (see page 192)
- **Certificates** (see page 193)
- **Letting fate decide** (see page 114): With this intervention it is important to develop the solution options together with the client so that they are doable and attractive for the client and are aimed at supporting him in his further development: *Here is a coin that you should toss every morning in front of your parents. It will decide if you should concentrate more on numbers that you encounter throughout the day, or if you should concentrate on the moments when you are particularly focused.*

"Luxury Generation"

This is really a societal phenomenon for which there is not (yet) a specific diagnosis. Generally it affects children, adolescents, and young adults who are materially well provided for and lead very shielded and fairly unchallenging lives. This phenomenon is encountered increasingly in outpatient as well as clinic contexts and encompasses a variety of problems of varying intensity.

The child or adolescent encountered by the therapist or counselor often has massive social and emotional problems, is often in a state of deep despair, and feels stuck in a rut. Aggressive outbursts, suicidal tendencies, or dissocial behavior are common symptoms, as are forms of addiction (e.g., media addiction), a sharp decline in productivity, and concentration disorders. Parents and other caregivers find themselves in a similarly desperate situation. They often feel overwhelmed and at a loss in the face of massive resistance or fundamentally contrary ideas and seem to have "given up" and thereby inadvertently exacerbate the problem. They often continue to use methods that stopped working long ago.

It is, of course, particularly important to study the patient's case history and to carry out an extensive diagnosis with a special focus on the situation at home, the parenting style, and potential stress factors and other possible causes.

Fortunately, there are many interventions at our disposal.

Interventions to address the "luxury generation"

- **Metaphors** (see page 60): Everyone is familiar with the story of the "Princess and the Pea." But there are at least as many *princes* who also feel the uncomfortable pea, despite the fact their bed has 20 mattresses.
- **Signed and sealed: Contracts with clients** (see page 184)
- **Therapeutic homework** (see page 110)
- **Observation tasks** (see page 98) are a very good way of providing valuable support and simultaneously helping the reflection process and modification of behavior.
- **Playing with hypotheses** (see page 161)
- **Exaggeration** (see page 179): Question to a mother of a mollycoddled 16-year-old: *I am just imagining your son in 20 years' time, still living at home, accusing you of not cleaning his shoes properly . . . What on earth will you do?*
- **The pocket helper** (see page 166): Here it is the *parents* who need the pocket helper to remind themselves to change things in their day-to-day routine in order to solve the problem.

- **A chair is (not) a chair** (*see page 145*): A role play with a chair invites the client(s) to see the problem from another perspective and to try possible solutions.
- **Scaling** (*see page 81*)
- **Reframing** (*see page 84*)
- **Circular questioning** (*see page 85*)
- **Asking about exceptions** (*see page 79*)
- **Breaking the pattern** (*see page 97*): *If you were to bring up another child, what would you do differently?* or *Could you try that— or something else—out between now and our next meeting?*
- Other questions: *What else does your son need to learn to be equipped for life?* or *What should your parents have taught you?*
- Provocative questions: *Mr. X, how do you like the way your daughter treats your wife?* or *Can I just ask who is in charge here?*

Lying

Lying is a common and persistent symptom among children and adolescents but can be successfully tackled with a solution-oriented approach.

Interventions to address lying

- **Prescribing the symptom** (*see page 100*), in combination with a detective task (see ***The change detective***, *page 104*) for the other members of the family. **Tip:** The task works very well in combination with oppositional behavior: *I always do the opposite of what I'm told to do!* By being given the task of lying, the client finds himself in the following dilemma: either to stop lying but not do the task, or to do the task and lie as he has been told to do—the opposite of the lie is the truth.
  - ° *You should lie at least four times a day. But you should try and make your lies so blatant that they will be obvious to everyone else.*
  - ° *The task of the others is to guess the lies, because otherwise nobody knows if you have completed your task or not.*
  - ° For the patient, lying thereby becomes boring and a chore—and is no longer fun.
- Questions: "If what you just said was a lie, or if the others say it is a lie, what would be the opposite—the truth?" A variation of **Prescribing the symptom** is to ask the client to think of a really colossal lie.

Media Overconsumption/Addiction

Nowadays it is hardly possible to imagine our lives without screens—whether computer or TV screens. Even many preschool children know how to use electronic media and by school age are often better at using them than their parents.

Precisely for this reason it is important to talk about it with children and adolescents, and to try to stop it from turning into an addiction.

Behaviors that should set alarm bells ringing
- If the child develops a sleep disorder or has nightmares or concentration problems
- When films and such become a more important topic of conversation than personal experiences
- When a child constantly escapes into his TV, Internet, or gaming world
- When a child plans his day around the TV, computer, or gaming schedule and has no more time for his friends or hobbies

Interventions to address media overconsumption and addiction

- **Therapeutic homework** (*see page 110*), for example, getting the child to write a little report after every film he watches or online game he plays.
- **Asking about exceptions** (*see page 79*): *Are there also times when you watch less TV? How is this time different?*
- Other questions: *What do you do when you turn the computer/TV off?*
- **Certificates** (*see page 193*): *Fantastic—you've managed to always turn off the computer at the right time!*
- Psychoeducation (see ***Systemic and creative psychoeducation***, *page 174*): Children, adolescents, and adults are always impressed when we explain how the brain works, how new "networks" are created, how memory works, and so on.

The golden rules for parents
1. Talk to each other!
2. Join in with playing! Show understanding and interest.
3. Encourage and promote other interests.

4. Take care with using TV or computer time as a reward or punishment!

5. Clear rules for everyone!

A case example: Jonah

Jonah, a 15-year-old high-school student, was brought to therapy by his parents because he could not keep up with the work in class.

He was inattentive, often in a bad mood, and refused to do his homework. He was also neglecting his friends and hardly went out. At school he was often unengaged, and his teachers were concerned because in the past, Jonah had had no problem keeping up with the rest of the class.

During the session, it emerged that Jonah planned his day around his favorite TV programs and had specially organized "online times" to play in virtual worlds; sometimes he did not even find the time to eat.

Neither he nor his family was convinced by the suggestion, on "diagnostic" grounds, that the whole family have two screen-free weeks, but they finally agreed.

Three weeks later the parents reported that the screen-free time had got them all thinking: The whole family had found it difficult to fill up their free time but were reminded that things had once been different.

Jonah seemed more relaxed but did not want to continue cold turkey. A discussion about goals for school and home time, combined with set screen times for the whole family, was a first step.

Mentally (or Physically) Ill Parents

According to a study conducted by the University of Massachusetts Medical School, more than five million children in the United States have a parent with a severe mental illness (Nicholson, Biebel, Williams, & Katz-Leavy, 2002). In Western countries it is estimated that, depending on the criteria applied, between 4 and 12 percent of parents suffer from a chronic physical illness (Sieh, Meijer, Oort, Visser-Meilly, & Van der Leij, 2010).

Children and adolescents with mentally ill parents are often described as a "forgotten" risk group because they have an increased risk of developing a mental disorder themselves later in life. It appears that children from families with a parent suffering from schizophrenia are more vulnerable than children of parents suffering from depression (Lenz, 2008).

Compared with their peers, the occurrence of clinically significant mental abnormalities doubles in children with one parent with a severe physical illness (Barkmann, Romer, Watson, & Schulte-Markwort, 2007). Experience has shown that children and adolescents with mentally or physically ill mothers or fathers take on the role of caregiver at a young age. They tend to be very loyal to their parents and do not reveal any family secrets; the affected parents, on the other hand, often suffer from feelings of guilt.

Stress management and the activation of resources are among the most important interventions with children and adolescents who have to deal with the everyday burden of having one or two mentally or physically ill parents. Other interventions include psychoeducation (adapted to the client's age and stage of development) and the support of an "open, familial climate that provides room for questions, anxieties and childish imagination" (Wiegand-Grefe, Romer, & Möller, 2008).

The timely identification of psychosocial and individual risk factors is an important preventative measure, as is the introduction of measures to help the entire family system so that the afflicted parents can continue to be parents and not just patients. Furthermore, the establishment of day-to-day routines and rituals is important.

Interventions to address issues with mentally (or physically) ill parents

- **Metaphors** (see page 60)
- Resource activation (see **Activating and working with resources**, page 68): *Can you also find something positive in the situation?*

- **Relaxation and imagination** (see page 154)
- **Family coat of arms** (see page 158)
- **Reflecting positions** (see page 143)
- **Redesigning the past** (see page 160): How did you manage to prevent things turning out even worse?
- Psychoeducation (see **Systemic and creative psychoeducation**, page 174)
- **Signed and sealed: Contracts with clients** (see page 184)
- Marking progress (see **Improvisation, movement, and more**, page 136): What have you achieved so far? Is the client also able to recognize his achievements?
- **Asking about exceptions** (see page 79)
- **Timeline work** (see page 126)
- **Circular questioning** (see page 85)
- **Scaling** (see page 81)
- **Reframing** (see page 84): These children are all experts in dealing with people with a chronic illness.
- **Therapeutic homework** (see page 110), such as writing a letter from the future or producing videos and films of the family or a self-portrait film to bring along to the next session (particularly effective with adolescents).
- **Rituals** (see page 94): Establishing new and reinforcing daily rituals that take the pressure off the children.

TIP. Group settings seem to have a particularly bolstering effect, as Vogt, Nelle, Eberling, Burr, and Decker (2003) have been able to prove in their work with the children of drug-addicted parents.

Mutism

Mutism is a disorder in which a person is unable to speak in certain or most everyday situations. Often the affected children speak only in safe or familiar environments with their family or friends. Mutism usually starts in preschool age. A short period of selective silence, for example, when the child starts kindergarten, usually normalizes itself after a few weeks.

Children with mutism usually have age-appropriate language skills and no significant speech development problems.

Mutism is often accompanied by social and other anxieties, oppositional defiant disorder, and self-esteem problems.

Several approaches can work with mutism. Above all,

- Create an environment in which the child feels comfortable and encouraged.
- Show a lot of patience and apply no pressure.
- Offer nonverbal communication, and praise and encourage any attempts at vocalization.

Interventions to address mutism

- Showing empathy, for example, through body language, such as sitting in the same way . . . or, be silent! This approach is, of course, deliberately unsettling . . . (see **Provoking**, page 91).
- **Glove puppets** (see page 118) to instigate a conversation, or talk with the child's favorite soft toy or doll.
- **Asking about exceptions** (see page 79): Are there situations when the child speaks outside of the home? . . . Maybe just whispers?
- Read together or listen to CDs
- Boost the child's confidence, such as with **Therapeutic stories and fairy tales** (see page 130) or **Drawing together** (see page 119)

A case example: Ned

Eight-year-old Ned, the youngest of four siblings, was referred by his family doctor because he had not spoken with strangers for three years. His parents reported that while he was at kindergarten this was still tolerated—the teachers accepted his behavior and never forced him to speak. After he started school things got more difficult, his teacher wanted him to read aloud to assess his progress.

When asked about exceptions, his father said that he spoke with other children but stopped when an adult appeared. Within his immediate family, talking wasn't a problem. In everyday situations—for example, if he was offered a piece of ham or salami at the meat counter in the supermarket—his parents would answer on his behalf.

During the first meeting Ned was very reserved and did not react to the therapist's greeting or when he was addressed directly. During the conversation, he sat beside his parents, listened attentively, but remained uninvolved and looked at the floor most of the time.

After a few minutes, Ned disappeared under the table at which the meeting with the family was taking place and remained crouched there. When the therapist also suddenly got up and disappeared under the table, it was not just the parents who were surprised!

Down there it was possible to achieve the first eye contact, and with the help of a glove puppet, a conversation started between Ned and the puppet.

Nail-biting

Nibbling at, biting off, and tearing fingernails (and occasionally toenails) and cuticles is something that approximately every third child or adolescent does and can lead to painful inflammation of the nail bed.

In most cases, nail-biting is harmless and temporary. It is particularly prevalent among children between 8 and 12 years of age, especially among girls, and can be a sign of stress or anxiety.

This symptom becomes a problem only if it is persistent and compulsive and causes more serious injury of a self-harming nature (Trapmann & Rotthaus, 2003).

Besides sports, relaxation techniques, and a closer examination of possible causes, several techniques can be effective.

Interventions to address nail-biting

- **Asking about exceptions** (see *page 79*), for example, *Are there days when you don't bite your nails? What's different about these times?* or *Do you sometimes manage not to bite all of your nails?*
- **Praise** (see *Compliments, praise, and such, page 168*)—this is very important when the client isn't biting his nails!
- Increasing physical activity to relieve tension, or listening to music/stories and taking time to cuddle together.
- **Activating resources** (see *page 69*)
- Choosing a problem-free finger (see *Prescribing problem-free times and rooms, page 106*): *Which finger are you giving a break this week?* or *Which is your favorite finger?* or *If you were your finger . . . ?* combined with appropriate praise or a reward for nails that have grown back! This can be combined with tossing a die to determine which finger will be spared (see *Dice: "Playing with possibilities," page 182*).
- **The pocket helper** (see *page 166*): A small, tactile object to use as a helper or talisman, which can be used instead of the fingernails in times of stress or anxiety, for example, a smooth pebble or horse chestnut.
- **Therapeutic stories and fairy tales** (see *page 130*): Worth a try, especially with young children!

Nightmares, Fear of Going to Sleep, and So On

Trapmann and Rotthaus (2003) describe nightmares in children as dreams that wake them up and that they usually remember well. Most adults have also experienced sleep disorders of one kind or another. In children, nightmares are most common between the ages of four and seven, and usually they involve dark chasms and abysses, murky figures, monsters, and the like.

While sleepwalking, also known as somnambulism, and night terrors, or pavor nocturnus, usually occur in the first third of the night, nightmares usually occur in the last third of the night (Resch & Richterich, 2004).

Nighttime panic attacks that resemble daytime attacks can also occur, particularly among children and adolescents with developmental delays.

Different kinds of sleep disorder are commonly associated with psychiatric disorders, including depression and ADHD, but also with physical ailments, for example, affecting the lungs. They can range from insomnia and slumps in efficiency to daytime tiredness.

With children and adolescents, especially, too much TV as well as gaming consoles, laptops, tablets, and smart phones, can lead to sleep disorders and sleep deprivation, which is why it is a good idea to carry out a media anamnesis with the client.

Interventions to address nightmares and sleep fears

- **Dream your dream** (see page 177): *Turn your nightmare into a nice dream . . .* or *How would the dream continue if you could finish dreaming it here in our meeting? Would you like to tell me what happens in your dream?* If the child is willing, he can then recount the terrible story. After he has finished recounting his dream, you can ask him to change a little detail of the story so that it is more positive. The next day he changes the detail even more and writes down the changed story—or draws it or gets somebody else to write it down (if the child cannot write yet). Even more changes are added, written down, or drawn the next day. (See *also* **Redesigning the past**, page 160.)
- **Relaxation exercise: 5-4-3-2-1** (see page 156) following a night terror or nighttime panic attack.
- Marking progress (see **Improvisation, movement, and more**, page 136)

- **Therapeutic homework** (see page 110)
- Resource activation (see **Activating and working with resources,** page 68): Which of your strengths do you value in particular?
- **Rewind → Reset** (see page 181)
- **Therapeutic stories and fairy tales** (see page 130)
- **Metaphors** (see page 60): Knight's armor or the hibernation cave
- **Externalization** (see page 89)
- **The anti-anxiety thread** (see page 189)
- **The forecast calendar** (see page 108)
- **Drawing together** (see page 119)
- **Asking about exceptions** (see page 79)

Obesity

In the United States an increasing number of children and adolescents, as well as adults, are affected by obesity. A 2009–2010 survey of child and adolescent health carried out by the Centers for Disease Control and Prevention revealed that 16.9 percent of the surveyed two- to nineteen-year-olds have a body mass index (BMI) above the 95th percentile, up from 5.1 percent in 1971–1974 (Ogden, Carroll, Kit, & Flegal, 2012). [Note that adult BMI values are based on international BMI standard values, while with children and adolescents, BMI values are based on age- and sex-specific BMI percentiles (Nitzko, 2010).]

Overall, the prevalence of obesity is increasing worldwide and increases with age; from puberty on it is very stable. As a whole, obese people are getting heavier (Warschburger, Petermann, & Fromme, 2005).

In addition to chronic physical ailments with a high risk of long-term damage such as cardiovascular and musculoskeletal disorders, psychosocial stress and psychological symptoms are also very prevalent. Ostracism and emotional stress resulting from a negative body image and lack of self-esteem should be treated in a targeted way in order to prevent a further reduction to quality of life, as well as typical concomitant illness, such as eating disorders and depression.

Apart from physical exercise and an improved diet, behavioral medicine programs have also proven to be effective. These include token programs, impulse control techniques, relapse prevention, and more (Reinehr, Dobe, & Kersting, 2003). However, somatic causes of obesity need to be ruled out at the start.

It is also important to discuss beneficial lifestyle factors, eating behavior, and the risk posed by other members of the family affected by obesity. Training programs usually work only if they incorporate family or caregivers, who ensure that the modified behavior is put into practice on a daily basis (Nitzko, 2010).

Several systemic solution-oriented approaches have also proven to be effective.

Interventions to address obesity

- **Compliments, praise, and such** (see page 168)
- **Therapeutic homework** (see page 110), for example, *Write yourself a letter from the future* or *Between now and next session, make a note of situations in which you are already able to behave in the way you want.*
- **Therapeutic stories and fairy tales** (see page 130)

- Resource activation (see **Activating and working with resources,** page 68): *Which of your strengths do you value in particular?*
- **Metaphors** (see page 60), such as **The filling station metaphor** (see page 66)
- **Exaggeration** (see page 179) in relation to the system strategy: *Do you want to feed the whole class with your daughter's packed lunch?*
- Psychoeducation (see **Systemic and creative psychoeducation,** page 174)
- Marking progress (see **Improvisation, movement, and more,** page 136)
- **Perspective goggles** (see page 152)
- **The power of the unexpected: Moving improvisations** (see page 136)
- **Relaxation and imagination** (see page 154)
- **The pocket helper** (see page 166)
- **A chair is (not) a chair** (see page 145)
- **Externalization** (see page 89)
- **Scaling** (see page 81)
- **Circular questioning** (see page 85)
- **Observation tasks** (see page 98)
- **The change detective** (see page 104)
- **The what's-it-good-for question** (see page 28). Excessive eating, which leads to obesity, often happens "naturally." The question *Why do you eat at this time?* can be used with children but is particularly effective for changing thinking processes in adolescents. It is important not to let clients get away with answers like "I eat, because I enjoy it" or "Because I'm hungry!" but to continue probing: *Why else do you do it?* combined with the question: *If you don't really know, who else in your family could I ask?*
- **Rituals** (see page 94): Rituals can be an important intervention to use with obese children, adolescents, and adults—in many cases, habits that stand in the way of long-term weight loss have become a fixed part of the family's daily routine. That's why there should be joint discussion about the way in which new rituals could help, and what these might be. For example, if food is used in the family as a form of reward or punishment (which is often the case), the discussion could be steered in the direction of alternatives. To

encourage more exercise, the family could be asked to plan some activities away from home.

- Learning how to give *praise* without a reward of sweets can even be practiced in a role play (see **Compliments, praise, and such**, *page 168*).

Playing the Clown

Playing the clown and wisecracking refer to age-inappropriate, goofy behavior that can occur in certain everyday contexts like kindergarten, school (class clown), or the family, as well as generally and unspecifically (Trapmann & Rotthaus, 2003).

Children and adolescents with this symptom tend not to exploit their intellectual capabilities, risk being excluded from the group (e.g., in sport or when learning), and often have few real friends but many admirers and a regular audience.

Even if humor and wittiness, occasional clowning around, and wisecracking are desirable qualities that can relieve tension and strengthen family or group bonds, it is important to help the person find the right balance.

Interventions to address children who play the clown

- **Relaxation and imagination** (see *page 154*)
- Resource activation (see ***Activating and working with resources***, *page 68*)
- **Emotion cards and such** (see *page 141*)
- Psychoeducation (see ***Systemic and creative psychoeducation***, *page 174*)
- **The inner team** (see *page 163*): *Are there situations when it would be better to leave the clown at home?*
- **Metaphors** (see *page 60*)
- **The pocket helper** (see *page 166*)
- **Exaggeration** (see *page 179*)
- **Asking about exceptions** (see *page 79*)
- **The change detective** (see *page 104*)
- **The forecast calendar** (see *page 108*)
- **Magic tricks** (see *page 134*)
- **Letting fate decide** (see *page 114*)

Posttraumatic Stress Disorder (PTSD)

Very stressful events such as accidents, subjection to violence, or natural catastrophes can lead to PTSD. In general, traumatic experiences are considered to be risk factors for a variety of reactions and clinical pictures (Stein & Rosner, 2009).

However, a distinction is drawn in terms of the duration of the symptoms between acute forms such as an acute stress disorder, and chronic forms such as a profound personality change. In contrast to adults, however, other forms of unusual behavior can also be very apparent in children and adolescents. In all cases of newly occurring or unusual symptoms, it is important to take these into consideration. Symptoms in children can manifest in a wide range of ways, such as sleep disorders and nightmares, very aggressive behavior or indifference, or social withdrawal. In some cases, the patient displays a recurrent behavior that incorporates elements of the traumatic experience without him being consciously aware of it.

Adolescents may reveal self-harming tendencies, a sharp decline in motivation, and concentration problems. Physical problems often include headaches and stomachaches, as well as a greater susceptibility to infections.

Von Schlippe and Schweitzer (2007) describe the danger of the therapist (or counselor) getting caught in a "problem trance" due to the gravity of the problem, and advocate, among other things, the establishment of a stable relationship between client and therapist, the restoration of a "secure foundation," and attempts to draw on the family's resilience potential.

Incorporating a functioning social network, and particularly the parents, in the therapeutic process is an important factor. Together with the child or adolescent, the parents can also obtain proper information through psychoeducation, which can help to counteract their anxieties and feelings of helplessness (Pfeiffer, 2008).

A sound basis for effective therapy or counseling is a reliable and confidence-building framework for conversations with a stable and secure relationship, as well as an open approach to the client's experiences. Here, too, it is vital to show patience and understanding and to communicate with the patient in an age-appropriate way and adapted to his developmental level. Trauma-centered strategies aimed at trauma exposure should remain in the hands of experienced and specially trained therapists.

Having a good rapport with the patient is extremely important and can be therapeutically valuable by changing the patient's focus or context. Sometimes showing over-the-top rapport can be particularly effective—but it requires the therapist to listen very carefully and to be "tuned in" to the situation.

A case example: PTSD

Martina, 12 years old, had to be moved from a psychotherapeutic open unit to a secure unit due to escalating violent behavior: She had injured a member of staff and threatened others.

She had been admitted to the clinic because she had broken all social bonds due to her negative and destructive behavior. Presumably she was traumatized; the girl complained about a throbbing in her vagina, could not bear the feeling of long trouser legs on her body, and seemed to have lost all sense of self-dignity. The girl was of average intelligence and good at school. Her parents were desperate because they could not get through to their daughter anymore. Moreover, her behavior was becoming increasingly compulsive. During a meeting with the whole family, she clearly showed her hostile attitude when asked about her clothing: "I don't want to because I don't want to."

The therapist responded: *You don't want to because you don't want to! I'm asking myself because I'm asking myself. I'm your therapist because I'm your therapist. We are having a conversation because we are having a conversation. And I'm pleased that you're here because I'm pleased that you're here.*

Martina responded to this statement with a very quizzical look.

You look rather confused, because you look rather confused! I'm asking myself again, because I'm asking myself again!

The patient reacted with a mixture of indignation and laughter.

I'm asking myself if you know where I come from? Suddenly the patient was very attentive and open, and contributed constructively to the rest of the discussion.

Age, the type and duration of the trauma, a possible physical infirmity, as well as the current symptomatology all need to be taken into consideration when working with a patient. Supportive interventions can also be used for stabilization. (Note that these solution processes may require a lot more therapy time than they would with other indications!)

Interventions to address PTSD

- Resource activation (see **Activating and working with resources**, page 68): *Which of your strengths do you value in particular?* Here the aim is to increase self-confidence. Lots of patience is required!
- **The power of the unexpected** (see page 136)
- **Emotion cards and such** (see page 141)

- **Relaxation and imagination** (*see page 154*): Of special significance here is the "safe inner sanctum."
- Psychoeducation (see **Systemic and creative psychoeducation**, *page 174*): Providing information about prevalence, forms, and effects, for example, of violence as well as about possible symptoms helps prevent misconceptions forming and provides some initial relief.
- **Redesigning the past** (*see page 160*)
- **Asking about exceptions** (*see page 79*)
- **Externalization** (*see page 89*)
- **Scaling** (*see page 81*)
- Genograms (see **The resources family tree**, *page 71*)
- **Timeline work** (*see page 126*)
- **Therapeutic homework** (*see page 110*), for example, *Write yourself a letter from the future.*
- **Circular questioning** (*see page 85*)
- **Prescribing change** (*see page 102*)
- **The change detective** (*see page 104*)
- **Glove puppets** (*see page 118*): Initial contact with children is best made with the help of glove puppets, drawing, or favorite toys; conveying messages nonverbally can be effective.

Another PTSD case: Alina

Sixteen-year-old Alina came to the first consultation with her father, at which point she had not been to school for about a year. This had been preceded by a car accident in which, unusually, members of the family had been sitting in both cars. Alina's brother had been critically injured and died at the scene, while her mother was still traumatized and was confined to a wheelchair. Alina and the other people involved in the accident had suffered only minor physical injuries, which had all healed quickly. And yet Alina still suffered from chronic pain, especially in her legs, which was sometimes so bad that she was unable to get out of bed. As a result, she stopped going to school, but medication could not alleviate the pain.

Alina's father had also been profoundly affected and suffered from other symptoms like insomnia and withdrawal. The question of blame had still not been resolved, and the family was also struggling financially, as neither of the parents had been able to continue their jobs as before.

Because the family was unable to come to the therapy sessions together and the two younger siblings came only occasionally, the therapist worked a lot with interventions such as circular questioning and scaling. The subject of the past and the future were frequently addressed, as were the family's roller-coaster emotions.

A significant step was made with a resource-focused collective timeline. In an individual setting with Alina, the timeline was complemented with homework (observing changes/exceptions) and work on a "life picture" in the form of a collage.

Further important steps, besides Alina's return to school, were getting legal support and claiming compensation; here the family was supported by an advisory center specializing in legal issues and was finally able to get some clarification.

Refusal to Eat and Picky Eating

Total refusal to eat is rare among children and is often the result of a traumatic experience such as forced intake of food or an extreme choking incident, a medical intervention (e.g., a gastrointestinal infection or operation), or a role model in the child's immediate environment. Many preschool children will eat only certain foods (picky eaters), often as a result of being spoiled (Scheer et al., 2007). Parents and caregivers often complain that a child hardly eats or does not eat at all, or eats only the wrong things or too much. In this case it helps to ask for detailed information about the child's eating habits and to ask the parents/caregiver to carefully observe the situation, for example, in the form of a diary.

Among adolescents and adults, a refusal to eat is usually linked to psychiatric clinical pictures such as anorexia or psychosocial stress caused, for example, by imminent deportation. Extremely picky eating, on the other hand, is usually the result of too much leniency on the part of the parents, or results from an underlying illness. It can also be the symptom of a mental illness, for example, paranoid psychosis. In this case, a comprehensive diagnosis is required before beginning therapy.

Interventions to address picky eating and refusal to eat

- Resource activation (see ***Activating and working with resources,*** *page 68*): *Which of your strengths do you value in particular?* Affection, encouragement, and praise also work.
- **Relaxation and imagination** (see *page 154*)
- **Playing with hypotheses** (see *page 161*)
- Psychoeducation (see ***Systemic and creative psychoeducation,*** *page 174*)
- **Signed and sealed: Contracts with clients** (see *page 184*)
- **Asking about exceptions** (see *page 79*)
- **Therapeutic stories and fairy tales** (see *page 130*)
- Helper figures (see ***Cartoon therapy,*** *page 125*)
- **Traffic-light cards** (see *page 190*)
- **Scaling** (see *page 81*)

School-Related Problems: Reluctance to Go to School, Truancy, and School Phobia

Dealing with these three problems in the same section does not mean that they are the same. On the contrary, it is important to differentiate between them in order to reach a diagnosis. However, the initial symptoms are often identical: The child has a problem with going to school.

At the root of school phobia is fear, which often becomes apparent in the fact that the problems begin the evening before.

With truancy, this is often not so clear. A reluctance to go to school is often a wolf in sheep's clothing: at the root of it may be a problem with schoolwork, lack of self-confidence, or conflict situations connected to school.

The baseline symptom should be examined first: A child does not want to go to school.

Careful: Problems at school often have little to do with school!

Interventions to address school-attendance-related problems

- **Asking about exceptions** (see page 79): *When do you manage to go to school? What is different on those days?* or *How do you decide whether or not to go to school?* Often children have a "feeling" that prevents them from going to school. This "feeling" is a good starting point.
- **Prescribing the symptom** (see page 100) in two respects:
  - You can ask the client to describe the feeling and prescribe it three times a day—after first checking that the student is able to elicit the feeling. Prescribing the symptom shows that you can have the feeling without playing truant from school.
  - You can also forbid a student to go to school. There is nothing to lose and you achieve—temporarily at least—good compliance.
- **The forecast calendar** (see page 108): If the student manages to go to school now and again, the forecast calendar works well: *What do you think you will do tomorrow? Do you think you will manage to go to school?* The calendar is an even more important tool in cases of school phobia, because the client often feels overwhelmed by a feeling of powerlessness. With the forecast, he can regain some control.

- **Circular questioning** (see page 85): *If you were a teacher and you had a student who didn't like school, what would you do?* or *If your teacher was sitting here, what would he say is missing from the class when you are not there?* (This question can also be diagnostically useful)
- Reinforcing self-confidence (or courage) can be accomplished particularly well with ***Talismans, courage stones, and other helpers*** (see page 186). **Tip**: With younger children it can also be combined with **Therapeutic stories and fairy tales** (see page 130).
- Questions: Get the client to describe the problem in detail:
   ° *Who does what, when, and why . . . ?*
   ° *How do your parents/siblings react . . . ?* The "family dance" is often revealing, and the family often only becomes aware of it as a result of the question.
- **Letting fate decide** (see page 114)

Self-Esteem Problems

Patients with a self-esteem problem are encouraged to (re)discover or use their resources and abilities.

Interventions to address self-esteem problems

- **The resources family tree** (*see page 71*): Ask the client to draw a family tree, either during the session or as homework, showing the special abilities of certain family members, dead or alive (e.g., grandparents, favorite aunt). This is combined with the question: *Where are these abilities in you?*
- **The resources barometer** (*see page 71*): Of the many resources that emerge out of the family tree, one of them is chosen and the client has to decide on a scale of 0 ("not at all") to 10 ("always") how often he currently uses this ability (*see also* **Scaling**, *page 81*). For example, patients with self-esteem problems may rate their ability "courage" at level 3. The question is then: *What would you be doing differently if you said 4?* Whatever the client describes in response can be prescribed as **Therapeutic homework** (*see page 110*): *Between now and next week, please act as if you were at level 4!*
- **Prescribing change** (*see page 102*)
- **Letting fate decide** (*see page 114*): For example, about which resources the patient would like to practice using in the following week: each of the six sides of a die can correspond to an ability. Here the motto "*Doing is knowing*" applies (see Berg & De Shazer, 1998). By doing something, the patient knows that he can do it.
- **Cartoon therapy** (*see page 125*): Particularly with elementary-school-age children and up, drawing a cartoon dealing with the subject of self-esteem can take things in a positive direction by means of a helper figure. This intervention can be enlarged upon with **Therapeutic stories and fairy tales** (*see page 130*) in the next session; it can also be combined with **Talismans, courage stones, and other helpers** (*see page 186*).
- **Externalization** (*see page 89*): A child's favorite doll or an adult's talisman can serve as a constant reminder of the abilities he could use to increase his self-esteem. And of course, once the

fundamental problem is externalized, the doll or talisman stays at home.

- **Working with the child's name** (*see page 122*): The name exercise, in which positive qualities are associated with each letter, is a good intervention for all age groups. The sheet of paper with the name exercise can be hung up in a special place at home, as a constant reminder to the client of his abilities.
- **Certificates** (*see page 193*): Particularly with clients lacking in self-esteem, a certificate is a good way of acknowledging the steps that the client has taken to utilize his abilities to overcome his self-esteem issues.
  - ° *You managed to give a presentation all on your own at school!*
  - ° *We are proud that you . . . !*
  - ° *Congratulations for showing courage in settling a dispute!*

Self-Harming

According to Petermann and Winkel (2009), self-harming behavior can be defined as such if it involves direct and deliberate harming, if there are no suicidal intentions, and if it is socially unacceptable.

Self-harming can be inflicted in many ways and on different parts of the body. Skin cutting usually occurs on the limbs and is carried out with some kind of sharp object (e.g., glass shards, razor blades, broken bits of CD). Other forms of self-harming include biting, burning, and scratching.

Prevention and timely interventions are important for treatment, as is differentiating the symptoms from suicidal behavior. Psychiatric help and inpatient treatment may be required.

It should also be remembered that severe self-harming may also be an early symptom of a disorder (a borderline or schizoid personality disorder) that requires intensive psychiatric-psychotherapeutic treatment.

Interventions to address self-harming

- Resource activation (see *Activating and working with resources*, *page 68*)
- **Reflecting positions** (see *page 143*): *If you saw somebody who also did this, what would you think?*
- **Redesigning the past** (see *page 160*)
- Psychoeducation (see *Systemic and creative psychoeducation*, *page 174*): With some clients it helps to provide a precise anatomical description of the self-inflicted injury.
- **The inner team** (see *page 163*)
- **The pocket helper** (see *page 166*)
- **Metaphors** (see *page 60*)
- **Therapeutic homework** (see *page 110*)
- **Timeline work** (see *page 126*)
- **Asking about exceptions** (see *page 79*)
- **The forecast calendar** (see *page 108*)

Separation and Divorce

Children and adolescents who experience the separation or divorce of their parents can find themselves developing parental alienation syndrome due to conflicts of loyalty and the pressure of taking sides (Schmidt, 2008).

Gaulier, Margerum, Price, and Windell (2007) describe the often massive strain on everybody involved in a separation or divorce. Difficult separations can lead to frustration, stress, and emotional distress over a protracted period of time.

Interventions to address issues with separation and divorce

- Resource activation (see *Activating and working with resources, page 68*): *Which of your strengths could you really do with now?*
- **Reflecting positions** (see *page 143*): *If you were to put yourself into the position of your wife . . .*
- **Family coat of arms** (see *page 158*): Completely rethinking a coat of arms after first imagining what it looked like before can be a helpful approach for some affected families, also with patchwork families, and in combination with developing family **Rituals** (see *page 94*), **The rule of the month** (see *page 192*), and so on.
- **Mottos, mantras, and myths** (see *page 171*): The attempt to create a family picture together often results in some welcome laughter. It is important to take into account the perspectives of everyone involved.
- **Therapeutic stories and fairy tales** (see *page 130*)
- **The power of the unexpected** (see *page 136*)
- **Metaphors** (see *page 60*), such as **The filling station metaphor** (see *page 66*)
- **Reframing** (see *page 84*)
- **Prescribing change** (see *page 102*)
- **Circular questioning** (see *page 85*)
- **Asking about exceptions** (see *page 79*)
- **Drawing together** (see *page 119*)
- **Observation tasks** (see *page 98*)
- **Talismans, courage stones, and other helpers** (see *page 186*)
- **Rituals** (see *page 94*)
- **Scaling** (see *page 81*) of confidence and probability

Separation Anxiety

According to Schmidt (2008), clinical pictures involving separation anxiety fall under the spectrum of interaction disorders that are atypical of the expected developmental level.

In contrast to a fear of strangers that typically occurs in the second half of the first year of life, or normal separation anxiety among young children, extreme forms of separation anxiety involve excessive crying, clinginess, and protestation, often lasting a long time, and sometimes in combination with other symptoms such as headaches or stomachaches, vomiting, problems falling asleep, or nightmares.

School phobia is a special form of separation anxiety, in which fear of being separated from a parent or caregiver can lead to truancy.

Interventions to address separation anxiety

- **Dream your dream** (see page 177): *How could the dream continue in a different way?*
- **Relaxation exercise: 5-4-3-2-1** (see page 156)
- Resource activation (see **Activating and working with resources**, page 68): *Which of your strengths do you value in particular?*
- **Metaphors** (see page 60)
- Marking progress (see **Improvisation, movement, and more**, page 136)
- **Therapeutic stories and fairy tales** (see page 130)
- **Scaling** (see page 81)
- **Asking about exceptions** (see page 79)
- **Drawing together** (see page 119)
- **The forecast calendar** (see page 108)
- **Talismans, courage stones, and other helpers** (see page 186)

Sibling Rivalry

Siblings are often ignored in therapy, although they can be a rich source of ideas and knowledge about each other. Competitive siblings ensure that all siblings are included in the therapy. (That was an example of reframing!)

With sibling rivalry it is a good idea to ask the "opponents" to observe each other in a *resource-focused* way, to write down their observations, and not talk about it with each other until the next session.

Interventions to address sibling rivalry

- Questions:
  - *What is good about having a brother/sister?*
  - *Imagine your rivalry didn't exist, what would be different?*
  - *Imagine you had to search for a treasure that you could only find together, because if one of you turned up alone, it would disappear. What would you do?*
- **Asking about exceptions** (see page 79): *Are there times when you get on well together? Are there times when you take care of each other?*
- **A chair is (not) a chair** (see page 145): Role reversal—if the siblings are willing to participate, you can ask the antagonists to act each other in a role-play. If this works, set it as a homework in which the parents have to guess when the children have swapped roles.
- **The Miracle Question** (see page 87): often works and provides an insight into the whole family!
- **Reframing** (see page 84): *Siblings who argue such a lot must have a high opinion of each other—otherwise they wouldn't be able to fight like that. What do you know about the abilities of your brother/sister?*

Sleep Disorders

During childhood and adolescence the following types of sleep disorder are most common:

- Problems falling asleep
- Problems sleeping through the night
- Events that disturb sleep (sleepwalking, nightmares, teeth gnashing, or talking in one's sleep)
- Excessive need of sleep

It is very important to look out for other symptoms that could indicate a possible apnea syndrome (e.g., snoring or abnormal pauses in breathing) or seizures (e.g., abnormal muscle twitching).

Because sleep disorders are often connected to other physical ailments (e.g., asthma) or go hand in hand with psychic disorders (depression, anxiety disorders, ADHD), these problems should also be addressed—that is, clarified and treated.

Sleep disorders are common and often temporary, but it is important to take into account other possible problems in the client's life, such as conflicts with family or friends, anxiety about a separation, a house move, financial problems, and so on (Rabenschlag, 1998).

In every case, the client should provide detailed information about his sleeping disorder, as this often provides information that is useful for the therapy.

An example: Lucas

Lucas is 10 years old and comes to therapy with his mother. He describes his nightly bedtime routine, and when asked what time he goes to bed, he says 8 p.m.—a time appropriate for his age. But when asked when he actually falls asleep, he is surprised and thinks about it. Then he admits:

"Usually only at around 11, because after mom has said good night, I usually turn the light back on and read."

In answer to the question *What else?* he says:

"Sometimes I also play a bit . . . "

What else? And what do you do then . . . ?

"Sometimes I turn the computer back on."

What else? What do you do next . . . ?

"Or sometimes the TV in my room . . . "

What else?

"Usually my parents take away my cell phone in the evening, but if they forget, I send text messages to my friends . . . "

What else . . . ?

It is always worth getting the client to explain his going-to-bed and sleeping routine in detail. In some cases it is helpful to get the client to write a *sleeping journal* for one to three weeks.

It is also important to determine what needs the child/adolescent satisfies during the time he should be sleeping, and whether these needs could be met during the day.

Several interventions can provide additional support.

Interventions to address sleep disorders

- **Rituals** (see *page 94*) for bedtime (and wake-up time): With some clinical pictures (e.g., ADHD), waking up is almost more problematic than going to sleep, so an early waking-up ritual with plenty of time for the morning routine, including "cuddle time," can provide substantial relief.
- **Asking about exceptions** (see *page 79*): *Are there days when you are able to fall asleep quickly? What is different on these occasions?*
- **The anti-anxiety thread** (see *page 189*)—particularly when the child is afraid of going to sleep.
- **Therapeutic stories and fairy tales** (see *page 130*) work particularly well with younger children.
- **Cartoon therapy** (see *page 125*), particularly with elementary-school-age children who have problems falling asleep or sleeping through the night; this can also be used with nightmares.
- Psychoeducation (see **Systemic and creative psychoeducation**, *page 174*): Sometimes it is necessary to explain sleep hygiene and facts about sleep, such as individual sleeping needs, stages of sleep, and so on.
- Helper figures (see **Cartoon therapy**, *page 125*)

Snitching

Children who snitch, or tattle, are good at telling on others. So they are also very good observers and have a strong need to talk. This is an example of reframing: an effective means of changing the focus of the observation.

This is also important in relation to snitching: How can you get away from the problem and introduce new ideas without pathologizing the patient? Several approaches offer avenues to explore.

Interventions to address snitching

- **Metaphors** (see page 60)
- Resource activation (see **Activating and working with resources**, page 68)
- **Perspective goggles** (see page 152): Which strengths do you particularly appreciate in . . . ?
- **Reframing** (see page 84): If you are good at snitching, then you must be a good observer. Could you imagine using your powers of observation to only snitch on people who have done something really well? (Somebody—perhaps one of the parents—should make sure that the task is fulfilled.)
- Marking progress (see **Improvisation, movement, and more**, page 136)
- **Relaxation and imagination** (see page 154)
- **Letters from the Fairy Kingdom** (see page 133)
- **The pocket helper** (see page 166)
- **The change detective** (see page 104)
- **Asking about exceptions** (see page 79)
- **Scaling** (see page 81)
- **Prescribing the symptom** (see page 100): Over the next two weeks I would like you to snitch on somebody three times a day!

Social Phobias and Social Anxiety

Insecurity, shyness, and anxiety when dealing with unfamiliar people or dealing with people in certain situations, are the criteria of this behavioral disorder (Petermann & Suhr-Dachs, 2008). Affected persons use special avoidance strategies that affect their relationships with outsiders; however, they are socially competent with people they know and trust.

Depending on the person's situation, age, and the demands made by his environment—for example, the need to perform well at school—the condition can become a burden in different ways. Family or social and cognitive factors, as well as character or temperament, can influence the risk of social phobia or anxiety.

Therapeutic interventions should be age appropriate, with a focus on behavior therapy and training programs to boost social skills. Several interventions are also worth trying.

Interventions to address social phobias and anxiety

- **Metaphors** (see page 60)
- Resource activation (see **Activating and working with resources,** page 68)
- **Relaxation and imagination** (see page 154)
- **Reflecting positions** (see page 143)
- **The power of the unexpected** (see page 136)
- **Emotion cards and such** (see page 141)
- **Compliments, praise, and such** (see page 168)
- **The pocket helper** (see page 166): The "helper" should remind the client that he wanted to overcome his social phobia: *In difficult situations the pocket helper will remind you that you wanted to remember this.*
- **Reframing** (see page 84): *When you have a social phobia, you are very careful about who you include in your circle of acquaintances.*
- **Prescribing change** (see page 102)
- **The change detective** (see page 104)
- **Drawing together** (see page 119)
- **Cartoon therapy** (see page 125)
- **Asking about exceptions** (see page 79)
- **The forecast calendar** (see page 108)
- **Timeline work** (see page 126)

TIPS. With socially anxious clients, a lot can be achieved with finely dosed "social" homework, for example, *What kind of homework would I have to set to make you realize it is helping you?*

Soiling

Soiling is a problem that occurs primarily among children and adolescents, usually boys, mostly during the day.

Important basic interventions incorporate self-awareness and relaxation exercises, as well as explanations of the digestive system and psychoeducation, with the active cooperation of parents particularly with younger children (Fuhrmann, Schreiner-Zink & von Gontard, 2008).

We have had positive experiences in clinical practice with promoting several interventions.

Interventions to address soiling

- Bathroom culture: With soiling, attention should be paid to a special bathroom culture. For the purpose of clarification, always ask about the usual family routines: *When? Where? How? For how long?* Be sure to ask *What else?*
- **Rituals** (*see page 94*) around visits to the bathroom always take place after main meals and last at least 5–10 minutes in a pleasant atmosphere, with a comfy seat, feet on the ground. A favorite book or comic provides diversion and relaxation. There should also be a stool next to the toilet for putting the book down.
- Promoting independence, increasing responsibility after the soiling, by getting the child to put his dirty underwear in the washing machine.

Careful: The paradoxical intervention of prescribing the symptom can work but can also have the opposite effect!

Stammering, Stuttering, and Such

Speech or language development problems are very common among children. According to a 2008 report by the American Speech-Language-Hearing Association, around 9 percent of young children have speech or language problems, and by the first grade 5 percent have noticeable speech disorders. The majority of these problems have no known cause; they can be temporary or permanent, and they can be an isolated symptom or part of a more complex developmental problem or clinical picture (Castrogiovanni, 2008). As a rule, speech disorders need to be treated with the help of specialist doctors, speech-language pathologists, and speech therapists (Strassburg, 2000).

An early diagnosis of speech and language disorders includes general physical and neurological testing. Hearing and oral motor skills are checked, as are eating and drinking behavior and the developmental level in all of these areas. Specific computer-aided and laboratory tests may also be necessary depending on the symptom.

Age-appropriate language skills are evaluated based on vocabulary and syntax, comprehension, and pronunciation, in order to classify the disorder as an expressive, receptive speech disorder, an articulation disorder, or a mixed or global clinical picture.

Developmental stuttering is common among young children and signifies a temporary fluency disorder. "Real" stuttering goes far beyond the physiological stages of inarticulate speaking, usually begins in preschool age, and is classified as either clonic or tonic stuttering. The stuttering may also be accompanied by breathing or muscular coordination problems, as well as by other facial movements or movements of the upper body, for example, furrowed brow or arm flapping.

Other speech impairments include stumbling over words and having problems with clear articulation, while stammering, or dyslalia, is a speech impairment causing the person to have difficulties correctly pronouncing certain words or sounds, for example, consonants.

Each condition requires specialist treatment, notably speech therapy, but a variety of interventions can be used to complement this treatment.

Interventions to address stammering and stuttering

- Resource activation (see **Activating and working with resources**, *page 68*): The strengthening of particular skills and abilities can be worked on in a targeted way to boost the client's self-esteem and also to support oral motor skills, for example, spitting far, spouting water, blowing, or blowing air into something (e.g., a balloon).

 ° *Which other abilities would help you . . . ?*
 ° *Which of your strengths do you value in particular?*

- **Relaxation and imagination** (see page 154)
- Psychoeducation (see ***Systemic and creative psychoeducation***, page 174)
- **The pocket helper** (see page 166)
- **The inner team** (see page 163): *Which member of your team could help you at school when you don't want to put your hand up to answer a question?*
- Marking progress (see ***Improvisation, movement, and more***, page 136)
- **Emotion cards and such** (see page 141)
- **The power of the unexpected** (see page 136)
- **Metaphors** (see page 60)
- **Therapeutic stories and fairy tales** (see page 130)
- **Asking about exceptions** (see page 79)
- **Talismans, courage stones, and other helpers** (see page 186)
- **Glove puppets** (see page 118)
- **Drawing together** (see page 119)
- **Prescribing the symptom** (see page 100)
- **The forecast calendar** (see page 108)

Stealing, Playing with Fire, Running Away

Forms of dissocial behavior diagnosed as antisocial personality disorder due to their intensity and frequency include the stealing of money and other objects, mostly at home or from particular people (Baving, 2006, 2008). Similarly to frequent lying, cheating, running away, temper tantrums, or aggression toward living beings or innate objects, this kind of behavior violates existing social rules and can make coexistence with other people extremely difficult.

In order to understand what lies behind the stealing or other behavior, and in order to categorize the situation of the affected person more effectively, Trapmann and Rotthaus (2003) recommend initially clarifying what is being stolen and from whom, and perhaps with whom, for whom, and how. Aspects such as social pressure, conspicuous thefts, or the desire for recognition and attention can play a significant role. It is also important to clarify to what extent the act serves the purpose of self-protection.

A variety of factors can significantly contribute to the emergence and perpetuation of all of these symptoms, including the kind of parenting the affected person experiences, as well as lack of interest and positive feedback from caregivers, particularly in the case of children. When treating the patient, it is also important to consider his development and case history, as well as current problems and personal circumstances (Baving, 2006).

The key objective of therapeutic measures is to reduce the problematic behavior, as well as the conditions that are perpetuating it, and to strengthen functionality within the family:

Interventions to address stealing, playing with fire, running away

- **Reflecting positions** (see page 143)
- Marking progress (see **Improvisation, movement, and more**, page 136)
- **The inner team** (see page 163)
- **The pocket helper** (see page 166)
- **Compliments, praise, and such** (see page 168)
- Resource activation (see **Activating and working with resources**, page 68): Which of your abilities could help you to . . . ?
- **Metaphors** (see page 60)
- **Rewind → Reset** (see page 181): What could you do differently next time?

- **The Miracle Question** *(see page 87)*: Stealing does not happen all the time; it is almost always opportunistic: *When the miracle occurs, the opportunities to steal are still there but you don't steal anymore. What do you do instead?*
- **Scaling** *(see page 81)*
- **Circular questioning** *(see page 85)*
- **Asking about exceptions** *(see page 79)*
- **The change detective** *(see page 104)*
- **The forecast calendar** *(see page 108)*
- **Therapeutic homework** *(see page 110)*, for example, *Write yourself a letter from the future.*

Stomachaches

Abdominal pains are one of the most common psychosomatic disorders in child-hood and adolescence, that is, clinical pictures involving subjectively intense suffer-ing without any indication of concrete physical ailments (Noeker, 2008).

Of course, it is important to first rule out an underlying physical ailment. Stom-ach pains are also often an indication of a predisposition to constipation.

Initial questioning should focus on an exact assessment of the symptoms, for example, *Tell me more about your stomachaches.*

Besides asking about the modalities—that is, when, how often, where, in what context—you can also ask *what else* questions.

Interventions to address issues related to stomachaches

- **Asking about exceptions** (see *page 79*)
- **The forecast calendar** (see *page 108*)
- **Externalization** (see *page 89*), for example, drawing the pain (see ***Drawing the problem,*** *page 90*)
- **Rituals** for relaxation (see *page 94*)
- **Circular questions** (see *page 85*) with dolls or favorite toys can be used with stomachaches, as well as other pain syndromes, to elicit a more precise description of the problem, for example, the doll as the expert:
  ° *I think your doll knows you best. What do you think she would say you could do to make the tummy ache go away?*
  ° *Do you think your doll can forecast when your pains are going to start?*
- **Observation tasks** (see *page 98*)
- **The change detective** (see *page 104*)

Substance Abuse and Addiction

The consumption of alcohol and nicotine is widespread, especially among young people, and adolescents in particular tend toward risk taking and experimentation in their peer groups.

Addiction encompasses harmful use of psychotropic substances, for example, alcohol and drugs, which can lead to problematic conditions such as acute poisoning, harmful substance misuse, or a substance addiction (Horn, 2009). In a broader sense, addiction can also include being addicted to the Internet, to work, or to sports.

Children and adolescents with behavioral disorders or growing up with parents suffering from addiction are at a higher risk of developing an addiction themselves. Timely preventative measures, parent counseling, and risk minimization are extremely important. Several techniques can be helpful.

Interventions to address substance abuse and addiction

- Psychoeducation (see *Systemic and creative psychoeducation*, page 174)
- **Reflecting positions** (see *page 143*)
- **Emotion cards and such** (see *page 141*)
- **Activating and working with resources** (see *page 68*)
- **The inner team** (see *page 163*)
- **The pocket helper** (see *page 166*)
- **Biography work** (see *page 128*)
- Sculpture work (see *Improvisation, movement, and more*, page 136)
- **Metaphors** (see *page 60*)
- **Observation tasks** (see *page 98*)
- Stress management and relaxation (see, e.g., *Relaxation and imagination*, page 154)
- **Circular questioning** (see *page 85*)
- **Asking about exceptions** (see *page 87*)
- **The forecast calendar** (see *page 108*)
- **Timeline work** (see *page 126*)
- **Scaling** (see *page 81*)
- **Therapeutic homework** (see *page 110*), for example, *Write a letter to the illness.*

Suicidality

A case example: "I wish I were dead . . . "

A mother reported that she woke up her eight-year-old son Ethan on a Thursday at the beginning of September. He started to scream and cry and told her that he could not go to school. Up to this point it had been difficult to get him to go to school in the morning, because he always cried, but eventually he would go.

On this Thursday morning she could not calm him down and decided to go to the doctor with him. The doctor gave him a sick note for two days, to try to smooth the situation out.

But on Monday the same thing happened, and once again, it wasn't possible to get Ethan to go to school. He developed massive anxieties. He was afraid of storms, wind, and some kind of fantasy characters. He didn't leave his room for days on end, the curtains were constantly closed, and he had music playing the whole time.

He had constant crying fits and came out with things like

- "Help, I can't bear my life anymore."
- "My head is bursting."
- **"I wish I were dead."**
- "Why won't anybody help me?"
- "I'm freaking out."

These are just a few examples. This kind of "attack" occurred again and again. They did become less frequent, but according to his parents, as soon as they told Ethan he had to do something, he would have an attack or his anxieties would return.

After another visit to the doctor, a decision was reached to give him another week's sick leave. The doctor wanted to work with Ethan intensively during this time and to treat him primarily homeopathically.

Neither course of action worked. The doctor then decided to refer Ethan to a child and adolescent psychiatric clinic. While they waited for an appointment, Ethan remained on sick leave and continued to receive homeopathic treatment. His mother explained: "Luckily his teacher has been a great support. During the initial phase she came three times a week to bring Ethan all the material from the lessons he was missing at school." At the clinic, the decision was made to treat Ethan as an inpatient for child depression.

The term *suicidality* encompasses a broad spectrum of causes, thoughts, and deeds, starting with suicidal thoughts all the way through to the act of trying to commit suicide. Suicidal tendencies occur in connection with a variety of psychiatric clinical pictures and behavioral syndromes (von Schlippe & Schweitzer, 2007).

However, self-harming behavior is not automatically a sign of suicidality. Thinking about how it would be to be dead is normal in certain age groups; it becomes difficult only if these thoughts begin to dominate the person's day-to-day life or become obsessive.

Suicidal behavior can also be a form of attention seeking, which then leads to others taking notice.

As a therapist, it is important to maintain sufficient distance and not to take on the role of minder—however threatening the suicidal thoughts or behavior of the patient may be.

With the right care, often the patient's serious intention of suicide can turn into a less threatening cry for help.

Along with the interventions described here, it is especially important to divert the focus of the suicidal patient away from suicide toward a will to survive.

Interventions to address suicidality

- Resource activation (see ***Activating and working with resources***, page 68): *Which of your strengths do you value in particular?*
- **Relaxation techniques** (see ***Relaxation and imagination***, page 154)
- **"Life" contract** (see ***Signed and sealed: Contracts with clients***, page 184)
- **Exaggeration** (see *page 179*)
- **Reflecting positions** (see *page 143*)
- **Asking about exceptions** (see *page 79*)
- **Externalization** (see *page 89*)
- **Scaling** of the nonsuicidality/will to live (see *page 81*): There is little point in scaling suicidality. This would only lead the patient to concentrate even more on his suicidality and to scale it even higher than it really is. We therefore recommend scaling the *nonsuicidality*, for example, the patient's belief in himself. This can be combined with asking the patient what he would be doing differently in terms of mastering the problem, if he was at level 5.5 instead of 5. Scaling is particularly effective because it enables a hypothetical and perspective-changing approach—something that is generally very difficult with suicidal patients.

- The pie scale is a variation of scaling: You get the client to draw a round pie to represent himself as a person. The patient then draws in the slice that represents the part of him that is not suicidal. This visual representation often leads to surprising realizations. It opens up the way for such questions as *What is the nonsuicidal slice of pie filled with? How is this slice different from the others—which abilities are there in this slice?*
- **Therapeutic homework** (see page 110), for example, *Write yourself a letter from the future.*
- **Timeline work** (see page 126)
- **The forecast calendar** (see page 108)
- **Circular questioning** (see page 85)
- Coping questions, for example,
    - *Where do you get your energy from to keep on living, despite everything?*
    - *Why are things not much worse than they are?*
    - *What prevented you from turning your ideas into reality?*
    - *Why do you find it so difficult to cope and how have you managed to cope up to now?*
- **Observation tasks** (see page 98)
- **Asking about exceptions** (see page 79): *What is different about the times when you are not feeling suicidal?*

Thumb-sucking

Most children start sucking their thumb during their first year; among children between three and five years of age, 86 percent suck their thumb occasionally. Renewed, intensive thumb-sucking can be triggered, for example, by emotional distress or psychological strain.

Focusing on relieving tension and fears through conversation and maximizing stimulation and physical activity can be very effective interventions. Several approaches can be helpful.

Interventions to address thumb-sucking

- **Asking about exceptions** (see page 79)
- Cuddle times and praise (see also below) as a reward for not sucking.
- **Externalization** (see page 89): Personifying the thumb: *Imagine you are your thumb!*
- *Paradoxical interventions* (see **Prescribing the symptom**, page 100): *If you desperately need to suck your thumb, then please also suck your other thumb at the same time!* (But don't forget to check the client's willingness to cooperate, or ask for permission to set an unusual task!)
- **Prescribing problem-free times and rooms** (see page 106), for example, the "thumb room," to increase the client's control over the symptom: You can stipulate rooms in the house in which thumb-sucking is allowed or not allowed. It is important to extend this task step by step: When the first step has been achieved and the child is able to stick to the thumb-sucking-free rooms, the child should be given plenty of praise, and the number of thumb-sucking-free rooms is gradually increased.
- **Traffic-light cards** (see page 190): Not sucking a thumb has to be worthwhile, too, so work with the green as well as the red card!

Trichotillomania (Hair Pulling)

Compulsive pulling out of hair, or trichotillomania, is classified as deliberate self-harming (Resch & Brunner, 2004).

This type of behavioral disorder stereotypically occurs among children and adolescents with a mental disability, especially in relation to certain genetic syndromes (Petermann & Winkel, 2009), and usually follows a regular and fairly rigid pattern. Related automatisms include eye boring, lip biting, and head hitting.

A special case: Jasmine

Jasmine had just turned 12 when she came to a consultation with her parents because she was constantly tearing her hair out. The dramatic extent of this behavior became apparent only when she entered the room. On her head were just a few clumps of hair—the rest of her head was bald.

In total contrast to this striking appearance, Jasmine was physically and intellectually well developed for her age and on the threshold of puberty, and at the first meeting she added a note of easy-going humor to the proceedings. She was talkative and open; the only thing she refused to discuss was her hair.

She was not experiencing any particular stress at school or in her free time, or at home with her family; neither she nor her parents could explain her problem.

Working with a family sculpture and the intervention "a chair is (not) a chair" enabled first steps toward a reduction of the symptom. Feelings and emotions were addressed in an individual session, and the girl discovered the "yelling bag"—having a paper bag with her into which she could yell when she felt the need further minimized the problem.

Interventions to address trichotillomania

- Resource activation!!! (see **Activating and working with resources**, page 68): Which of your strengths do you value in particular?
- **Reflecting positions** (see page 143)
- Sculpture work (see **Improvisation, movement, and more**, page 136)
- **A chair is (not) a chair** (see page 145)
- **Relaxation and imagination** (see page 154): Imagination exercises are a possible coping strategy and can help to reduce stress.

- **Perspective goggles** (see page 152)
- **Metaphors** (see page 60)
- Marking progress (see **Improvisation, movement, and more**, page 136)
- **Emotion cards and such** (see page 141)
- **Signed and sealed: Contracts with clients** (see page 184)
- **Glove puppets** (see page 118)
- **Scaling** (see page 81)
- **Asking about exceptions** (see page 79)
- **Prescribing problem-free times and rooms** (see page 106)
- **Observation tasks** (see page 98) and **Therapeutic homework** (see page 110): Between now and next session, make a note of when you manage not to pull your hair out. In the next session, this could be followed up with How exactly did you manage that? All of these interventions can be used prior to medical treatment or as a simultaneous backup.

Part 4

Seemingly Hopeless: Mastering Particularly Tricky Situations

In this section of the book we describe some tricky situations frequently encountered by therapists and counselors. In each case we provide suggestions of how to make progress.

Even if these situations don't repeat themselves exactly, there are often similarities. Perhaps some of the following will seem familiar to you.

When the Parent Always Answers Questions Addressed to the Child

This is a very common problem! If, after the second or third question, the concerned parent is still answering on behalf of the child, the therapist should intervene:

- *Tell me, Ronny, how is this for you? I'm noticing that when I ask you a question, your mother always answers! What would you say to me?*
- *Thank you, Mrs. X! I can see that you are very concerned. But sometimes it helps if I can also hear what the child has to say about the matter.*
- *Can I demonstrate to you what I am seeing?*

"You Are Our Last Hope!"

This sentence reveals how much pressure the patient is under, but also how great the pressure could become on the therapist. You should eradicate this pressure!

Possible interventions include:

- *How will you notice that it was a good thing to invest your last hope in me?*
- *I think we should compromise and say I'm the "second-to-last" hope!*
- *I can assure you that, if need be, there can be someone else after me!*

"We've Tried Everything Already!"

Along with the last point—"You are our last hope!"—clients will often claim that they have already tried everything. Often this is true. But "tried everything . . . " unfortunately also often means " . . . and gave up too early."

It is worth examining the issue more closely, using the following types of question:

- *Which approach worked best? And how exactly? And what did you do differently that time?*
- *What do I not need to suggest again?*

The problem with failed attempts is that often the client was given a tip that quickly proved to be ineffective, either because it wasn't the client's own solution or because the affected person was more of a customer or complainant than a client (de Shazer, 1997). (See **The Miracle Question**, page 87.)

The therapist may also be concerned that compliance is not particularly good—which is why, with such patients, it is especially important to proceed in a resource-focused way and for them to work out their own "solution."

But when the client says "I've tried everything!" you may of course actually be thinking "I doubt it!"

"Things Are Never Going to Improve!"

Parents are often in despair and yet at the same time can't stop complaining about their child's behavior. This reveals that they are at the end of their rope—and this is exactly what you should pick up on:

- *I'm impressed that you want to make a fresh start despite your obvious frustration.*
- *When we are exhausted, it is difficult to come up with ideas. Can I make a suggestion? Tell me about when everything was still good.*
- *What makes you so hopeful that we can work this out?*
- *How do you cope with the situation day in and day out?*

"Typical"

This word is seldom meant in the positive sense and is often used in conflict-ridden relationships, which is why the following questions can be helpful:

- *Are there also nice things that are typical?*
- *What exactly is typical? And how do you deal with it? Would you like to deal with it differently?*

"If My Wife Didn't Do That, We Wouldn't Have a Problem"

This is a classic complaint in couple conflicts. Possible interventions might be:

- *What would you be doing differently if you didn't have a problem?*
- *Would you mind starting with the change and then observing what happens?*

This is a classic indication for **The change detective** (see page 104).

When the Client/Patient Has a Concern but the Therapist Has No Time

It is a surprisingly common occurrence for a patient to have a very important and time-consuming issue that they want to "quickly" discuss with the therapist. The therapist is pressed for time as he has another client waiting or because it is getting late and he needs to get back to his own family. But he doesn't want to leave the suffering patient in the lurch, because he notices that it is really important.

The conversation should lead to some kind of result: *Mr. X, unfortunately I only have 10 minutes. At the end of those 10 minutes, how would you know that our conversation has been worthwhile?*

"Ideally, I Would Just Leave Him Right Here!"

This response comes in several different versions:

- "Can't you just keep him here? Ideally, for good!"
- And then there is the young mother who in the first consultation says in front of her son: "I never wanted to have him anyway!"
- A foster father: "Sometimes I'm shocked by my own thoughts . . ."

These kinds of remarks—which are usually expressed at the start of a therapy—are not uncommon: The parents or caregivers are clearly out of their depth with the child's problem. The brutal objectivity of these statements is nothing more than a sign of deep-rooted despair.

Behind this sentence is a very different one: "I can't cope anymore! And I want to do something good for my child by bringing him here and giving us a break from each other." We are familiar with these kinds of reactions from parents who are exhausted.

And then there are parents who find it hard to say anything at all in the presence of their child (or a teacher or social services worker).

An appropriate reaction might be to express surprise at this resentment: *I'm wondering about all the things that must have happened for a parent to develop such feelings? You've obviously been through some very difficult times.*

When a parent comes out with this kind of statement, the first thing to do is to take the child out of the firing line—and not by saying something like "How can you say such a thing?!" In this kind of situation, rapport and empathy are required: *The fact that you express your despair so openly suggests that you must be really exhausted!* or *How have you coped with this continuous stress?*

This takes the focus away from the child and puts it instead on exploring the intensity of these emotions—which can be an extreme burden on the child—and thinking about alternatives. This also prevents the child from thinking that he is being admitted to a clinic because he is a burden to the parent ("the child has to go away so that I can feel better") and provides assurance that this is a mutually beneficial measure ("Perhaps some time in a clinic would be a good opportunity for us both to recover, so that we can subsequently work on finding a solution together").

"Everyone Says We've Got a Problem. But What Is It?"

This may manifest as "I don't understand, we don't have any problems at home!" or "It's the school's fault. If only the teacher would be a bit more understanding."

The message behind this message is usually: *We don't know why we're here* or *If it weren't for the school we wouldn't be here* or *The school sent us but we don't think it's necessary.* These are the kinds of ideas that parents come with.

To start with, then, there is no real problem to solve. The art of handling these kinds of unclear or nonexistent assignments is to start the therapy or counseling while also working out what needs to be specifically dealt with. This works with such questions as

- *Which of you thought that it might be a good idea to come here today?*
- *The teacher (or other person) must have had the child's best interests at heart. What could have been the reason for him to seek out help for you, although you don't know why you need it?*
- *What would you have to do now so that nobody else comes up with the idea of sending you here?*
- *If the teacher were sitting here now, and I asked him his reasons for sending you here, what would he say?*

Parents often feel that they are being treated unfairly and are caught in a cycle of self-justification that has prevented any meaningful change. These questions are all invitations to escape this cycle.

"I Give Up—I Can't Stand It Any More!"

This sentence is also an expression of pure despair. Again, it is important to strongly empathize with the client and to reformulate the sentence:

- *You can see no way out. Neither backward nor forward.*
- *You've ground to a halt. And your reserve fuel supplies have run out, too.*

With these sentences you pick up on the client's state of mind and prepare the ground for solution-oriented and resource-focused interventions. The empathetic stage can be followed by such questions as

- *May I ask something? When was the last time that you had an idea of what to do, and what was your idea?*
- *How would you notice that you are no longer completely stuck in a rut? What would you be doing differently?*

People who describe their situations with sentences like the one above are focused on their immobility and exhaustion. These seemingly hopeless situations often have more "ways out" than initially meets the eye. The above questions provide an opportunity to act against this paralysis and find new sources of strength.

When Even Focusing on Resources Does Not Bring Things into Focus

Clients are sometimes so afflicted with their problem that even the idea that there might be a solution does not motivate them.

This often means that a person is no longer able to imagine a life without his problem, which in turn means that the problem fulfills a purpose or has advantages. It is then the job of the therapist not to help the client get rid of the problem but to find a middle way between the problem and the solution. It will not help the client if you want to get rid of something that he wants to keep. Finding a middle way means carefully balancing the scales to reach an equilibrium.

In terms of **Scaling** (*see page 81*), this means that you have to scale downward as well as upward in order to find the stable value on the scale (how much of the problem is necessary to remain stable?). Up to now, scaling has usually been about taking steps toward getting better. Scaling downward, on the other hand, means taking steps toward the problem.

How can this work? Based on the presumption that maintaining the problem serves a function and is aided by many resources, then the point of scaling in the direction of the problem becomes clearer: to activate these (and other) resources to find a solution.

The Belgian hypnotherapist Paul Koeck impressively demonstrated how this can work: The patient is given an insight into the microdynamics (fine-tuning) of his problem as well as solution models.

Example: Traveling down the scale

A client wanted to move to Paris but was afraid of doing so. Because she really wanted to take this step, she sought help.

The therapist asked the client to choose a number on a scale of 1 to 100 that best corresponded to her current situation. With a combination of hypnosis and scaling, he asked her to concentrate on her number 43 and to feel herself into it. Then he asked her: *If you want to take a step forward it might also be good to take a step back, for example, to number 42. Can you imagine how it feels to be at number 42? Take your time when you get to number 42, and then give me a sign.*

He kept on going down the scale with his client, always asking her to take note of her reactions to these numbers.

When she reached the point where she was blocked, he asked her how she had managed to move so far down the scale and asked her to repeat this. He pointed out everything she had done in order to take this step backward, which suddenly revealed resources.

This form of resource-focusing makes it very clear that you also need resources to have a problem. Toward the end of the session, he went up the scale again with his patient and again asked her to concentrate on her reactions, which gave her a very good sense of which physical reactions corresponded to which points on the scale.

"He Can't Get Himself Organized—
Please Teach Him How!"

Parents sometimes express this concern to a therapist/counselor. Some responses might be

- *What would be different if he was able to organize himself? What would he do differently, and what would you do differently?*
- *What's good about being organized?*
- *What does he manage to get done despite being disorganized? How does he manage that?*

These are all questions that can be added to as needed and that almost imperceptibly throw the ball back into the parents' court.

When Somebody Is Not Present

There is always a reason that somebody is not present. However, it is still possible to include this person with the aid of **Circular questioning** (*see page 85; see also **A chair is (not) a chair**, page 145*) and in combination with various sculpture techniques (see ***Sculpture work: Understanding without words***, *page 144*).

You can try to bring about as much change as possible with those who are present, in order to arouse the curiosity of the absent member of the system. Sometimes this has such an effect on the system that things actually begin to change.

When One Person Won't Join In

For example, a highly motivated family comes to therapy: Everyone wants to bring about change—apart from Ryan, who doesn't get involved.

The therapist can set Ryan the following kind of task: *Ryan, it's great that you've joined the rest of the family, but I think it's very important that you just listen and don't get involved* (a paradoxical intervention: **Prescribing the symptom** within the conversation setting; *see page 100*). Together with the rest of the family, you negotiate changes that they should try before the next session, here too with the instruction that Ryan should absolutely not try these changes. *Every family needs somebody who makes sure that progress is not made too quickly.* At the next session you ask Ryan if he wants to continue restricting himself to being the listener and not involving himself, or if he has something to say on the matter. Either is okay, but whichever way he decides, he always has the option of getting involved.

You continue working with the family to find out how they managed to bring about the changes, and to what extent Ryan was involved. If Ryan was involved—great. If he held back, then he acted in accordance with the therapist's instructions. In either case he is involved in the therapeutic process.

This intervention is about giving the "refusenik" a role that he couldn't *not* take on, or else ensuring that there was so much change in the family that he has to change himself in some way in order not to be at a disadvantage.

"I Will Not Sit Down at the Same Table with That Person!"

This is a definitive statement that seems to rule out a discussion, unless:

- *Could there be a reason why you should sit down at the same table?*
- *If your ex-partner were sitting here, what would he have to say on the matter?*
- *Would you be willing to try an experiment if I guarantee that nothing will happen to you?*

If need be, such conversations can be carried out using a one-way glass window or a video, or in separate rooms but at the same time. The therapist moves back and forth between the two rooms and, for example, reports to the child (in a third room) what is being discussed.

When an Argument Flares Up in the Consulting Room

Before you know it, the couple or family reveal why they are there: they start arguing, and everyone immediately wants the therapist or counselor to give his opinion: Who is right?

Of course, this question should not be answered. Instead, **Reframing** works well (*see page 84*). The therapist thanks the clients:

- *Thank you for showing me why you came!*
- *Does this also happen at home?*
- *Can I describe to you what I have observed?*

If the argument flares up again:

- *Can I interrupt?* (Usually some body language is required, too—for example, you may need to raise your arms to attract attention.)
- *Can somebody else tell me how this started?*
- Or simply: *Why do you need an answer to the question "who is right?"*

"That's Right, Isn't It?"

This is a common tactic to try to break down the impartiality of the therapist. While this question should not be answered, it should be acknowledged:

- *And what if it was right?* complemented by
- *And what if it wasn't right?*

When the Patient Does Not Have a Concern

Sometimes patients—young and old—come to therapy and claim not to have a problem or not to know why they are there.

The only kinds of question that need to be asked is:

- *What could you do so that nobody would come up with the idea of sending you here?*
- *What could we both do so that you don't have to come here anymore?*
- *Why do you think that the others are concerned about you? What could you do so that they stop worrying?*

These questions deserve an answer too!

When the Problem Is the Marriage, Not the Child

Sometimes parents come with a troubled child and the therapist assumes they are having a marital crisis. This is a very common trap: the parents are the clients but come as parents. But when the therapist suspects marital problems, he sees them as a couple and no longer as parents. Systemically, the therapist moves from the parent to the couple level.

It is okay to do this, but not without asking for permission first—and of course, the parents might say no. Their decision should be respected, even if you have made a correct evaluation. A question might be:

- *Excuse me, but I think I need to ask a question that is not directly related to the problem with your daughter. May I?*
- *What you just told me has more to do with you as a couple than as parents. Can I delve a bit deeper?*

But in our experience, parents rarely refuse such a request. Secretly they may even have hoped that this underlying problem would come to light.

The Client Remains Skeptical

It is not unusual for clients to have a reserved or even hostile attitude to possible solutions: "That's just pie in the sky!"

Here, too, it is important to connect with the patient: *Yes, but a pie in the sky is still a pie!*

You can give free reign to your creativity here by emphasizing this sentence through, for example, gesticulation or a special intonation.

Indication "X": When the Problem Cannot Be Addressed

Sometimes one of the people involved in the problem system will not allow a problem or certain facts to be addressed. This situation arises frequently:

- Parents are going through a relationship crisis and do not want their children to find out about it.
- Adolescents have a secret that they do not want their parents to find out.
- In couples therapy one partner doesn't want the other to know about certain things.

There are many other constellations in which secrets suddenly crop up that can block a therapy process because the others—who up to now have not known about the secret—insist on it being revealed.

As a therapist or counselor you can encourage this demand, or protect the keeper of the secret. In either case, you take up the position of one of the parties and are no longer a neutral intermediary. How do you get out of this dilemma?

Here, too, there are a plethora of possible interventions.

Ask, Ask, Ask

By taking on the position of questioner, it is possible to maintain your neutrality. A possible question might be:

- *If we had talked about the problem, what would be different now?*
- *Can I call the problem "X"? If "X" were no longer a problem, what would be different?*

These questions are addressed both to the person with the secret and to those who do not know the secret, and they open up the perspective that this unknown problem is resolvable, and that it does not have to block communication between the people involved.

Bound to Secrecy

A second scenario is that the keeper of the secret wants to reveal the secret to the therapist, but usually only on the condition that he will not tell anybody else. Of course, the therapist then runs the risk of becoming the ally of one person and the opponent of the others. So before allowing the person to share his secret, it is important to clarify the following:

> *Before you tell me your secret, you should know that your secret is safe with me, but that I have to tell your parents that I know your secret. Is that okay with you?*

Dangerous Secrets

As a therapist or counselor, you need to be clear about whether you are ethically willing to keep a secret. For example, if during a one-on-one session an adolescent reveals that he is taking drugs but does not want his parents to find out, then it is the job of the therapist to tell the client that it is his responsibility to let his parents know. If they do not know, they do not even have the possibility of trying to fulfill their role as parents. In this way, appropriate therapy measures can be initiated for everyone involved. And of course, the therapist should continue to provide the adolescent with one-on-one support.

Sometimes there are also secrets in teams, and the same approach can be taken. But it is quite possible that part of the team knows about the problem, and the other part does not. Then you could ask the part of the team that is initiated in the secret to reflect on what might be different if those who were uninitiated were let in on the secret. The uninitiated team members watch and listen, observe the discussion from a solution-oriented and resource-focused perspective, and in the next step reflect on what they have heard.

The secret usually comes out during these kinds of sessions, and the setting protects those involved, as the secret loses its threatening nature by tacitly becoming the focus of attention. Hypotheses are developed about what the secret might be, and these inevitably come up during the reflecting stage. This gives the initiated team members the possibility of having their say during their own reflection (see **Reflecting positions**, *page 143*).

But the goal of such reflective settings is in this case not to reveal the secret but to learn how to deal with the secret. If the secret *is* revealed during the process of finding a suitable way of dealing with it, it does not pose a threat, as it has been revealed in a safe environment.

When Nothing Seems to Work

Occasionally there are conversation situations in which nothing seems to work. Before stopping completely, the therapist or counselor still has the option of doing the impossible, for example:

- *Unsettle* the client, by doing something very unusual or completely unexpected.
- *Provoke*, by admitting that you don't know what to do anymore: *Do you have an idea, perhaps?*
- *Do something completely differently*—whatever you think of on the spur of the moment!
- *Mimic or exaggerate* what the client (usually a child) is doing, for example, also refuse to cooperate, look dismissive or dissatisfied, cross your arms in the same way, or be really loud . . .

The following interventions can also help get things back on track. However, with all interventions it is very important to proceed with respect—respect based on concern for the client's well-being and his future. Part of this respect involves, for example, asking for permission to try certain interventions, or to provoke the client:

- When tough decisions have to be made, tried and tested methods include **Resource memory** (see page 74) or rolling a die to make the decision and then testing out if the decision is the right one.
- When somebody constantly complains that he always makes the same decision in certain situations and is then annoyed by the decision, the **Rewind → Reset** (see page 181) intervention is indicated for the most recent annoying decision. This can also be adapted to the behavior of others, for example, in teams.

There are no limits to what you can do, as long as you respect the client!

The Concluding Question

At the end of a first session, but also at the end of subsequent sessions, it is a good idea to ask whether there is anything else important that the therapist should know about:

> *Thank you for letting me be involved in your situation. Is there anything that has not yet been discussed that I ought to know about? And if there is something, why would it be good to tell me about it?*

Sometimes this question brings about a surprising turn in events. But the question is by no means reserved for the first meeting. It can be asked at any stage of the therapy that seems appropriate.

Other Challenges

"I've Finished!": Determining When the Therapy or Counseling Should End

When therapy or counseling should come to an end is a frequently discussed issue. In fact, it is good when participants, for example, the parents, ask at the beginning how long the treatment is likely to last, as the question usually cannot be answered straight away and opens up the discussion.

As hard as many clients, family members, or other participants often find it to take the first step and make an appointment, it is often equally hard to end the therapy after they have waited so long to finally begin it. *How would you notice that it was a good thing to have been here?*

Some interventions, like **Scaling** (see page 81) or **The Miracle Question** (*see page 87*) can give an impression of how the participants rated their progress.

Oaklander (1999) points out a variety of criteria that indicate when a decision should be made to end therapy/counseling: parents/teachers notice a change in behavior, the child develops new interests or hobbies, or the sessions have come to seem a nuisance.

Of course, a lack of interest in the therapy or counseling can equally be a sign that the process should *not* end, but these signs at least invite all of the participants to take stock and to decide on the best course of action.

The reverse situation can of course also arise; that is, the therapist or counselor thinks the time has come to end the meetings, but the parent or child, or both, absolutely want to continue. *Can you explain why I might think our meetings can come to an end—while you are convinced we should continue?*

Sometimes it is the school or kindergarten teachers, or caregivers in other institutions, who have a completely different view about whether to end therapy or not. Then it is important to ask why this might be so.

Of course, it can also be that the therapy or counseling has been a success and the clients do not return because everything is going well. This is a hypothesis that the therapist or counselor should allow himself to have when patients do not return—until proven otherwise!

Last but Not Least

- If you get stuck in a rut, have patience. And faith.
- Change needs time. (And also a start!)
- Everything has more than two sides . . .
- Sometimes you have to/are allowed to take things literally!

- You don't need to know what the problem is in order to find a solution . . .

We wish you every success!

A case vignette: Short-term therapy spanning 16 years

Amy, 30 years old at the time and a resident in a facility for people with intellectual disabilities, came with a case history of a psychosis, "emotional incontinence" (characterized by uncontrollable displays of emotion), and a pronounced desire to be treated fairly. She had been living in the facility for over 10 years.

The acute reason for her referral was that she was constantly getting into fights in her residential unit, was not fulfilling her duties, and talked to herself, especially with a cassette recorder. In the first session she was very fearful, but it did not take long to dispel her fears, and she soon participated in the conversation.

The first step was a purely psychiatric diagnosis and treatment with appropriate medication, which worked well. Eight drops of a highly potent neuroleptic drug (four in the morning, four in the evening) were sufficient, and she stopped talking to herself.

This was the start of a short-term therapy that ended up lasting 16 years.

Once Amy had these psychotic aspects of her behavior under control, attention was turned to the group dynamic: There were lots of arguments in the group, and everybody watched everybody else to check whether they were doing what they were supposed to be doing.

Because Amy suffered most of all as a result of these fights, and the group suffered mostly as a result of Amy, the therapist gained Amy's permission to work with the whole group. A consensus was reached that everybody would do the duties they had been assigned, and Amy was given an **Observation task** as homework: *Please check that all of your housemates keep an eye on you to make sure that you fulfill your duties on time!*

The problem disappeared almost immediately and didn't recur for a long time. But other problems kept arising, or new problems took the place of old ones. For example, Amy suddenly started having uncontrollable crying fits and, at the same time, laughing fits. But as there were days when she did not have such episodes, she was asked to forecast whether she would have an episode the next day or not (*see The forecast calendar, page 108*). This resulted in a double success: She was able to make accurate forecasts, and the attacks abated.

Other Challenges   317

The basic requirement for a forecast intervention to be effective is, first, that the patient understands what a forecast is and, second, that the problem is not always present: There must be exceptions to the problem (*see **Asking about exceptions**, page 79*).

Subsequent reasons for Amy's repeated referral by the facility staff were sudden violent tantrums. The intervention used to relieve this situation was **Prescribing the symptom** (*see page 100*): Amy was asked to have a tantrum at least twice a day.

Several years later the crying fits returned, and this time they were even more persistent. As a placebo, she was prescribed a medication called "Pleurex," which is completely free of active ingredients. It was already a well-known fact that Amy was extremely fussy about taking her medication, and it was very important to her that her dosage was not increased. For example, oncoming psychotic attacks could be nipped in the bud by discussing a possible increase in the number of drops she had to take. She saw this as such a threat that she did everything she could to get her symptoms under control—and succeeded.

The intervention here was to ask a coping question: *How did you manage that?* Her simple answer: "I just carried on doing what I was doing and didn't think about it any more."

Another method used with Amy was the pie chart as a form of **Scaling** (*see page 81*). The scaling pie chart method was carefully explained to her, and despite her intellectual disability, she quickly got the hang of it. The pie chart can also be used for psychotherapeutic purposes, along the lines of *How happy are you with yourself at the moment, and can you cut out this piece from the pie?*

She did this very willingly and was also able to think about what she had to do to increase the size of the piece of pie. For example, she wanted to be friendlier to her housemates in the mornings, because she had noticed that they were then also friendlier to her.

There were also frequent group crises. At another group meeting about five years ago, one of the members of the group who was currently drawing negative attention to herself was asked to change something about her behavior so that everybody would notice an improvement (*see **Prescribing change**, page 102*). Because the affected person could not write, she whispered her intention into the therapist's ear. The others were given the **Observation task** of finding out what she had changed.

The atmosphere in the group changed immediately, and this also led to

The Therapist's Treasure Chest

the group thinking up these kinds of measures on their own. (Not to forget: all of the housemates had an intellectual disability!)

Amy is still receiving psychotherapeutic treatment, with meetings approximately every quarter, with the therapist sometimes being invited to the residential unit, for example, for dinner. The caregivers in the unit all confirmed that the group was very adept at organizing its microcosm.

For a therapist with many years' experience, this again impressively proved that mental disabilities and resource- and solution-oriented therapy are by no means a contradiction in terms. On the contrary, there is a strong synergy effect because these seemingly simple interventions increase the self-confidence of people with an intellectual disability to such an extent that they quickly get the feeling that they can deal with things themselves. Up to this point, they have grown up thinking "we need to be helped." They may have even experienced that others did not like it when they tried to come up with solutions themselves.

Achieving this also requires a solution-oriented team that is willing and able to see past the intellectual disability to the treasure trove of abilities that these people possess, and to be positively surprised on a daily basis.

And on that note: Prepare to be amazed!

Select Bibliography

Andersen, T. (Ed.) (1990). *Das Reflektierende Team. Dialoge und Dialoge über die Dialoge* [*The reflecting team. Dialogues and dialogues about the dialogues*]. Dortmund: Verlag Modernes Lernen.

Andrecht, U., & Geiken, G. (1999). Ressourcenorientierte Familiendiagnostik in der Kinder- und Jugendpsychiatrie [Resource-oriented family diagnostics in child and adolescent psychiatry]. In Vogt-Hillmann, M., & Burr, W. (Eds.), *Kinderleichte Lösungen: Lösungsorientierte Kreative Kindertherapie* [*Simple solutions: Solution-oriented creative child therapy*]. Dortmund: Borgmann.

Antonovsky, A. (1997). *Salutogenese. Zur Entmystifizierung der Gesundheit* [*Salutogenesis: On demystifying health issues*]. Tübingen: DGVT-Verlag.

Backhausen, W., & Thommen, J. P. (2006). *Coaching. Durch systemisches Denken zu innovativer Personalentwicklung* [*Coaching: Using systematic thinking to achieve innovative personnel development*]. Wiesbaden: Gabler Verlag.

Banner, A. S. (1986). Cough. Physiology, evaluation, and treatment. *Lung, 164,* 74–92.

Barkley, R. A., Murphy, K. R., & Fischer, M. (2008). *ADHD in adults: What the science says.* New York: Guilford.

Barkmann, C., Romer, G., Watson, M., & Schulte-Markwort, M. (2007). Parental Physical Illness as a risk for psychosocial maladjustment in children and adolescents: Epidemiological findings from a national survey in Germany. *Psychosomatics, 48,* 476–481.

Bauer, C., & Hegemann, T. (2010). *Ich schaffs!—Cool ans Ziel: Das lösungsorientierte Programm für die Arbeit mit Jugendlichen* [*I can do it! Achieving goals the cool way: The solution-oriented program for working with adolescents*] (2nd ed.). Heidelberg: Carl-Auer.

Baving, L. (2006). *Störungen des Sozialverhaltens* [*Social behavior disorders*]. Heidelberg: Springer.

Baving, L. (2008). Aggressiv-dissoziales Verhalten [Aggressive-dissocial behavior]. In Petermann, F. (Ed.), *Lehrbuch der Klinischen Kinderpsychologie* [*Handbook of clinical child psychology*] (6th ed.). Göttingen: Hogrefe.

Beaulieu, D. (2010). *Impact-Techniken für die Psychotherapie* [*Impact techniques for psychotherapy*] (4th ed.). Heidelberg: Carl-Auer.

Berg, I. K., & de Shazer, S. (1998). *Kurzzeittherapie—Von Problemen zu Lösungen* [*Brief therapy—from problems to solutions*] (DVD). Düsseldorf: Auditorium Netzwerk.

Beushausen, J. (2010) Ressourcenorientierte stabilisierende Interventionen [Resource-oriented Stabilizing Interventions]. Kontext, 41, 287–307.

Bode, H. (2009a). Hochbegabung [Giftedness]. In Bode, H., Straßburg, H. M., & Hollmann, H. (Eds.), Sozialpädiatrie in der Praxis [Social pediatrics in practice]. Munich: Urban & Fischer Verlag.

Bode, H. (2009b). Soziale Lage und Gesundheit von Kindern und Jugendlichen [Social background and health of children and adolescents]. In Bode, H., Straßburg, H. M., & Hollmann, H. (Eds.), Sozialpädiatrie in der Praxis [Social pediatrics in practice]. Munich: Urban & Fischer Verlag.

Bonney, H. (2003). Kinder und Jugendliche in der familientherapeutischen Praxis [Children and adolescents in family therapeutic practice]. Heidelberg: Carl-Auer.

Brett, D. (1998). Anna zähmt die Monster: Therapeutische Geschichten für Kinder [Anna tames the monster: Therapeutic stories for children] (5th ed.). Salzhausen: Iskopress.

Brock, I. (2010). Geschwister und ihr Einfluss auf die Entwicklung sozialer und emotionaler Kompetenz [Siblings and their influence on the development of social and emotional competency]. Familiendynamik, 35, 310–317.

Caby, A., & Caby, F. (2010a). Eltern stärken [Empowering parents]. In Romeike, G., & Imelmann, H. (Eds.), Eltern verstehen und stärken. Analyse und Konzepte der Erziehungsberatung [Understanding and empowering parents. Analysis and concepts of parenting counseling]. Weinheim and Munich: Beltz Juventa.

Caby, A., & Caby, F. (2010b). Psychotherapeutische Kniffe für den ergotherapeutischen Alltag. Erfahrungen aus der systemisch-lösungsorientierten Arbeit mit Kindern, Jugendlichen und Familien [Psychotherapeutic tricks for everyday occupational therapy. Experiences from systemic solution-oriented work with children, adolescents, and families]. Praxis Ergotherapie, 23(1), 18–22.

Caby, A., Hubert-Schnelle, C., & Caby, F. (2005). Ressourcen- und lösungsorientierte Sprache im Tagesklinischen Setting am Beispiel von Reflektierender Gruppentherapie [Resource- and solution-oriented language in a day unit setting using the example of reflecting group therapy]. Zeitschrift für Systemische Therapie und Beratung, 23(3), 187–192.

Caby, A., Vrdoljak, S., Hubert-Schnelle, C., & Caby, F. (2009). Reflektierende Familien (RF) im Tagesklinischen Setting [Reflecting families (RF) in a day unit setting]. Forum für Kinder- und Jugendpsychiatrie, Psychosomatik und Psychotherapie, 3, 6–13.

Caby, F. (2001). Aspekte einer systemischen Gruppentherapie [Aspects of a systemic group therapy]. In Rotthaus, W. (Ed.), Systemische Kinder- und Jugendlichenpsychotherapie [Systemic child and adolescent psychotherapy]. Heidelberg: Carl-Auer-Systeme.

Caby, F. (2002). Die Gruppe als System [The group as a system]. In Vogt-Hillmann, M., & Burr, W. (Eds.), Lösungen im Jugendstil: Systemisch-lösungsorientierte Kreative Kinder- und Jugendlichentherapie [Child-appropriate solutions: Systemic solution-oriented creative child and adolescent therapy]. Dortmund: Borgmann.

Caby, F. (2008). Reflektierende Familien oder: Bench-Marking für Familiensysteme [Reflecting families or: Bench-marking for family systems]. Forum für Kinder- und Jugendpsychiatrie, Psychosomatik und Psychotherapie, 4, 46–59.

Castrogiovanni, A. (2008). Incidence and prevalence of communication disorders and hearing loss in children. American Speech-Language-Hearing Association. Retrieved from http://www.asha.org/research/reports/children.htm.

De Jong, P., & Berg, I. K. (2008). Interviewing for solutions (3rd ed). Belmont, CA: Brooks/Cole.

Delfos, M. F. (2004). *"Sag mir mal . . ." Gesprächsführung mit Kindern* [*"Tell me . . ." conversations with children*]. Weinheim and Basel: Beltz.

Delfos, M. F. (2007). *"Wie meinst Du das?" Gesprächsführung mit Jugendlichen (13–18 Jahre).* [*"What do you mean by that?" Conversation techniques with adolescents (aged 13–18)*]. Weinheim and Basel: Beltz.

De Shazer, S. (1989). *Wege der erfolgreichen Kurztherapie* [*Effective brief therapy methods*]. Stuttgart: Klett-Cotta.

De Shazer, S. (1997). *Der Dreh: Überraschende Wendungen und Lösungen in der Kurzzeittherapie* [*Clues. Investigating solutions in brief therapy*] (5th ed.). Heidelberg: Carl-Auer.

De Shazer, S. (1998). *Das Spiel mit den Unterschieden: Wie therapeutische Lösungen lösen* [*Putting difference to work*]. Heidelberg: Carl-Auer.

De Shazer, S., & Berg, I. K. (1992). *Solution-focused therapy.* Classes at the Brief Therapy Institute. Milwaukee, WI.

De Shazer, S., & Dolan, Y. (2008). *Mehr als ein Wunder: Lösungsfokussierte Kurztherapie heute* [*More than miracles: The state of the art of solution-focused brief therapy*]. Heidelberg: Carl-Auer.

Döpfner, M., Banaschewski, T., & Sonuga-Barke, E. (2008). Aufmerksamkeitsdefizit-/Hyperaktivitätsstörungen (ADHS) [Attention deficit/hyperactivity disorders (ADHD)]. In Petermann, F. (Ed.), *Lehrbuch der Klinischen Kinderpsychologie* [*Handbook of clinical child psychology*] (6th ed.). Göttingen: Hogrefe.

Duncan, B. L., & Miller, S. D. (2003). Die Veränderungstheorie des Klienten: Den Klienten im integrativen Prozess beratend um Rat fragen [The client's theory of change: Consulting the client in the integrative process]. In Schemmel, H., & Schaller, J. (Eds.), *Ressourcen: Ein Hand- und Lesebuch zur therapeutischen Arbeit* [*Resources: A therapy handbook*]. Tübingen: DGVT-Verlag.

Durrant, M. (1996). *Auf die Stärken kannst du bauen: Lösungsorientierte Arbeit in Heimen und anderen stationären Settings* [*You can build on your strengths: Solution-oriented work in homes and other inpatient settings*]. Dortmund: Verlag Modernes Lernen.

Färber, H. (1983). Preface to *Integrative Therapie mit geistig und psychisch behinderten Kindern und Jugendlichen* [*Integrative therapy with mentally and intellectually disabled children and adolescents*]. Dortmund: Verlag Modernes Lernen.

Fehm, L., & Helbig-Lang, S. (2009). Hausaufgaben in der Psychotherapie [Homework in psychotherapy]. *Psychotherapeut, 54*(5), 377–392.

Foerster, v. H. (1993). *KybernEthik* [*Cyberethics*]. Berlin: Merve.

Freud, S. (1969–1975). Der Humor [Humor] (1927). In Mitscherlich, A., et al. (Eds.), *Freud—Studienausgabe Volume 4. Psychologische Schriften* [*Freud—student edition, Vol. 4, Psychological writings*]. Frankfurt am Main: Nabu Press.

Fuhrmann, P., Schreiner-Zink, S., & von Gontard, A. (2008). Störungen der Ausscheidung: Einnässen und Einkoten [Excretion disorders: Enuresis and encopresis]. In Petermann, F. (Ed.), *Lehrbuch der Klinischen Kinderpsychologie* [*Handbook of clinical child psychology*] (6th ed.). Göttingen: Hogrefe.

Furman, B. (2008a). *Es ist nie zu spät, eine glückliche Kindheit zu haben* [*It's never too late to have a happy childhood*] (5th ed.). Dortmund: Borgmann.

Furman, B. (2008b). *Ich schaff! Spielerisch und praktisch Lösungen mit Kindern finden—Das 15-Schritte-Programm für Eltern, Erzieher und Therapeuten* [*Kids' skills—playful and practical solution-finding with children*] (3rd ed.). Heidelberg: Carl-Auer.

Furman, B. (2011). Ich schaffs! [I can do it!] Workshop presented in Aschendorf, May 16.

Gaulier, B., Margerum, J., Price, J. A., & Windell, J. (2007). *Defusing the high-conflict divorce. A treatment handbook for working with angry couples.* Atascadero, CA: Impact Publishers.

Görlitz, G. (2005). *Psychotherapie für Kinder und Familien: Übungen und Materialien für die Arbeit mit Eltern und Bezugspersonen* [Psychotherapy for children and families: Exercises and materials for working with children and caregivers]. Stuttgart: Pfeiffer bei Klett-Cotta.

Grabbe, M., & Wilson, J. (2010). Seminar presented at the ten-year anniversary of the North German Institute of Brief Therapy, Berlin, June 19.

Günter, M. (2004). Chronische Krankheiten und psychische Beteiligung [Chronic illnesses and psychological aspects]. In Eggers, C., Fegert, J. M., & Resch, F. (Eds.), *Psychiatrie und Psychotherapie des Kindes- und Jugendalters* [Psychiatry and psychotherapy of children and adolescents]. Heidelberg: Springer.

Haley, J. (1991). *Problem-solving therapy* (2nd ed.). Hoboken, NJ.

Hargens, J. (2000). Von Lösungen, Möglichkeiten, Ressourcen und Problemen. Respektieren und Infragestellen von Unterschieden [Solutions, possibilities, resources and problems. respecting and questioning differences]. In Hargens, J., & Eberling, W. (Eds.), *Einfach kurz und gut. Teil 2. Ressourcen erkennen und nutzen* [Short and sweet. Part 2. Recognizing and using resources]. Dortmund: Borgmann.

Hargens, J. (2003). *Systemische Therapie . . . und gut. Ein Lehrstück mit Hägar* [Systemic therapy . . . and good. A lesson with Hägar]. Dortmund: Verlag Modernes Lernen.

Hargens, J., & Eberling, W. (Eds.) (2000). *Einfach kurz und gut, Teil 2: Ressourcen erkennen und nutzen* [In a nutshell: Recognizing and using resources]. Dortmund: Borgmann.

Hargens, J., & v. Schlippe, A. (Eds.) (2002). *Das Spiel der Ideen. Reflektierendes Team und systemische Praxis* [Playing with ideas. Reflecting teams and systemic practice] (2nd ed.). Dortmund: Verlag Modernes Lernen.

Hirschberg, R. (2007). Das Problem-Lösungsbild [The problem-solution picture]. In Vogt, M. (Ed.), *Wenn Lösungen Gestalt annehmen: Externalisieren in der kreativen Kindertherapie* [When solutions take on a form: Externalization in creative child therapy]. Dortmund: Borgmann.

Hobday, A., & Ollier, K. (2001). *Helfende Spiele: Kreative Lebens- und Konfliktberatung von Kindern und Jugendlichen* [Helpful games: Creative life and conflict coaching for children and adolescents]. Weinheim and Basel: Beltz.

Höfkes, A., Trahe, U., & Trepte, A. (2004). *Alltagssituationen spielend meistern* [Simple ways of mastering everyday situations]. Dortmund: Verlag Modernes Lernen.

Holtz, K. L., & Mrochen, S. (2005). *Einführung in die Hypnotherapie mit Kindern und Jugendlichen* [Introduction to hypnotherapy with children and adolescents]. Heidelberg: Carl-Auer.

Holtz K. L., Mrochen, S., Nemetschek, P., & Trenkle, B. (Eds.) (2007). *Neugierig aufs Großwerden: Praxis der Hypnotherapie mit Kindern und Jugendlichen* [Excited about growing up: Using hypnotherapy with children and adolescents] (3rd ed.). Heidelberg: Carl-Auer.

Horn, W. R. (2009). Spezielle Jugendmedizinische Aspekte [Special pediatric aspects]. In Schlack, H. G., Thyen, U., & von Kries, R. (Eds.), *Sozialpädiatrie. Gesundheitswissenschaft und pädiatrischer Alltag* [Social pediatrics, health sciences, and everyday pediatric practice]. Heidelberg: Springer.

Isebaert, L., et al. (2005). *Kurzzeittherapie—ein praktisches Handbuch: Die gesundheitsorientierte kognitive Therapie* [Brief therapy—a practical handbook: Health-oriented cognitive therapy]. Stuttgart: Thieme.

Johnson, L. D. (2001). Strategic and solution-focused treatment of depression. In Geary, B. B., & Zeig, J. K. (Eds.), *The handbook of Ericksonian psychotherapy.* Phoenix, AZ: Milton H. Erickson Foundation Press.

Kindl-Beilfuß, C. (2008). *Fragen können wie Küsse schmecken. Systemische Fragetechniken für Anfänger und Fortgeschrittene [Questions can taste like kisses. Systemic questioning for beginners and advanced practitioners]*. Heidelberg: Carl-Auer.

Kriz, J. (2008). Systemische Grundlagen der Eltern-Kleinkind-Beratung [Systemic foundations of parent-young child counseling]. In Borke, J., & Eickhorst, A. (Eds.), *Systemische Entwicklungsberatung in der frühen Kindheit [Systemic development counseling in early childhood]*. Stuttgart: UTB.

Krowatschek, D., Albrecht, S., & Krowatschek, G. (2007a). *Marburger Konzentrationstraining für Schulkinder [Marburg concentration training for school children]*. Dortmund: Verlag Modernes Lernen.

Krowatschek, D., & Hengst, U. (2006). *Mit dem Zauberteppich unterwegs. Entspannung in Schule, Gruppe und Therapie für Kinder und Jugendliche [Working with a magic carpet. Relaxation at school, in groups, and in therapy with children and adolescents]*. Dortmund: Verlag Modernes Lernen.

Krowatschek, D., Krowatschek, G., & Wingert, G. (2007b). *Marburger Konzentrationstraining für Jugendliche (MKT-J) [Marburg concentration training for adolescents (MCT-A)]*. Dortmund: Verlag Modernes Lernen.

Lange, K. (2011). Schulung und psychosoziale Betreuung von Kindern und Jugendlichen mit Diabetes [Instruction and psychosocial care of children and adolescents with diabetes]. *Kinderärztliche Praxis, 82*, 29–34.

Lauth, G. W., Grünke, M., & Brumstein, J. C. (2004). *Interventionen bei Lernstörungen. Förderung, Training und Therapie in der Praxis [Interventions for learning disorders. facilitation, training, and therapy in practice]*. Göttingen: Hogrefe-Verlag.

Lee, S.-H., von Stülpnagel, C., & Heinen, F. (2006). Therapie der Migräne im Kindesalter—Update [Therapy of migraines in children—update]. *Monatschr Kinderheilkd, 154*, 764–772.

Lenz, A. (2008). *Interventionen bei Kindern psychisch kranker Eltern. Grundlagen, Diagnostik und therapeutische Maßnahmen [Interventions with children of mentally ill parents. Essentials, diagnostics and therapeutic measures]*. Göttingen: Hogrefe-Verlag.

Levold, T. (2006). Metaphern und Resilienz [Metaphors and resilience]. In Welter-Enderlin, R., & Hildenbrand, B. (Eds.), *Resilienz—Gedeihen trotz widriger Umstände [Resilience—thriving despite adverse circumstances]*. Heidelberg: Carl-Auer.

Ludewig, K. (2002). *Leitmotive systemischer Therapie [Leitmotifs of systemic therapy]*. Stuttgart: Klett-Cotta.

Ludewig, K. (2005). *Einführung in die theoretischen Grundlagen der systemischen Therapie [Introduction to the theoretical foundations of systemic therapy]*. Heidelberg: Carl-Auer.

Ludewig, K., & Wilken, U. (Eds.) (2000). *Das Familienbrett. Ein Verfahren für die Forschung und Praxis mit Familien und anderen sozialen Systemen [The family board. An approach to research and practice with families and other social systems]*. Göttingen: Hogrefe.

Minuchin, S. (1997). *Familie und Familientherapie. Theorie und Praxis struktureller Familientherapie [Families and family therapy—structural family therapy in theory and practice]* (10th ed.). Freiburg: Lambertus-Verlag.

Mrochen, S. (1997). In Mrochen, S., Holtz, K. L., & Trenkle, B. (Eds.) *Die Pupille des Bettnässers: Hypnotherapeutische Arbeit mit Kindern und Jugendlichen [The Eye of the bed-wetter: Hypnotherapy work with children and adolescents]* (3rd ed.). Heidelberg: Carl-Auer.

Mrochen, S., & Bierbaum-Luttermann, H. (2007). Beziehungsaufbau und Beziehungsgestaltung. Rapport mit Kindern . . . [Establishing and structuring relationships. Rapport with children . . .]. In Holtz, K. L., Mrochen, S., Nemetschek, P., & Trenkle, B. (Eds.), *Neugierig aufs Großw-*

erden. *Praxis der Hypnotherapie mit Kindern und Jugendlichen* [*Excited about growing up. Using hypnotherapy with children and adolescents*] (3rd ed.). Heidelberg: Carl-Auer.

Nagy, G. (2006). s.v. Figurative idioms. *Thesaurus of English Idioms*. Puchong: Tinta..

Nardone, G. (2003). *Systemische Kurztherapie bei Zwängen und Phobien. Einführung in die Kunst der Lösung komplizierter Probleme mit einfachen Mitteln* [*Systemic brief therapy with compulsions and phobias. Introduction to the art of solving complicated problems using simple means*] (2nd ed.). Bern: Verlag Hans Huber.

Nemetschek, P. (2006). *Systemische Familientherapie mit Kindern, Jugendlichen und Eltern: Lebensfluss-Modelle und analoge Methoden* [*Systemic family therapy with children, adolescents, and parents: Stream of life models and analog methods*]. Stuttgart: Klett-Cotta.

Neumeyer, A. (2000). *Mit Feengeist und Zauberpuste—Zauberhaftes Arbeiten in Pädagogik und Therapie* [*Fairy spirits and magic dust—working with magical methods in pedagogy and therapy*]. Freiburg: Lambertus.

Nicholson, J., Biebel, K., Williams, V. F., & Katz-Leavy, J. (2002). Prevalence of parenthood in adults with mental illness: Implications for state and federal policy, programs, and providers. In Manderscheid, R. W., & Henderson, M. J. (Eds.), *Mental health, United States, 2002*, pp. 120–137. Rockville, MD: Substance Abuse and Mental Health Services Administration.

Nicolai, T., & Griese, M. (Eds.) (2011). *Praktische Pneumologie in der Pädiatrie—Diagnostik* [*Practical pneumology in pediatrics*]. Stuttgart: Thieme.

Nitzko, S. (2010). Übergewicht und Adipositas in Kindheit und Jugend. [Obesity and adiposity in childhood and adolescence]. *Praxis der Kinderpsychologie und Kinderpsychiatrie, 59*, 831–851.

Noeker, M. (2008). Funktionelle und somatoforme Störungen [Functional and somatoform disorders]. In Petermann, F. (Ed.), *Lehrbuch der klinischen Kinderpsychologie* [*Handbook of clinical child psychology*] (6th ed.). Göttingen: Hogrefe.

Oaklander, V. (1999). *Gestalttherapie mit Kindern und Jugendlichen* [*Gestalt therapy with children and adolescents*] (11th ed.). Stuttgart: Klett-Cotta.

Ogden C. L., Carroll M. D., Kit B. K., & Flegal K. M. (2012). Prevalence of obesity and trends in body mass index among US children and adolescents, 1999–2010. *Journal of the American Medical Association, 307*(5), 483–490.

Petermann, U., & Petermann, F. (2007). Aggressives Verhalten [Aggressive behavior]. *Monatsschrift Kinderheilkunde, 155*, 928–936.

Petermann, U., & Suhr-Dachs, L. (2008). Soziale Phobie [Social phobia]. In Petermann, F. (Ed.), *Lehrbuch der Klinischen Kinderpsychologie* [*Handbook of clinical child psychology*] (6th ed.). Göttingen: Hogrefe.

Petermann, F., & Winkel, S. (2009). *Selbstverletzendes Verhalten* [*Self-harming behavior*]. Göttingen: Hogrefe.

Pfeiffer, U. (2008). Die Behandlung von traumatisierten Kindern und Jugendlichen [The treatment of traumatized children and adolescents]. *Kinder- und Jugendmedizin, 8*, 13–17.

Prior, M. (2009). *Minimax—Interventionen* [*Minimax—interventions*] (8th ed.). Heidelberg: Carl-Auer.

Rabenschlag, U. (1998). *Kinder reisen durch die Nacht* [*Children travel through the night*]. Freiburg: Herder.

Reichelt-Nauseef, S., & Heidbreder, C. (2009). *Weiterbildungskurs WB-S7* [*Further training FT-S7*]. Hamburg: Institut für Systemische Studien.

Reinehr, T., Dobe, M., & Kersting, M. (2003). *Therapie der Adipositas im Kindes- und Jugendalter. Das*

Adipositas-Schulungsprogramm OBELDICKS [*Therapy of adiposity in children and adolescents. the adiposity training program obeldicks*]. Göttingen: Hogrefe.

Renner, C. (2005). *Stark fürs Leben—Geistiges Karate für Kinder. Ein lösungsorientierter Ansatz in der Kindertherapie* [*Strong for life—mental karate for children. A solution-oriented approach in child therapy*]. Stuttgart: Klett-Cotta.

Resch, F., & Brunner, R. (2004). Posttraumatische Belastungsstörung, Anpassungsstörungen und Selbstbeschädigungserkrankungen [Posttraumatic stress disorder, adjustment disorders, and self-harming disorders]. In Eggers, C., Fegert, J. M., & Resch, F. (Eds.), *Psychiatrie und Psychotherapie des Kindes- und Jugendalters* [*Psychiatry and psychotherapy of children and adolescents*]. Heidelberg: Springer.

Resch, F., & Richterich, A. (2004). Weitere psychische Störungen mit körperlicher Symptomatik [Other psychiatric disorders with physical symptoms]. In Eggers, C., Fegert, J. M., & Resch, F. (Eds.), *Psychiatrie und Psychotherapie des Kindes- und Jugendalters* [*Psychiatry and psychotherapy of children and adolescents*]. Heidelberg: Springer.

Retzlaff, R. (2008). *Spiel-Räume: Lehrbuch der systemischen Therapie mit Kindern und Jugendlichen* [*Play-rooms: Handbook of systematic therapy with children and adolescents*]. Stuttgart: Klett-Cotta.

Retzlaff, R. (2010). *Familien-Stärken. Behinderung, Resilienz und systemische Therapie* [*Family strengths. Disabilities, resilience, and systemic therapy*]. Stuttgart: Klett-Cotta.

Rieger, C., v. d. Hardt, H., Sennhauser, F. H., Wahn, U., & Zach, M. (Eds.) (1999). *Pädiatrische Pneumologie* [*Pediatric pneumology*]. Berlin: Springer.

Ronan, K., & Kazantzis, N. (2006). The use of between-session (homework) activities in psychotherapy: Conclusions from the *Journal of Psychotherapy* [Electronic version]. *Journal of Psychotherapy Integration, 16*(2), 254–259.

Rosen, S. (2009). *Die Lehrgeschichten von Milton H. Erickson. Herausgegeben und kommentiert von Sidney Rosen* [*The teaching tales of Milton H. Erickson*]. Edited and annotated by Sidney Rosen (8th ed.). Salzhausen: Iskopress.

Rotthaus, W. (1996). Systemische Therapie mit geistig behinderten Menschen [Systemic therapy with mentally disabled people]. *Behinderte in Familie, Schule und Gesellschaft, 19*, 45–52.

Rotthaus, W. (Ed.) (2005). *Systemische Kinder- und Jugendlichenpsychotherapie* [*Systemic Child and Adolescent Psychotherapy*]. Heidelberg: Carl-Auer.

Rutter, M. (2000). Resilience reconsidered. Conceptual considerations, empirical findings, and policy implications. In Shonkoff, J. P., & Meisels, S. J. (Eds.), *Handbook of early childhood intervention*. Cambridge: Cambridge University.

Ryan, T., & Walker, R. (2004). *Wo gehöre ich hin? Biografiearbeit mit Kindern und Jugendlichen* [*Where do I belong? Biographical work with children and adolescents*] (3rd ed.). Weinheim and Munich: Beltz.

Sarimski, K. (2005). *Psychische Störungen bei behinderten Kindern und Jugendlichen* [*Mental disorders in disabled children*]. Göttingen: Hogrefe.

Sarimski, K., & Steinhausen, H. C. (2008). *Psychische Störungen bei geistiger Behinderung* [*Mental disorders in disabled children*]. Göttingen: Hogrefe.

Scheer, P., et al. (2007). Essstörungen des Kindes- und Jugendalters [Eating disorders in childhood and adolescence]. *Monatsschrift Kinderheilkunde, 155*, 804–810.

Schemmel, H., & Schaller, J. (2003). *Ressourcen: Ein Hand- und Lesebuch zur therapeutischen Arbeit* [*Resources: A handbook and reading book of therapeutic work*]. Tübingen: DGVT-Verlag.

Select Bibliography

Schiepek, G., & Cremers, S. (2003). Ressourcenorientierung und Ressourcendiagnostik in der Psychotherapie [Resource orientation and resource diagnostics in psychotherapy]. In Schemmel, H., & Schaller, J. (Eds.), *Ressourcen: Ein Hand- und Lesebuch zur therapeutischen Arbeit* [Resources: A handbook and reading book of therapeutic work]. Tübingen: DGVT-Verlag.

Schmidt, M. H. (2008). Interaktionsstörungen [Interaction disorders]. In Petermann, F. (Ed.), *Lehrbuch der Klinischen Kinderpsychologie* [Handbook of clinical child psychology] (6th ed.). Göttingen: Hogrefe.

Schneider, S. (2004). Angststörungen [Anxiety disorders]. In Eggers, C., Fegert, J., & Resch, F. (Eds.), *Psychiatrie und Psychotherapie des Kindes- und Jugendalters* [Psychiatry and psychotherapy with children and adolescents]. Berlin: Springer.

Schone, R., & Wagenblass, S. (2006). *Wenn Eltern psychisch krank sind . . . Kindliche Lebenswelten und institutionelle Handlungsmuster* [When parents are mentally ill . . . children's experiences and institutional patterns of action] (2nd ed.). Weinheim and Munich: Beltz Juventa.

Schulz von Thun, F. (1998). *Miteinander reden: 3. Das "Innere Team" und situationsgerechte Kommunikation. Kommunikation, Person, Situation* [Talking to each other: 3. The "inner team" and appropriate communication. Communication, person, situation]. Reinbek bei Hamburg: Rororo.

Selekman, M. D. (1997). *Solution-focused therapy with children: Harnessing family strengths for systemic change.* New York: Guilford.

Sickinger, G. (2000). Behindert—na und? Systemisch-lösungsorientiertes Arbeiten mit Mitarbeitern im Behindertenbereich—ein Erfahrungsbericht [And? systemic solution-oriented work with employees working with the disabled—a report]. In Hargens, J., & Eberling, W. (Eds.), *Einfach kurz und gut. Teil 2. Ressourcen erkennen und nutzen* [Short and sweet. Part 2. Recognizing and using resources]. Dortmund: Borgmann.

Sieh D. S., Meijer A. M., Oort F. J., Visser-Meily J. M., & Van der Leij D. A. (2010). Problem behavior in children of chronically ill parents: A meta-analysis. *Clinical Child and Family Psychology Review, 13*(4), 384–397.

Simon, F. B., & Rech-Simon, C. (2001). *Zirkuläres Fragen. Systemische Therapie in Fallbeispielen: Ein Lehrbuch* [Circular questioning. Systemic therapy in case studies: A handbook] (4th ed.). Heidelberg: Carl-Auer.

Steil, R., & Rosner, R. (2009). *Posttraumatische Belastungsstörung. Leitfaden Kinder- und Jugendpsychotherapie* [Posttraumatic stress disorder. A handbook for child and adolescent psychotherapy]. Göttingen: Hogrefe.

Steiner, T., & Berg, I. K. (2005). *Handbuch Lösungsorientiertes Arbeiten mit Kindern* [Handbook of solution-oriented work with children]. Heidelberg: Carl-Auer.

Strassburg, H. M. (2000). Logopädische Beurteilung und Therapie [Speech assessment and therapy]. In Strassburg, H. M., Dacheneder, W., & Kreß, W. (Eds.), *Entwicklungsstörungen bei Kindern* [Developmental disorders in children] (2nd ed.). Munich: Jena.

Taussig, L. M., & Landau, L. I. (Eds.) (1999). *Pediatric respiratory medicine.* St. Louis, MO: Mosby.

Thyen, U., Szczepanski, R., Krötz, V., & Kuske, M. (2009). Chronische Gesundheitsstörungen [Chronic health disorders]. In Schlack, H. G., Thyen, U., & von Kries, R. (Eds.), *Sozialpädiatrie. Gesundheitswissenschaft und pädiatrischer Alltag* [Social pediatrics. Health sciences and everyday pediatric practice]. Heidelberg: Springer.

Titze, M., & Eschenröder, C. T. (2007). *Therapeutischer Humor* [Therapeutic humor] (5th ed.). Frankfurt: Grundlagen Anwendungen.

Trapmann, H., & Rotthaus, W. (2003). *Auffälliges Verhalten im Kindesalter. Handbuch für Eltern und*

Erzieher—Band I [*Conspicuous behavior in children. A handbook for parents and teachers*, Vol. I]. Dortmund: Verlag Modernes Lernen.

Vogt, M., & Caby, F. (2010). *Ressourcenorientierte Gruppentherapie mit Kindern und Jugendlichen* [*Resource-oriented group therapy with children and adolescents*]. Dortmund: Verlag Modernes Lernen.

Vogt, M., Hubert-Schnelle, C., & Clavée, S. (2010). Brüderchen und Schwesterchen. Geschwisterbeziehungen als Kraftquellen nutzen [Brothers and sisters. Using sibling relationships as sources of strength]. *Familiendynamik, 35,* 318–326.

Vogt, M., Nelle, A. C., Eberling, W., Burr, W., & Decker, R. (2003). Ressourcenorientierte Gruppentherapie für Kinder suchtkranker Eltern—Skizze eines Angebots [Resource-oriented group therapy for children of addicted parents—outline of an offer]. In Schemmel, H., & Schaller, J. (Eds.), *Ressourcen: Ein Hand- und Lesebuch zur therapeutischen Arbeit* [*Resources: A handbook and reading book of therapeutic work*]. Tübingen: DGVT-Verlag.

Vogt-Hillmann, M., & Burr, W. (2009a). *Kinderleichte Lösungen. Lösungsorientierte Kreative Kindertherapie* [*Simple solutions: Solution-oriented creative child therapy*]. Dortmund: Verlag Modernes Lernen.

Vogt-Hillmann, M., & Burr, W. (Eds.) (2009b). *Lösungen im Jugendstil. Systemisch-lösungsorientierte Kreative Kinder- und Jugendlichentherapie* [*Child-appropriate solutions. Systemic solution-oriented creative therapy for children and adolescents*]. Dortmund: Borgmann.

Vogt-Hillmann, M., Eberling, W., & Burr, W. (1999). Kinderleichte Lösungen [Simple solutions for children]. In Vogt-Hillmann, M., & Burr, W. (Eds.), *Kinderleichte Lösungen: Lösungsorientierte Kreative Kindertherapie* [*Simple solutions: Solution-oriented creative child therapy*]. Dortmund: Borgmann.

von Kisbed, V. (2008). Foreword. In de Shazer, S., & Dolan, Y. (Eds.), *Mehr als ein Wunder. Lösungsfokussierte Kurzzeittherapie heute* [*More than miracles: The state of the art of solution-focused brief therapy*]. Heidelberg: Carl-Auer.

von Schlippe, A., & Schweitzer, J. (1999). *Lehrbuch der systemischen Therapie und Beratung* [*Handbook of systemic therapy and counseling*] (6th ed.). Göttingen: Vandenhoeck & Ruprecht.

von Schlippe, A., & Schweitzer, J. (2007). *Lehrbuch der systemischen Therapie und Beratung II. Das störungsspezifische Wissen* [*Handbook of systemic therapy and counseling II. Disorder-specific knowledge*]. Göttingen: Vandenhoeck & Ruprecht.

von Schlippe, A., & Schweitzer, J. (2009). *Systemische Interventionen* [*Systemic interventions*]. Göttingen: Vandenhoeck & Ruprecht.

Walter, J. L., & Peller, J. E. (1994). *Lösungsorientierte Kurztherapie. Ein Lehr- und Lernbuch. Band 9, Systemische Studien* [*Solution-oriented brief therapy. A handbook and study guide*, Vol. 9, *Systemic studies*]. Dortmund: Verlag Modernes Lernen.

Walter, J., & Schmid, G. (2009). Kinder und Jugendliche mit psychischen Störungen und Entwicklungsauffälligkeiten [Children and adolescents with mental disorders and developmental problems]. In Schlack, H. G., et al. (Eds.), *Sozialpädiatrie. Gesundheitswissenschaft und pädiatrischer Alltag* [*Social pediatrics. Health science and everyday pediatric practice*]. Heidelberg: Springer.

Warschburger, P., Petermann, F., & Fromme, C. (2005). *Adipositas. Training mit Kindern und Jugendlichen* [*Adiposity. Training with children and adolescents*] (2nd ed.). Weinheim and Basel: Beltz.

Watzlawick, P. (1983). *Anleitung zum Unglücklichsein* [*A guide to unhappiness*]. Munich: Piper Taschenbuch.

Select Bibliography

Watzlawick, P. (1999). In Döring-Meijer, H. (Ed.), *Ressourcenorientierung— Lösungsorientierung: Etwas mehr Spaß und Leichtigkeit in der systemischen Therapie und Beratung* [Resource-oriented—solution-oriented: More fun and humor in systemic therapy and counseling]. Göttingen: Vandenhoeck & Ruprecht.

Welter-Enderlin, R. (2004). In Welter-Enderlin, R., & Hildenbrand, B. (Eds.), *Rituale— Vielfalt in Alltag und Therapie* [*Rituals—diversity in daily life and therapy*] (2nd ed.). Heidelberg: Carl-Auer.

Wendlandt, W. (2002). *Therapeutische Hausaufgaben. Materialien für die Eigenarbeit und das Selbsttraining. Eine Anleitung für Therapeuten, Betroffene, Eltern und Erzieher* [*Therapeutic homework. Materials for independent work and self-training. An instruction manual for therapists, caregivers, parents, and teachers*]. Stuttgart: Thieme.

White, D., & Epston, D. (1990). *Narrative means to therapeutic ends.* New York: Norton.

Wiegand-Grefe, S., Romer, G., & Möller, B. (2008). Kinder psychisch oder körperlich kranker Eltern. Forschungsstand und Perspektiven indizierter Prävention bei einer kinder- und jugendpsychiatrischen Risikobelastung [Children of mentally and physically ill parents. The state of research and perspectives on indicated preventative measures for alleviating the burden of risk on children and adolescents]. *Kinder- und Jugendmedizin, 8,* 38–44.

Wilson, J. (2003). *Kindorientierte Therapie: Ein systemisch-kooperativer Ansatz* [*Child-oriented therapy: A systemic-cooperative approach*]. Heidelberg: Carl-Auer.

Winnicott, D. W. (1971). *Therapeutic consultation in child psychiatry.* London: Hogarth Press.

Zeig, J. (2006). *Confluence: The selected papers of Jeffrey K. Zeig.* Phoenix, AZ: Zeig, Tucker & Theise.

Index